WELSH
CALVINISTIC METHODISM

ANGLESEY

Bangor
Conwy
Rhuddlan
St Asaph
FLINT
Caernarfon
CAERNARVON
Llansannan
Tal-y-sarn
Rhuthun
DENBIGH
Clynnog
Beddgelert
Wrexham
Pwllheli
Penrhyndeudraith
Bala
Llanfair
MERIONETH
MONTGOMERY
Tywyn
Llanidloes
Aberystwyth
Lledrod
Rhaeadr
CARDIGAN
RADNOR
Llangeitho
Tregaron
Tŵr-gwyn
Hay
Nevern
Cil-y-cwm
Pantycelyn
Farm
Talgarth
Llansawel
Llandovery
Trefeca
St David's
CARMARTHEN
Llandeilo
BRECKNOCK
PEMBROKE
Llandeilo
Abergavenny
Llanddowror
Carmarthen
GLAMORGAN
MONMOUTH
Swansea
Tonyrefail
Watford
Cardiff
Llan-gan

MAP OF WALES
showing the old counties
and the more important
centres mentioned

WELSH CALVINISTIC METHODISM

A HISTORICAL SKETCH
OF THE
PRESBYTERIAN CHURCH OF WALES

by
THE REV. WILLIAM WILLIAMS
Swansea

THIRD EDITION ENLARGED
With introduction and notes by Gwyn Davies
and an appendix by D. Martyn Lloyd-Jones on
"William Williams and Welsh Calvinistic Methodism."

BRYNTIRION PRESS
1998

First published, London 1872. Second impression, 1884.
Third edition is published by Bryntirion Press, 1998.

ISBN 1 85049 147 X

Cover design:
Phil Boorman @ burgum boorman ltd.

Typeset by Tentmaker Publications, Stoke-on-Trent.

Published by Bryntirion Press,
Bryntirion, Bridgend, CF31 4DX, Wales, UK

Printed by WBC Book Manufacturers, Bridgend, Wales.

PREFACE

H AS the Principality of Wales been really benefited by the Methodist Reformation of the last century? This is a question which has, of late, been much canvassed, and to which some have given a negative answer. It has been the means of multiplying places of worship, and of enormously swelling Nonconformist congregations, but it has been asserted that it has caused little or no improvement in the morals of the people, and that they were as contented, peaceful, and pure, or very nearly so, before "all the sects" had swollen to their present proportions, and when they had scarcely any religious instruction, but such as was furnished by the "Clergy of their own Church," as their descendants are in the present generation. Statements to this effect are made by men of some weight, and repeated on their authority by more humble individuals. It is to meet such assertions that I have prefixed to the present edition of my historical sketch a chapter on the moral and religious state of the Principality during the last hundred years or so before the rise of Methodism. The authorities which I quote cannot be charged with partiality to Dissenters, for, with one or two exceptions, they were Clergymen, and some of them very distinguished clergymen, of the Church of England.

I have made a few other additions, besides such changes as were necessary to give an accurate idea of the present state of the Church, the history of which I have endeavoured to trace.

WILLIAM WILLIAMS

SWANSEA, July *3rd*, 1884.

5

CONTENTS

CHAPTER V

CHAPTER VI

CHAPTER VII

CHAPTER VIII

CHAPTER IX

CHAPTER X

CHAPTER XI

CHAPTER XII

CHAPTER XIII

CHAPTER XIV

CHAPTER XV

CHAPTER XVI

INTRODUCTION TO THE THIRD EDITION

WHY republish a work which first appeared over a century ago? Has not our knowledge increased during this period? Have not more facts emerged to provide a fuller and more accurate picture of the events described in this book? At a different level, why draw attention again to what seems in many respects to be a spent force, a subject of interest to the odd historian but to very few others at the end of the twentieth century?

There are a number of answers to such questions as these. In the first place, an understanding of Methodism, both in its early stages and in its later development, is essential to an understanding of the history, literature, and culture of modern Wales. That history, that literature (in both Welsh and English), and that culture in large measure reflect the influence of Methodism and the other 'Methodized' religious bodies, either positively or in the various attempts to shake off what was considered to be an unwelcome and even oppressive yoke. The virtue of the present volume is that it provides us not so much with what are by now the well-known facts of the story of Methodism as with an insight into the inner workings of the movement, its inner dynamism, its inner power. For all the importance of knowing what, say, Howel Harris did in a particular place on a particular day, it is that much more important to know why he did it, what constrained him to act as he did, what end he had in view. This volume affords us such a peep behind the scenes, and in so doing helps us to understand the spiritual forces which have shaped and moulded modern Wales.

The mention of spiritual forces leads us to consider the specifically spiritual value of the work. There is here no mere catalogue of dates; the author is rather at pains to trace the hand of God, to demonstrate the reality of lives transformed by the living Christ, to draw attention to the courage, the perseverance, the ingenuity, the zeal—and the weaknesses—of men and women, most of whom were quite ordinary as regards their talents and circumstances. For the ordinary Christian of today, whose knowledge of history may be for some reason quite limited, this book has particular value. To adapt the author's final sentence, a careful and prayerful reading of this book will help us 'to retain the ground which our fathers won with their sword and their bow, and to march on to greater and still greater victories over ungodliness and sin'.

That sentence is set firmly In the context of a plea for an outpouring of the Holy Spirit, and here too the book is particularly important. The growth of 'revivalism' in the middle of the last century and the spread of the Charismatic Movement from the middle of the present century have to a large extent obscured the meaning of, and need for, true revival. In this volume we see what true revival really is. We see its origins in the sovereignty of God, its development not through man-made gimmicks but through Spirit-empowered preaching and holy boldness, its lasting effect on individuals, on churches, on neighbourhoods, almost on a whole nation. This is not to suggest for a moment that revivals cure all problems overnight; there is no place for empty romanticising when the present volume shows only too clearly that even where God is evidently at work tensions and errors still abound among mortal men. But a true understanding of the nature of revival should nevertheless lead us to agree with Jonathan Edwards—a contemporary of the early Welsh Methodists—that 'It may be observed that from the fall of man to our day, the work of Redemption in its effect has mainly been carried on by remarkable communications of the Spirit of God'. And there should be only one genuine response from the Christian - a fervent and persevering prayer that God would revive his work once more.

But what of those periods when there are no 'remarkable communications of the Spirit of God'? It may well be that the history of Calvinistic Methodism has much to teach us even at times like these. Indeed, as Dr D. M. Lloyd-Jones reminds us in the lecture included in this present volume, the very term 'Calvinistic Methodism' is a particularly apt expression of the essence of the Christian faith. The word 'Calvinistic' reminds us of the doctrinal content of that faith, of the vital importance of 'the form of sound words', of the need to define closely and carefully that which is to be believed. More particularly, it draws attention to God's sovereignty, especially in redemption, and displays a holy jealousy for God's rights, his honour, and his glory. The word 'Methodist', on the other hand, speaks of heart-warming Christian experience, a religion of genuine spiritual vitality allied to a disciplined and devoted pursuit of holy living. There have been professed 'Calvinists' who have not been 'Methodists', and who have consequently lost their way in sterile intellectual debates. There have been professed 'Methodists' who have not been 'Calvinists', and who have consequently displayed 'a zeal of God, but not according to knowledge', an unbiblical enthusiasm that has often led them and their followers into excessive subjectivism and emotional turmoil. Where 'Calvinist' is joined to 'Methodist', however, there is a fine balance which has always produced a mature, rounded, consistent Christianity. This was true of the Calvinistic Methodists of Wales as described in this volume; but it is also true of 'Calvinistic Methodists' of every nation and every period. And perhaps no period since the birth of Calvinistic Methodism in Wales urgently requires that combination of 'Calvinism' and 'Methodism' quite as much as the present day.

*   *   *   *   *   *   *   *   *

The present work, it must be admitted, is semi-polemical in nature. The second half of the nineteenth century saw a hardening of denominational attitudes in Wales, one aspect of which was a growing dispute over the spiritual condition of Wales before the birth of Methodism. It was not uncommon for Methodists to exaggerate the darkness before the dawn, and to give undue prominence to the contribution of Howel Harris, Daniel Rowland, and their colleagues in dispersing that darkness. Not unnaturally, the Established Church and the older Nonconformists resented what they considered to be at best the turning of a blind eye to the existence and activities of their representatives in the early eighteenth century. At the same time, the Established Church and the older Nonconformists were themselves not always free from prejudice in their historical writings.

It was against this background that William Williams wrote the present volume, and his preface, his introduction to the first edition, and his first chapter all reflect something of what was a burning (and not always honourable) debate. While endeavouring to be as fair as possible, his sympathies obviously lay with the Methodists, and he appealed to contemporary evidence, both Anglican and Nonconformist, for proof of the spiritual desolation of pre-Methodist Wales. In so doing he was probably unaware of the improvement in the quality and regularity of preaching, the substantial growth in the number of Bibles and devotional books published, the additional educational opportunities, and the increasing attention paid to the practical implications of Christian morality which characterised this period and which in some measure prepared the way for Methodism. But he was surely correct in drawing attention to both the quantitative and the qualitative impact of Methodism as such. While the endeavours of godly men in pre-Methodist Anglicanism and Nonconformity should in no way be ignored or belittled, it can hardly be denied that the spiritual climate in Wales in 1850 was vastly different from that in

1700, and that humanly speaking it was Methodism and Methodizing influences which were largely responsible for this change. In this connection it is at least pleasing to note that Thomas Rees, the Congregationalist historian who bore the brunt of Williams's criticisms for playing down the importance of Methodism, referred to him in the preface to the second edition of his *History of Protestant Nonconformity in Wales* as his 'valued friend and fellow-townsman'.

At the time of writing this book William Williams—not to be confused with the famous hymn-writer of the same name—was the minister of Bethany (English) Calvinistic Methodist Church, Swansea. Born in 1817 at Pen-llin in the Vale of Glamorgan—some two miles from Llan-gan, the scene of the remarkable ministry of David Jones recorded with obvious affection and respect in this volume—he was for a time a schoolteacher and was later in business at Cowbridge. He had been received into membership with the Calvinistic Methodists at the age of eighteen, and when twenty-one had begun to preach. He received a call from the Methodist Church at Pen-clawdd, Gower, in 1844, and took up his charge at Swansea in 1851. Apart from a five-year period at Crickhowell (during which he was responsible for erecting Whitefield's Chapel at Abergavenny) he remained at Swansea for the rest of his life. Bethany was eventually replaced by Argyle Chapel in St Helen's Road; it speaks volumes for the nature of the man that when, in his Jubilee year in the ministry, he received a testimonial of £500 from the church, he immediately gave it to the treasurer to clear the debt on the chapel. He was a most acceptable preacher noted for his Puritan doctrine, but it is as an author that he is best remembered. He edited the Welsh periodical *Y Cylchgrawn* between 1851 and 1855, and contributed many articles (particularly on the history of Methodism in Glamorgan) to various other Welsh-language periodicals. His first book was *Y Puritaniaid (The Puritans)*, published in 1860. Three years later he wrote an interesting

Memoir of Wm. Griffiths, Gower, known to history as 'the Apostle of Gower'. Although it is difficult to be certain in a land overflowing with men bearing the name of 'William Williams', he may well have been the one responsible for *Gair at y Prophwydi (A Word to the Prophets)*, published in 1870. The present volume was his last and most important work. It appeared first in 1872, and the second edition (here completely retypeset) was published in 1884. The author died in 1900, full of years and held in the highest respect among both Calvinistic Methodists and those of other orthodox denominations.

By modern standards of historical scholarship, his work is deficient in a number of respects. Apart from certain errors of fact, there is something almost whimsical about his attempt to portray the past which can not only give the non-Welshman the wrong impression about Wales and the Welsh but also embarrass his modern fellow-countrymen. It must be acknowledged, moreover, that he has a pronounced tendency to paraphrase when rendering Welsh quotations in English, and that even his quotations from English sources are not always accurate. In addition, he on occasion makes his own translation from Welsh sources to English when the original versions lying behind those sources are actually in English. Page references are something of a problem, too: sometimes he quotes the first page on which the original quotation appears, sometimes the last page, and sometimes no page at all.

It would be tedious for both editor and reader to see these deficiencies remedied by the incorporation of a host of minor corrections in this edition. Quotations and translations have therefore been left as they stand; significant departures from the original have been recorded in the notes at the end of every chapter. Serious students, or those who may want to quote the original words, are advised to turn to the sources quoted. One major problem in this respect is that sources are not always acknowledged by the author. Wherever possible these have been indicated in the notes, but on William Williams's own admission (p.19) he derived most of his material from John Hughes's three-volume *History of Welsh Methodism*, (written in Welsh), and it was deemed that constant reference to this work in the notes—except where the occasion demanded it—would be of little benefit. The notes endeavour to explain certain points of historical interest, however, and to correct a number of matters of fact.

The author's attempts to render Welsh personal names and place-names into English have been far from successful or consistent. Corrections to both personal names and place-names have been incorporated in the text. Appendix B contains details of books quoted in the text, and recent publications in English for further reading are given in Appendix C.

It would be a mistake to conclude that the errors and inconsistencies to be found in the original work have any material effect on the value of the volume as such. While obviously disconcerting to the historian, such errors and inconsistencies are almost entirely of minor significance and have virtually no bearing on the substance of the book. And that substance deserves no less notice now than when the book was first published. Attention has already been drawn to its importance in describing that Methodism which has exerted so strong an influence over Wales during the last 250 years, to its significance in demonstrating the reality of God at work in revival, and to its value in depicting the essential elements of vibrant Christianity in terms of "Calvinistic Methodism". These are not trifling themes even in what is an increasingly paganized Wales. On the eve of far-reaching political changes, it would be good to think that the people of Wales were also concerned to take a fresh look at the spiritual rock from which the nation has been hewn.

At the end of the volume there is included a notable lecture by D. Martyn Lloyd-Jones on "William Williams and Welsh Calvinistic Methodism". This lecture, given at the

Puritan and Reformed Studies Conference (now the Westminster Conference) in 1968, both summarises and extends the discussion of the essence of Calvinistic Methodism found in the main body of the book, and seeks to show its urgent relevance for today. No twentieth-century Welshman has embodied that essence more than Dr Lloyd-Jones, and the present work is much enriched by the inclusion of the lecture. (For the sake of clarity, it should be pointed out that the "William Williams" of the lecture is the preacher, author, and hymnwriter to whose name is normally added that of his home at Pantycelyn, and not the author of the book reprinted here.)

I should like to thank the staff of the National Library of Wales, Aberystwyth, and of the Library of the University of Wales, Aberystwyth (particularly Elgan Davies) for their kindness and co-operation in assisting the preparation of this edition. I am also grateful to Elaine Davies and Mair Jones for typing the original material included, to Lady Catherwood and The Banner of Truth Trust for permission to include the lecture on "William Williams and Welsh Calvinistic Methodism" by D. Martyn Lloyd-Jones, to Phil Roberts of Tentmaker Publications for scanning in the original book and typesetting this edition, to David Kingdon for his care in seeing the book through the various stages of publication, and to E. Wyn James for first suggesting the possibility of republishing William Williams's work.

GWYN DAVIES

INTRODUCTION TO THE FIRST EDITION

A *History of Welsh Methodism* was collected with vast labour, and written in the language of the Principality, by the late Rev. John Hughes of Liverpool, and published in three large octavo volumes, containing about six hundred pages each, the last of which came out in the year 1856.

This valuable work is greatly prized by a large number of the Welsh people, but is well worthy of a much wider circulation than it has hitherto obtained.

Though I have gathered considerable information from other sources, the principal part of my labour in the preparation of the following pages has consisted in searching for materials in Mr. Hughes's great treasury, arranging them in my own way, and writing them down in my own words.

I have not thought it necessary to enter into a minute description of the state of the Principality prior to the Methodist period, as the story which I tell cannot fail to enable the reader to draw a correct inference upon that subject for himself; but there are certain statements with reference to that period made in the *History of Protestant Nonconformity in Wales,* by the Rev. Dr. Rees of Swansea, which I feel I ought not to leave unnoticed.

Dr. Rees gives statistics to show that there were 50,000 Nonconformists in Wales before Howel Harris entered upon the work of an Evangelist.[1]

These statistics are partly based upon, and partly deduced from, returns collected about the year 1715 by Dr. John Evans, and still preserved at Dr. Williams's Library in London.[2] There is a table given in four columns; the first containing the names of churches, or pastoral charges, the second those of their respective ministers, the third gives the average number of attendants at each place, and the fourth the social and political standing of those attendants.

The number in the column in which the attendants are classified does in no case come near the number given in the preceding column as belonging to the congregation named in the first column. Thus, for example, at Abergavenny, the first place on the list, we have 280 attendants, classified in the next column as follows,—1 esquire, 16 gentlemen, 7 yeomen, 63 tradesmen, 1 farmer, 7 labourers, making in all 95; the remaining 185 I presume are made up of the females, young people, and children of the families belonging to that place of worship. This list contains 71 pastoral charges, but there were several from which no returns were obtained, and Dr. Rees says:—

"It will be observed that returns of the average number of hearers have been received from only 58 of the places or pastoral charges named, and that the aggregate amount of these is 20,007, or about 345 for each charge. By estimating the other 13, which made no returns, at 345 each, which would be rather below than above the mark (the author has in the preceding paragraph given a reason for this statement), the aggregate number would amount to 24,485. To this number again, at least 3,000 should be added, as the average of the attendants at the Meetings of the Friends, who were then comparatively numerous and influential in several parts of the Principality; thus the total would amount to 27,485. But as it is an admitted rule, in estimating the number of persons belonging to any place of worship, to regard the number of actual attendants at any ordinary service, as only a little more than one half of the people who consider such a place as their usual place of worship, we may safely calculate that *fifty thousand,* or about one eighth of the population of Wales in 1715, were Nonconformists." [3]

"Historians," says the author, "one after another, have been misled by the account given by Mr. Charles, of Bala, in the *Drysorfa* for 1799, of the weakness of Nonconformity in North Wales, and the prevalence of irreligion and superstition there as late as the year 1740. They have taken for granted that that graphic and telling description of the state of things in most parts of the North, was applicable to the *whole* of the Principality, which was a most unfounded assumption, quite as absurd as if a person assumed that the majority of the population of Ireland were Protestants, because it happens to be so in some districts of the Province of Ulster. It is well known that North Wales, in respect both of area and population, constitutes only a little more than one-third of the Principality, including Monmouthshire; and at that time its Nonconforming inhabitants scarcely amounted to one-twentieth of the whole body of Welsh Nonconformists." [4]

Wales, including Monmouthshire, according to Dr. Rees, contained a population of 400,000, of which he gives, say, 140,000 to North Wales, and 260,000 to the South, and since the Nonconforming inhabitants of the former province "scarcely amounted to one-twentieth of the whole body of Welsh Nonconformists," it follows that their number in the North would be scarcely 2,500, leaving 47,500 Nonconformists in the South, or considerably more than one in every six of the whole population. Dr. Rees has thus, by various processes of induction, addition, subtraction, and multiplication, ascertained that before the beginning of the Methodist Revival there were in South Wales and Monmouthshire as many as 47,500 Nonconformists; and yet so small was the influence for good that this great host exerted over their fellow-countrymen, that earnest preachers of the Gospel, who affectionately warned them to flee from the wrath to come, were received in every neighbourhood with stones and brickbats, and met with the worst treatment, as far as South Wales was concerned, in some of those very localities where, according to the statistics before us, Nonconformity had the greatest number of adherents.

Dr. Rees brings a very serious accusation against the

fathers of Methodism. "It seems," says he, on page 305, "that the early Methodists, either from prejudice against their Nonconforming brethren, *or a desire to claim to themselves the undivided honour of having evangelized the Principality, designedly misrepresented,* or ignored the labours of all other sects." If they had been capable of the baseness which the portion I have italicised of the above sentence supposes them to have been, their history would not have been worthy of being written, nor their names of being remembered; but those men of God were infinitely above such littleness, and, happily, their reputation is above being affected by this sweeping and groundless charge.

Exception has been taken to a couplet in the Rev. W. Williams's elegy on the death of Howel Harris, where it is said that "neither presbyter, priest, nor prophet was awake" when he went out to preach the Gospel. The Rev. Griffith Jones was awake and doing a great work long before Harris was heard of, so were some other Episcopal clergymen, and so were several Nonconformist ministers. The author of the elegy knew this to be the case, and was well aware that his readers knew it. It is evident, therefore, that he meant his words to be understood not in an absolute, but in a relative sense. Although a number of earnest men were endeavouring to do good in their various localities, the overwhelming majority of those who had undertaken the duties of watchmen were fast asleep.

But it should be borne in mind that at the beginning of the Methodist Revival numbers of the Nonconformists of Wales were Unitarians, and that many more were tending fast in that direction.[5] Dr. Rees assists us to form an estimate of the value to evangelical religion of much of the great mass of Nonconformity which he has brought before us:

"All the former controversies in which the Welsh Nonconformists had been engaged, sink to nothing in their importance and consequences when compared with the great Arminian controversy, which began about the year

1729" (seven years before Harris began to preach).[6] "Those were disputes about mere non-essentials, and whatever evil effects might have attended them at the time, they soon disappeared; but in this controversy, those points which are regarded as the essential and peculiar doctrines of revealed religion became the subjects of discussion; for though the advocates of the new views, at first, only professed Arminian sentiments, yet it was such a kind of Arminianism that led them direct to Arianism and ultimately to Unitarianism. This unhappy agitation, in the course of a few years, divided the Nonconformist body into two hostile, antagonistic, and irreconcilable parties."[7]

Thus, at the very time when the Methodist revival began, the enemy was coming in like a flood, but the Spirit of the Lord lifted up a standard against him, and numbers of the best Nonconformists, Independent ministers, and lay brethren of the same denomination, rallied around that standard, so far as to give to the Methodists their heartiest sympathy, and all the aid in their power. But there were others who stood aloof from the movement, and there were some who even bitterly opposed it. "There are more," says the Rev. Edmund Jones, the saintly Independent minister of Pontypool, in a letter to Howel Harris on the 7th of August, 1741,—"There are more of our Dissenting ministers who are friends to the Methodists than you mention, this side of the country, beside Mr. Henry Davies, Mr. Philip Pugh, and myself—viz., Mr. Lewis Jones, Mr. Joseph Simmons, Mr. Owen Rees, Mr. William Williams, Mr. Cole, etc.; but perhaps they will not act much. But you know our Lord's saying, 'He that is not against us is on our side; and I cannot but observe that they are our best men who are favourable to you, and that they are, for the most part, dry and inexperienced, or Arminians, that are against you—at least who are bitter."[8]

It is these "best men," saturated as they were with the same spirit as the Methodists, that gave to Welsh

Independency a new life, and gave it the impetus that made it the great power for good that it has been ever since, and still by God's grace continues to be. The Independents of Wales have adopted some of the peculiarities of Methodism, which make a marked distinction between them and their brethren in England, and which bring them within a little of being Methodists themselves under a different form of Church government. "The Societies" says Dr. Rees, "or *experience meetings,* which are peculiar to the Nonconforming churches of Wales, and are regarded by the most spiritually-minded members of all evangelical denominations as essential to the well-being of the churches, are of Methodist origin. So is also the *Association,* where twelve or fifteen sermons are delivered in the open air during two successive days, and where the congregations generally amount to five, ten, and even fifteen thousand. The Associations, or ministers' meetings in Wales, previous to the rise of Methodism, were similar to the county Associations in England, where only one or two sermons were delivered. They were comparatively cold and formal affairs, and excited no particular attention in any locality. Lay and itinerant preaching, catechetical meetings, and Sabbath-schools, though not originated by the Methodists, were reorganized, improved, and brought to their present state of efficiency chiefly by them."[9]

The two denominations are kept apart by a slender and not very high barrier of Church polity. They preach the same doctrines, and in the same spirit. A stranger could not, by listening to the best preachers of each, ascertain to which of the two they belonged. God has blessed both abundantly, and will yet bless them, while they strive for a victory, not over one another, but over ignorance, error, and sin, and labour not for themselves, but for the kingdom of our Lord Jesus Christ.

A few individuals in the Methodist body, in the early part of its history, set themselves up as teachers of

Antinomian, Sandemanian, and some other strange doctrines, which subverted the faith and corrupted the morals of a small number, but as their vagaries did not in any perceptible degree affect the Connexion, nor, as far as I could ascertain, form a subject of dispute at any one of its Associations, I have not thought it worth while to make any reference to them in the ensuing pages.[10]

The facts and incidents which I narrate have been selected from a great many more of a similar character. There were many sufferings endured and sacrifices made for conscience' sake which I have not been able to detail, and many earnest and successful labourers, whose history the limits I had prescribed for myself would not permit me to give. I trust, however, that I have written enough to enable the reader to form an accurate idea of the rise, progress, and character of Welsh Calvinistic Methodism; and I sincerely hope that the perusal of this narrative may be the means of inducing some to emulate the devout spirit and self-sacrificing zeal of those heroes and martyrs whose story I have thus briefly told.

WM. WILLIAMS.

November 9th, 1871.

NOTES

[1] Thomas Rees, *History of Protestant Nonconformity in Wales from its Rise to the Present Time* (London: 1861), pp.286-291.

[2] There is a useful discussion of the value of Evans's list in Michael R. Watts, *The Dissenters: I, From the Reformation to the French Revolution* (Oxford: Clarendon Press, 1978), pp.491-510.

[3] T. Rees, *Protestant Nonconformity*, p.292.

[4] *Ibid.*, p.305.

[5] This statement is rather misleading, as explicit Unitarianism did not appear in Wales until the early decades of the nineteenth century. D. Elwyn Davies, *"They Thought for*

Themselves" (Llandysul: Gomer Press, 1982), pp.46-47. It was the only statement in Williams's book to be criticized by Thomas Rees in the second edition of his *History of Protestant Nonconformity in Wales* (1883), p.vi.

[6] It would be better to replace 'seven' by 'six', although Harris was careful to distinguish between his original 'reading' or 'exhorting' and subsequent 'preaching'.

[7] T. Rees, *Protestant Nonconformity*, p.297.

[8] *Ibid.*, p.369.

[9] *Ibid.*, p.395.

[10] An Association held in 1744 expelled a Methodist who espoused Antinomianism. See p.83-84, and Eifion Evans, *Daniel Rowland and the Great Evangelical Awakening in Wales* (Edinburgh: Banner of Truth Trust, 1985), p.275. Sandemanians were also expelled at Association meetings. Gomer M. Roberts, *Y Pêr Ganiedydd [Pantycelyn]*, I (Aberystwyth: Gwasg Aberystwyth, 1949), pp.144-6.

WELSH CALVINISTIC METHODISM:

CHAPTER I

WALES BEFORE METHODISM

The Vicar of Llandovery—The Sleeping Bard's "Vision of the course of the World"—Trials of the Bishops of St. David's and St. Asaph—Dr. Erasmus Saunders's *View of the State of Religion in the Diocese of St. David's about the beginning of the Eighteenth Century*—Descriptions of the Period by Mr. John Evans, Bala, the Rev. Ioan Thomas, and the Rev. Griffith Jones, Llanddowror—Statistics of Nonconformists in 1715.

IF any one a hundred and fifty years hence will undertake to describe the moral and religious state of this country at the present time, he will have very great advantages over the writer who now attempts the same task with reference to a hundred and fifty years ago. He will have files of newspapers, reports of Registrars-General, and other official documents and records, to which to refer, and upon which to base his conclusions. But in writing of a century and a half ago, we have no such materials available; the immoralities of those times were not tabulated in Reports, and the oldest newspaper file in the Principality scarcely reaches back to the beginning of the present century. But from books, pamphlets, and letters, written by good and truthful men from the beginning of the seventeenth century up to the dawn of the Methodist Revival, we can form a moderately accurate idea of the state of Wales as to religion and morality during that period.

The Rev. Rhys Prichard was born at Llandovery in Carmarthenshire in the year 1579, was educated at Jesus College, Oxford, graduated as B.A. in 1602, became vicar of his native parish in the same year, and chancellor of the diocese of St. David's in 1626. He was a strict Conformist, and in his views and his spirit a thorough Puritan. He continued to reside at Llandovery, earnestly striving to do the work of the Master there and at other places up to his death in 1644; but so little was he appreciated in his day, that not a stone was placed to mark his grave, and no man *knows* where he was buried; but the writer of a brief memoir of him, which I have now before me, *"fully believed"* that he was buried in his own church.

A collection of poems written by him in the Welsh language, and entitled, *The Welshmen's Candle,* has passed through many editions; and an English translation of it by the Rev. W. Evans, Vicar of Llanhuadain, was published in London in 1815. That the good vicar found it hard to battle with the prevailing ignorance and immoralities of his time the following extracts from Mr. Evans's translation will abundantly show. I give the translation verbatim as I find it:—

"Women and men of low degree,
The very abjects of the land,
You always may in England see
Each with his Bible in his hand.

*   *   *   *   *   *   *

"They teach each tradesman's daughter there
To read the books that most excel;
Whereas the gentry's daughters here
Can scarce the Paternoster spell.

"'Tis to the Welsh a foul disgrace
They're in religion still so young,
That not a tythe[1] of all the race
The Scriptures read in their own tongue.[2]

*   *   *   *   *   *   *

"As filthy swine can feed on draff,
As thirsty oxen water quaff,
We swill and drench ourselves with heady drink;
We wallow in each foul desire,

As hogs delight to roll in mire,
And never of the consequences think.

"The Priest, the Farmer, and the Hind,
 With artisans of every kind,
 The Bailiff,[3] Judge, and Gentleman, each strives
 With most amazing insolence
 Which shall the Godhead most incense
 Nor can I say who worst among them lives.[4]

"In indolence the clergy live,
 The venal judges bribes receive,
 The gentry tipple in each paltry inn.

*　　*　　*　　*　　*　　*　　*

"There's not a hamlet to be found
 Or pretty village all around,[5]
 But that some monstrous crime appears
 Therein, to din the Godhead's ears.

*　　*　　*　　*　　*　　*　　*

"The sheriffs and their cormorant train
 On the fleec'd populace distrain,
 And, under veil of justice, prey
 Upon their wealth in open day.

"The wealthy glibly swallow down
 The little all the needy own,
 And by oppression drive the poor
 To beg their bread from door to door."[6]

Of Sabbath profanation we have the following:—

"Of all the days throughout the rolling year
 There's not a day we pass so much amiss,
 There's not a day wherein we all appear
 So irreligious, so profane as this.

"A day for drunkenness, a day for sport,
   A day to dance, a day to lounge away,
   A day for riot and excess too short,
   Amongst most Welshmen is the Sabbath day.

"A day to sit, a day in chat to spend,
   A day when fighting 'mongst us most prevails,
   A day to do the errands of the Fiend—
   Such is the Sabbath in most parts of Wales."[7]

There is much more to the same effect; and if any one takes the trouble to go through the book, he will find that very much worse things are said than I have quoted. Some have endeavoured to break the force of the author's descriptions by saying that they are instances of "poetic licence." I do not know how any one can find poetry in The *Welshmen's Candle.* It is rhyming prose, where the rhyme is neither smooth nor pleasant. It was not from his own imagination that the good man drew those lurid pictures, but from scenes of ungodliness which, to the intense sorrow of his soul, he was compelled daily to witness; and no one has a right to charge him with exaggeration, any more than to say that the inspired prophets of old exaggerated when describing the horrible abominations of the people of Israel.

In the year 1703 there appeared a remarkable book by the Rev. Ellis Wynne, Vicar of Llanfair in Merionethshire, which has passed through at least seventeen editions, the last of which came out in 1878, with explanatory notes by the Rev. David Silvan Evans, B.D., Rector of Llanwrin, Montgomeryshire.

It is entitled *The Visions of the Sleeping Bard,* and consists of three parts: "The vision of the course of the world," "The vision of Death in his lower courts," and "The vision of hell." It is very eloquent and very horrible. I can well remember the creeping sensation that came over me in reading portions of it many years ago. The reader is possessed by the conviction that the author describes that which he saw, and cannot help feeling now and again as if he saw it all himself.

It is only fair to say that the bard, in his dream of the course of the world, wandered far beyond the boundaries of his own country; and yet it is easy to identify those portions of it which relate to the Principality. The world is a vast city consisting of three streets, the control over which has been given to Belial's three daughters, Pride, Pleasure, and Lucre. Each street is called after the name of the particular princess that rules over it. In the street of Pride there were vanities innumerable, some standing before the glass for three hours together, to adjust their dress and to put their lips into proper shape; all endeavouring to set themselves off to the best advantage;—"a lady with a pedlar's shop on her back, and gems hanging by her ears that had cost enough to purchase a tolerable farm," and "a gentleman passing along with such a swagger that you could winnow beans in the breeze that was made by the tail of his coat."

The street of Lucre was full of oppression, extortion, and knavery of all kinds; magistrates, lawyers, doctors, merchants, shopkeepers, agents, stewards were all bent upon gain, and managing, by hook or by crook, to secure it.

In the street of Pleasure he saw gluttony and drunkenness and still grosser immoralities. He witnessed scenes which he did not feel at liberty to describe, and turning away in disgust from these, he and his angel guide came upon a place where they heard a great noise, "jabbering and thumping, crying and laughing, shouting and singing: 'Well,' said I, 'here *is* Bedlam to be sure.' When we entered the place the riot had ceased, and we saw men in all manner of positions lying amid the wrecks of bottles and cups and pots and tobacco-pipes. Upon inquiring what it was all about., we found that it was seven thirsty neighbours—a tinker, a dyer, a blacksmith, a miner, a chimney sweeper, a poet, and a parson, who had been having a carouse together. The last had come to preach on Temperance, and to show in his own person the hideousness of drunkenness. The quarrel began in a dispute that had arisen between them on the question which of them could drink the hardest; and it was the poet who had won the field over all but the parson, who, out of respect to his coat, was voted head and chief of the boon companions."[8]

Having visited a Quaker meeting, where all was wrong, and a Nonconformist meeting held in a barn, "where a man imitated preaching by rote, frequently saying the same thing three times over," the bard asked his guide, "Where, I pray thee, is the Church of England?" "That," said he, "is above, in the higher city, and constituting a large portion of the Church Catholic. But there are in this city some probationary churches belonging to the Church of England, where Welsh and English people are under training for a while, to fit them for having their names written on the book of the Church Catholic; and whoever obtains that privilege, happy is he. But, alas! there are only a few who care to qualify themselves for citizenship there." They visited the gallery of one of the churches of Wales during service, and found most of the congregation shamefully indecorous in their behaviour, while many of those who seemed very devout were only shamming. A Communion followed, when, through his guide's glass, he could see that most of the communicants received each some monstrous form with the bread and wine, while those who received a small ray of heavenly light were very few indeed.

The editor concludes a brief memoir of the author in the following words,—"No doubt the appearance of the book was as the piercing of a sword to a great many; but who can feel in his heart to blame the honest bard and pure-lived clergyman (for writing as he did) at that time? It was an age full of superstition, ignorance, and immorality that he lived in, and he strove hard to dispel the darkness that covered the Principality and to scatter the thick clouds that hung over the heads of its people; he exposed the oppression and hypocrisy, the vanity and folly of this world, and the numberless enchantments of the daughters of Belial in the City of Destruction, and exhorted all to a holy life, that they might be safely led to the City of Immanuel." The Rev. Rhys Prichard wrote in the first half of the seventeenth century, and the Rev. Ellis Wynne towards its close, or just at the beginning of the eighteenth; and it is evident that very little, if any, improvement had taken place in Wales in the interval between the days of the Vicar of Llandovery and those of the Vicar of Llanfair.

Near the close of the seventeenth century, proceedings were taken, on very grave charges, against two of the bishops of Wales, namely, Dr. Thomas Watson of St. David's and Dr. Edward Jones of St. Asaph; and the evidence adduced at their respective trials discloses a very sad state of things in those two dioceses, which comprised at the time by far the greater part of the Principality.

"*A summary view of the articles exhibited against the Bishop of St. David's and the proofs made thereon*" was published in London in 1701, and begins as follows: "In the month of July 1687, Dr. Thomas Watson was installed Bishop of St. David's, and though he had then, but very lately at his consecration, been instructed that a bishop should not be greedy of filthy lucre, but abhor covetousness, yet at his first coming down thither he declared *it was a poor bishopric, but that he was resolved to get money one way or other.* The *Tutor*[9] had long pursued that rule, and the *Bishop* so resolutely adhered to it that its pernicious effects appeared in every part of his episcopal administration, not in single instances, but in repeated acts of extortion, simony, and other crimes of the most enormous nature. As these were multiplied, so the fame of them increased, till, in the year 1694, it grew so loud and universal that it moved his Grace the Archbishop of Canterbury to visit the diocese of St. David's by commissioners. But that visitation ended, the Bishop's fears were so too, and he soon resumed his former practices, upon which, in the year 1695, a process was taken out against him at the promotion of Robert Lucy,

Esq., son of a former bishop of St. David's, and Registrar of
that diocese. By this process the Bishop was called to answer
certain articles concerning simony, and exactions of excessive
and illegal sums of money from his clergy, and concerning
divers other enormous crimes by him committed."[10] During
the trial that ensued a large number of witnesses, both clerical
and lay, gave evidence in support of the above charges, and
the result of it all is to show that the Bishop must have been a
very bad man, and that there were not a few in his diocese
who were not much better than he. "The proceedings were
slow and tedious, partly owing to the evasive and
procrastinating measures the Bishop had recourse to, and
partly, perhaps, owing to Archbishop Tennison's resolution
to hear and consider all that could possibly be alleged in
behalf of the Bishop, and so to leave him no ground of
complaint."[11]

The trial ended in the deprivation of the Bishop, which
sentence was pronounced against him by the Archbishop of
Canterbury, assisted by several of the Bishops of his Province,
on the 3rd of August 1699. He appealed against this sentence,
but it was confirmed unanimously by a very full court of the
King's Judges Delegates, on the 22nd of February 1700.[12]

Bishop Burnet, who was one of those who sat in the case,
says, "The Bishops who were present agreed to a sentence
of deposition; I went farther, and thought that he ought to
be excommunicated. He was one of the worst men, in all
respects, that I ever knew in holy orders,—passionate,
covetous, and false, in the blackest instances, without any
virtue or good quality to balance his many bad ones."[13]

Before the trial of the Bishop of St. David's had reached
its close, that of the Bishop of St. Asaph was commenced.
"A short narrative" of the proceedings against the latter was
published in London in 1702, a few extracts from which I
will place before my readers:—

"Dr. Edward Jones was translated from the Bishopric of
Cloyne to the see of St. Asaph in November 1692, but came

not to his diocese until April 1693… It must be owned that for the first summer, 1693, there are few exceptions to any of his collations. But the oftener his lordship returned to his diocese the years following, the more exceptionable were his collations; for one Mrs. Burdett, a relative of the Bishop's, who was left at St. Asaph, is proved to have tampered with the clergy in the Bishop's absence, which occasioned a public fame and report, within that diocese and elsewhere, which public fame is proved by twenty-one of the promoter's witnesses, that several dignities and livings were conferred upon the account of simoniacal contracts."

It does not appear that his lordship received money in *payment* for the benefices he conferred. All that he wished for was that his clergy should show their *gratitude* to him. Here is an instance. "George Williams and John Lloyd depose, almost in the same words, that Griffith Evans informed them to the effect following,—that when Tremeirchion became vacant he wrote to the Bishop to succeed in that vicarage; and in a few days afterwards he waited on Mrs. Burdett at the Bishop's house at St. Asaph, who asked him what he would give to succeed in Tremeirchion, intimating to him that she had been offered £20 for it; and shortly afterwards he had notice to come to Mrs. Burdett, who told him the Bishop was pleased to bestow upon him Tremeirchion, and then complained that the Bishop was very necessitous, and that then was a suitable time for him to show his gratitude to him; whereupon the said Evans delivered to Mrs. Burdett ten guineas for the Bishop's use, and three guineas for her and her husband; guineas then passing at thirty shillings apiece."[14]

This was not the first time for Griffith Evans to evince his *gratitude* to his diocesan, for "Edward Evans, Clerk, deposeth, that he heard the Bishop declare about the time that he preferred Evans to Llandrillo, that he, the said Evans, was the most grateful clergyman he has met with since he came to the diocese."[15] It is shown by a great number of depositions that many such expressions of gratitude, in sums of money of various amounts, were sometimes placed in the Bishop's own hands, but more frequently reached him either through his *lady* or through his relative Mrs. Burdett.

He was likewise charged "with great remissness in his government of his clergy, not only in neglecting the correction of such as had been complained of to him for their irregularities, but preferring several of them who his lordship must needs know were fitter for punishment than preferment."[16] Particulars are given of the bad deeds of some of those clergymen, but I do not care to mention them. The Bishop was in June 1701 suspended for six months, but at the end of that time it seems that the Archbishop was not satisfied with his purgation, "which made him continue the sentence without granting a relaxation until May 5th, 1702," when it was completely removed, after the Bishop had in the Archbishop's Court made an humble confession of his guilt in respect to several of the charges brought against him, expressed his deep contrition, and solemnly promised to offend no more.[17]

It is difficult to account for the difference in the punishment meted out to the two offending bishops. Referring to the Bishop of St. David's, Dr. Stoughton says, "He had been made a bishop by James II., whose policy he approved; and this circumstance seems to have had much to do with the issue of his trial... In a *Review* of his case published by a friendly hand, the charges brought against him are pronounced to be false, the veracity of the witnesses is impugned, and the whole process is described as a conspiracy carried on by 'subornation,' and inspired by 'political motives and inducements of pique and revenge.'"[18]

But if that were true, what are we to think of the great number of clergymen who bore witness against him? Things were in a deplorable state in that diocese if the bishop, who presided over it for twelve years, was as bad as the issue of his trial leads us to believe; but its condition must have been far worse if there could be found within it such a host of men in Holy Orders solemnly to swear to that which they knew to be false. If any dependence can be placed on their testimony, and on the admissions of some of those who came forward to bear witness in his defence, "when under interrogation," it is evident that, severe as his sentence was, it was not more than justice required; but at the same time we can imagine that it would have been lighter if he had not been such a pronounced Jacobite, and that that of his brother of St. Asaph would have been heavier if he had belonged to that party. The editor of the *Short Narrative* concludes his somewhat long preface in the following words:—"It was contrived that as Bishop Watson was sent to St. David's for the credit of one reign, Bishop Jones must be advanced to St. Asaph for the ornament of another, and though they are, it is thought, saints of the same calendar, yet they have been for some reason manifestly distinguished by the distributive justice of this world."

The diocese of St. David's at that time included the counties of Pembroke, Cardigan, Carmarthen, Brecknock, and Radnor, with a part of Glamorgan in South Wales, and Montgomeryshire in North Wales, besides portions of Monmouth and Hereford; and we have further light on the state of things over that wide district in "*A View of the State of Religion in the Diocese of St. David's about the Beginning of the Eighteenth Century,*" by Erasmus Saunders, D.D., published in London in 1721.[19]

At the Reformation the large estates which had got into the possession of the Church were taken from it, and either sold or given to laymen. With that the author does not find fault; but the wrong of which he complains is, that the tithes were not left in the possession of the Reformed Church. These had been disposed of to lay impropriators "to such an extent as to leave large portions of the country without any means, or very inadequate means, for the maintenance of religion." He refers to "the desolate remains of the old collegiate church at Llanddewi Brefi, in Cardiganshire, a church once endowed with handsome provision for a dean and twelve prebendaries; but the endowment is now alienated to that degree that the poor incumbent there, though the tithes of his parish are said to be worth four hundred pounds per annum, is obliged to content himself with about eight pounds salary.[20]

"Again, did you see what very sorry and mean cottages (if any) that are left for parsonages and vicarage houses... and where there are any, they are commonly so mean and inconvenient that the clergy, poor as they are, cannot think them habitable for themselves, and therefore are obliged to part with them to any that will please to rent them; but very often they fall to the sexton's lot, who, to get a sorry maintenance, is allowed the privilege of selling ale by the churchyard side.[21]

"In some places we have churches without chancels; in others we have but some piece of a church, that is, one end, or a side aisle that is remaining, and in some parishes even none at all... In some not only the bells are taken away, but the towers are demolished, and in many others there are scarce any seats, except here and there a few ill-contrived and broken stools and benches. Their little windows are without glass, and darkened with boards, mats, or lattices; their roofs decaying, tottering, and leaky; their walls green, mouldy, and nauseous, and very often without wash or plaster; and their floors ridged up with noisome graves, without any pavement, and only covered with a few rushes."[22]

The names of a large number of churches are given, "which had either been converted into barns or stables, or only served for the habitations of owls and jackdaws... The use for which they were intended is almost forgotten, unless it be at Llan-y-bri, where I am informed the impropriator or his tenant has let the church to the neighbouring dissenters, who are free to rent it for the desirable opportunity of turning a church into a conventicle."[23]

"As the Christian service is thus totally disused in some places, there are other some in which it may be said to be only half used, there being several churches where we but rarely, if at all, meet with preaching, catechising, or administering the Holy Communion. In others, the service of the Prayer is but partly read, and that, perhaps, but once a month, or once in a quarter of a year; nor is it indeed reasonable to expect that they should be better served while the stipends that are allowed for the service of them are so small that a poor curate must sometimes submit to serve three or four churches for ten or twelve pounds a year, and that, perhaps, when they are nearly as many miles distant from each other. And when it is thus with them, with what order or regularity (can it be supposed) are they capable of doing that service? Forced they are (now they are ordained) to submit to any terms; they must starve or even be contented with the meanest salaries, and yet trudge and labour for it as long as they are able; and having so little time and so many places to attend upon, how precipitately and as if out of breath are they obliged to read the prayers, or to shorten and abridge them! What time have either they or their congregations to compose themselves while thus forced to a kind of perpetual motion, or like hasty itinerants to hurry about from place to place? There is no time fixed for going to church, so it be on Sundays, so the poor man must begin at any time, with as many as be at hand, sooner or later as he can perform his round. He then abruptly huddles over as many prayers as may be in half an hour's time, and then returns again to his road, fasting (for how earnestly so ever his appetite may call for it, it is seldom that he has time, or that the impropriator's farmer can afford to give him dinner) till he has despatched his circuit, or that weariness or darkness obliges him to rest, or perhaps for the want of a little necessary refreshment at home, to go where he ought not, where it's odds but he will again meet with many of his congregation, who when their short service is over are too apt to think themselves at liberty to spend the remaining part of the day at an ale-house or at some pastime or diversion as they are disposed."[24]

Parishes where the tithe had not been alienated were as badly served as those where it had. Livings that were of any value were in "many cases given to clergymen who, however well qualified in other respects, were unable to speak to the people in their own language."[25] "What matters it who is the rector, an impropriator or an ecclesiastic, as to the edification or benefit of the people? Or what avails it to the curate who is patron, while they so far agree as to be equally sordid in their stipends and allowances?... It imports but little surely that they are not all impropriated, since the profits are carried off, and the pastoral care both in the one case and in the other left to be the business of any one, that is, perhaps of the cheapest that can be retained."[26] "It is not to be doubted but that the ordaining of persons that are themselves contemptible has an apparent tendency to derive contempt on their profession.; and it is so when any little A. B. C. Darian schoolmaster, a gentleman's butler, a mountebank, and what not, shall be so cheaply admitted to commence clerks, on the prevailing merit of some potent impropriator's recommendation, who may be solicitous for a cheap chaplain, or so to pack off a useless servant."[27]

Many of the people retained religious feelings and observed religious customs in spite of all. "They cross themselves," says the author, "as the first Christians were used to do, on many occasions, with a short ejaculation that through the Cross of Christ they might be safe or saved. In most mountainous parts, where old customs and simplicity are most prevailing, there we shall observe that when the people come to church, they go immediately to the graves of their friends, and there kneeling, offer up their prayer to God; but especially at the feast of the Nativity of our Lord; for they then come to church about cock-crowing, and bring either candles or torches with them, which they set to burn every one, one or more upon the grave of his departed friend, and then set themselves to sing their carols, and continue so to do, to welcome the approaching festival, until prayer-time.

"But with these innocent good old customs, they have also learned some of the Roman superstitious practices in the later ages, such as many times in their ejaculations to invocate, not only the Deity, but also the holy Virgin and other saints; for Mair wen, Iago, Teilaw Mawr, Celer, Celynog, and others, are often thus remembered, as if they had hardly yet forgotten the use of praying to them... In many parts of North Wales they continue in effect still to pay for obits, by giving oblations to the ministers at the burial of their friends, as they were formerly taught to do to pray them out of purgatory, without which useful perquisites the poor curates in many places would be very hard pushed to get their livelihood.

"And thus it is the Christian religion labours to keep ground here. Superstition and religion, error and truth, are so very oddly mixed, that it should in charity be concluded to be rather the misfortune of many that they are misled. For the generality are, I am afraid, more obliged, if not to their natural probity, to their religious observance of those ancient customs, or to the instruction that they get from their carols, or the Vicar of Llandovery's poems, than to any benefit received from the catechising and preaching of a regular ministry. So that if we have not yet unlearned the errors of our Popish ancestors, it is because the doctrines of the Reformation, begun about two hundred years ago in England, have not effectually reached us, nor is it likely that they ever should without a fit and learned clergy."[28]

In a Welsh periodical entitled *Drysorfa Ysbrydol*[29] (*The Spiritual Treasury*) for April 1799, Mr. John Evans, of Bala, an eminently good man and a preacher of many years' standing, then verging on eighty years of age, gives his recollections of the state of the country in his youth. Those recollections reached back to the year 1742; and I give a brief extract from that which he says:—

"There was great darkness in the country. Bibles were scarce, and there were few of the common people who could read at all. The habits of the people were most depraved and immoral. The gentry and commonalty, clergymen and laymen were very much alike; most were intemperate in their lives, without reverence for God's holy commandments, and neglecting His worship. Gluttony, drunkenness, and uncleanness had, like overflowing streams, covered the land... The common people were more disposed to attend church on Sabbath mornings than the gentry; but on Sabbath afternoons they would, like them, hasten to their amusements. There was scarcely a Sunday afternoon in which there was not some game in which young men displayed their prowess, and great numbers from all the adjacent neighbourhoods would gather together to see them."

The Rev. Dr. Rees, in his *History of Nonconformity in Wales,* intimates that "this graphic and telling description," while correct in regard to most of North Wales, could not be justly applied to the whole of the Principality.[30] But Mr. John Evans, of Bala, is not the only one who has spoken and written on that subject, and I will place before my reader a few extracts from that which was written about the time in question by two eminent men in South Wales. The Rev. Ioan Thomas, who became Independent minister at Rhaeadr and two other places in Radnorshire, in 1767, wrote an autobiography, which he entitled, *Free Grace: "A Short History of the goodness of God to His unworthy servant, Ioan Thomas, from his childhood until now."* He was born in 1730, in the parish of Myddfai, Carmarthenshire. From his early childhood he was under strong religious impressions, and while he was yet a lad his soul within him was sorely vexed in seeing the ungodliness of the people among whom he lived, and even then he began to rebuke them. Sabbath games were common in his neighbourhood, as they were everywhere else at the time, and for a while he took part in them himself; but, being convinced of their sinfulness, he desisted from them, and did all he could to persuade others to do the same. "I remember,"

says he, "on one Sabbath afternoon going near the church of
my native parish, where there were many playing quoits, and
great numbers, like a fair, looking on. In my childish way I
began to speak to them of the state of their souls; they
laughed, and seemed to regard me as a madman; and yet,
whether it was in consequence of my words, or because of
being threatened by others, or because of being pricked by
their own consciences, on being thus reproved by a child,
several of them ceased from their play in the churchyard. But
they would afterwards go to out-of-the way corners, where I
made it my business to follow them, and to speak to them of
the evil of thus profaning the Lord's Day. Sometimes I would
threaten to call the churchwardens, but I knew that that
would have been in vain, for they, regardless of their oath,
would not come out of the taverns, though I went to those
places to seek them. O ye perjurers, where are your oaths?"[31]

He began to preach in his twentieth year, travelled about
for that purpose, and met with rough treatment in several
places in South Wales. At Mynydd Ty'n-croes, near
Colwinstone, in the Vale of Glamorgan,[32] while preaching
in the open air, he was pelted with rotten eggs until his sides
were sore and his clothes in a most filthy condition. His head
was not touched, for a woman held a hat to protect it;[33] and
at Llangatwg,[34] Breconshire, a squire of the village, the
clergyman, and the sexton came out from the public-house
with the landlord to oppose him. The first of these collared
him and gave him a blow on the cheek, and then they all
returned to the place from which they had come.[35] At
Crickhowell the "howlings of the mob caused terror to his
flesh," and they smashed the window of the house in which
he was preaching.[36] "I was by the church of Ystrad, in
Glamorganshire, at one time when games were going on,
and I stood (to speak) by the churchyard wall. Then the ball
players and dancers left their work, and came to the other
side of the wall to hear, fiddlers and all. Then the clergyman,
who was there with them, having lost his company, said to

the fiddlers, 'If you expect to be paid, go on with your work; and you that are talking, go away from the churchyard, it is consecrated ground.'"[37]

The Rev. Griffith Jones, Vicar of Llanddowror, Carmarthenshire, and founder of the Welsh circulating charity schools, of which I will give some particulars in another chapter, published, from 1737 to 1760, an annual Report of his great work.[38] Preceding each Report there is a letter to some one whom the writer addresses as "Honoured Sir," in which he enlarges upon the necessity for such work as he was then doing, and gives instances of the good which, so far, had been done. In these letters we have glimpses of the state of Wales at the time when they were written. I will give some extracts:—

"The growing profaneness and open debauchery, the professed and practical infidelity, with the natural offspring of all this, the vices and immoralities of the time we live in, so daring and barefaced as publicly to triumph in our streets, and bid defiance to the laws of God and man; the infectious fumes of pernicious errors and deadly works of darkness, which have too much eclipsed the gospel light already, and threaten the total extinction of it in our land,—these dreadful calamities, I say, should awaken all the serious friends of religion to bestir themselves, and exert their zeal for the preservation and revival of it before it quite forsake us, or is taken away in judgment from us."[39]

"It has been found in several places, that where sixty or eighty young and old people came to these schools, not above three or four of them could say the Lord's Prayer, and they, too, in a very imperfect and unintelligible manner, not knowing so much as *who their Father in heaven is,* nor able to give a much better account of the easiest and more common articles of the Christian religion than those whom you kindly extend your charity to instruct in the Indies."[40]

"We hear of the great increase of venality and rapine, of debaucheries, perjuries, barbarous villanies, robberies in the light of the sun, unnatural, inhuman, and bloodthirsty cruelties. And shall we call ourselves still a Christian people, if we use not all profitable and proper methods to reform enormities grown to such a pitch, that our legislators have been justly alarmed to consider with great thoughts of heart, since loading the gallows with offenders and making a quick despatch of their lives will rather, it is justly feared, depopulate the country than mend it, what means to use, what laws to enact, that may be most likely to eradicate and remove the scandal of such enormous evils from a Christian country."[41]

These extracts are not translations, the letters from which they are taken having been written in English; and it will be observed that they date from nine to sixteen years after the beginning of the Methodist Revival. So far that movement was only in its infancy; and though a considerable number had been brought under its influence, they were few in comparison with the great mass who still continued in ungodliness.

There were many Nonconformists in Wales, especially in its southern counties, before Methodism began, and they were nearly all Independents, Presbyterians, and Baptists. In the middle of the seventeenth century, and for some time afterwards, it is difficult to distinguish the first of these from the last, for there were churches in which people, holding different views on the subject of baptism, communicated together, and which were designated Independent Churches. Richard Davies, the eminent Quaker of Welshpool, describing in his *Account of his Convincements*, etc., the change in his views which occurred about 1657, says, "Then as to water baptism, which I had under consideration, though I was no admirer of it, being not of the persuasion of re-baptising. Those who were Independents were not so much at first for re-baptising; but afterwards it prevailed more among them in these parts, when one Henry Jessey came here-aways, and about that time it was that I came from them."[42] But about the beginning of the eighteenth century the line of separation between them seems to have become more distinct. About 1715, Dr. John Evans collected the statistics of the Nonconforming Congregations in England and Wales, and the list, which he collected with great labour, is now in MS. in Dr. Williams's Library, Grafton Street, London. This list as given by Dr. Rees,[43] shows that there were at that time in Wales and Monmouthshire thirty-five Independent, nineteen Presbyterian, and fifteen Baptist Churches, which, with two others which were known to exist at the time, but are not mentioned in these statistics, make up seventy-one. Several of them had branches, which bring up the whole number of Congregations to one hundred and ten. The returns of "hearers" belonging to all these places show an aggregate of 20,007. But there were thirteen places, eleven of those that are given in the list and the two that were left out of it, from which no returns were received, and Dr. Rees, making reasonable allowance for these, brings up the number to 24,485. But I cannot feel that he is right in multiplying this number by two, on the ground "that it is an admitted rule to regard the actual number of attendants at any ordinary service as only a little more than one-half of the people who consider such a place as their usual place of worship." The column giving the number of adherents in the original list, a copy of which I have now before me, is headed, *"Number of hearers,"* and not *"Average Attendance;"* and opposite many of the Churches there is given a classification of those hearers, as, for example, "Abergavenny, Esq., 1; Gentlemen, 16 Yeomen, 7; Tradesmen, 63; Farmers, 1; Labourers, 7." There is likewise a column showing the number of voters belonging to each place. All this seems to me to lead inevitably to the conclusion that the people who furnished the returns meant them to include all whom they considered as belonging to the places of which they reported. But this is of little consequence, and is a mere matter of opinion. Dr. Rees could not have had any reason for wishing to make the

Nonconformists of the time appear more numerous than they were; and neither have I for wishing to make them appear less. Quality is much more important than numbers, and those thousands of Nonconformists, as the prevailing immoralities of their times abundantly prove, were, with a few noteworthy exceptions, very different, in moral weight and religious influence, from that which their successors of the same denominations became in after-years. The Rev. Ioan Thomas, from whose Autobiography I have already given some extracts, began his religious life among the Methodists. He worked with them for some years, but, in 1761, joined the Independents, or, as he designates them, the Dissenters. In reference to this change he says, "There were several who from time to time advised me to go to the Academy, that I might have a little more human learning... I saw that the Dissenters were in their discipline according to the Word of God, and nearer the Apostolic order of the New Testament than the Methodists; but I loved the life and zeal of the Methodists, and feared the lukewarmness of the Dissenters, lest, if I joined them, I should become lukewarm as they were; but some of them said to me that if I would come among them, I might be the means of warming them."[44]

He decided upon seeking admission into the Academy at Abergavenny, "and I mentioned this purpose to the Rev. Daniel Rowland, who said nothing against me... I arrived at Abergavenny about the end of 1761, and when I came to set about learning Latin books, and saw so much ungodliness in the town, and such lukewarmness in the congregation, I felt that it had become a change of climate with me, and fearing that I would lose ground in my spirit, I retired daily at noon to the plantations by the side of the river Usk to pray, where I often found it very sweet... During the four years that I stayed at the Academy I preached frequently here and at other places, and in the holidays I would go through several of the counties of Wales, especially Cardiganshire, preaching with the

Methodists and the Dissenters, when I got a little of the fire of Llangeitho to keep my soul from freezing in the region of Abergavenny. Mr. Rowland was very kind to me, and would sometimes ask me to preach at Llangeitho... The most earnest and experimental of the Dissenters loved me, but the lukewarm and formal regarded me as too much of a Methodist, especially when I had help from Heaven to preach; but when I was dry and dead, and spoke only from my own understanding, they would say that I was like a Dissenter."[45]

But by-and-by there came a blessed change. The fire kindled in the hearts of great numbers of the "Dissenters," and they became "like Methodists," and so like them in their entire consecration to Christ, in the holiness of their lives, and in the earnestness and power of their ministry, as to be enabled as efficiently as they to carry on the work of the Master. The Calvinistic Methodists, as a denomination, have no right "to claim for themselves the credit of having evangelised Wales," and I am not aware of any desire on their part to do so. The Principality is not yet all that we could wish it to be. There still remains in it much sin, and there is still within its borders not a little heathenism, but a great work has continued to be done in it for several generations, not by the Methodists or any other connexion alone; but impelled by the Methodistical spirit which came to permeate all the denominations, many good and devoted men, some belonging to the Establishment, and more to the various Nonconforming Churches, have worked mightily for Christ, and it is by the blessing of God upon their labours that the Wales of to-day is so very different from the Wales of a hundred and fifty years ago.

NOTES

[1] Williams has a footnote: "The original has 'one in a hundred'."

[2] Rhys Prichard, *The Morning Star, or the Divine Poems of Mr*

Rees Prichard . . . Translated into English Verse by the Rev. William Evans. (1771; new edition, Merthyr: 1815), p.11.

[3] Williams has a footnote: "The Magistrate."

[4] Rhys Prichard, *The Morning Star*, p.14.

[5] The original has 'petty', not 'pretty'.

[6] Rhys Prichard, *The Morning Star*, p.296.

[7] *Ibid.*, p.416.

[8] Ellis Wynne, *Gweledigaethau y Bardd Cwsg, gyda nodiadau eglurhaol gan D. Silvan Evans* (1853; new edition, Caerfyrddin: 1878), p.31.

[9] Williams has a footnote: "At St. John's College, Cambridge" i.e. Watson's previous post.

[10] *A Summary View of the Articles Exhibited against the Late Archbishop of St David's* (London: 1701), p.1.

[11] T. B. Howell, *A Complete Collection of State Trials*, XIV (London: 1816), p.453.

[12] *Ibid.*, p.467; Lord Raymond, *Reports of Cases Argued and Adjudged in the Courts of King's Bench and Common Pleas, in the Reigns of the Late King William, Queen Anne, King George the First, and King George the Second,* I (fourth edition, 1792), pp.447, 539.

[13] Howell, *State Trials,* XIV, p.467.

[14] [Robert Wynne], *A Short Narrative of the Proceedings against the Bp. of St. A[saph]* (London: 1702), p.16.

[15] *Ibid.,* p.15.   [16] *Ibid.,* p.56.

[17] *Ibid.,* p.75.

[18] John Stoughton, *History of Religion in England from the Opening of the Long Parliament to the End of the Eighteenth Century. V: The Church of the Revolution* (1874; revised edition, London: 1881), p.225.

[19] The description provided by Saunders, while certainly not without sound foundation, was no doubt coloured to some extent by the fact that his desire for a bishopric had been thwarted. Geraint H. Jenkins, *Literature, Religion and Society in Wales, 1660-1730* (Cardiff: University of Wales Press, 1978), p.305.

[20] Erasmus Saunders, *A View of the State of Religion in the Diocese of St David's about the Beginning of the 18th Century* (London: 1721), p.14.

[21] *Ibid.*, p.15.   [22] *Ibid.*, p.17.

[23] *Ibid.*, p.23.   [24] *Ibid.*, p.24.

[25] *Ibid.*, p.38. This is not in fact a quotation, although the words within the quotation marks convey accurately the gist of the original text.

[26] *Ibid.*, p.58.   [27] *Ibid.*, p.60.

[28] *Ibid.*, p.35.

[29] *Trysorfa Ysbrydol* is the correct title. John Evans's reminiscences have recently been published in Goronwy Prys Owen, ed., *Atgofion John Evans y Bala: Y Diwygiad Methodistaidd ym Meirionnydd a Môn* (Caernarfon: Gwasg Pantycelyn, 1997), 158pp.

[30] T. Rees, *Protestant Nonconformity*, p.305.

[31] Ioan Thomas, *Rhad Ras* (Abertawe: 1810), p.27. This work was republished, ed. J. Dyfnallt Owen, by the University of Wales Press in 1949 with different pagination.

[32] There is no mention of either Colwinstone or the Vale of Glamorgan in the original.

[33] Ioan Thomas, *Rhad Ras*, p.67.

[34] The place named in the original is Ffrwddog, near Crickhowell.

[35] Ioan Thomas, *Rhad Ras*, p.64.

[36] *Ibid.*, p.71.   [37] *Ibid.*, p.65.

[38] The reports were actually published from 1740 to 1761. While it would be unjust to accuse Griffith Jones of exaggeration in his reports, it should be borne in mind that he tended to dwell on some of the darker aspects of religious life in Wales in order to gain the sympathy and support of Christians in England.

[39] Griffith Jones, *Welch Piety, or, a Collection of the Several Accounts of the Circulating Welch Charity Schools*, 1745-46, p.12.

[40] *Ibid.*, 1748-9, p.5.   [41] *Ibid.*, 1751-2, pp.16-17.

[42] Richard Davies, *An Account of the Convincement, Exercises, Services, and Travels of . . . Richard Davies* (1710; fifth edition, London: 1794), p.42.

[43] T. Rees, *Protestant Nonconformity*, pp.286-291.

[44] Ioan Thomas, *Rhad Ras*, pp.85-86.

[45] *Ibid.*, pp.86, 88.

CHAPTER II

Howel Harris—Daniel Rowland—Howel Davies.

NEARLY one hundred and fifty years ago, on Lord's Day the 30th of March 1735, which was the Sabbath before Easter, in the parish church of Talgarth, in the county of Brecon, South Wales, the officiating clergyman, whose name we have not the happiness to know,[1] gave notice to his hearers of his intention to celebrate the Lord's Supper on the Sabbath next following. Seeing his people negligent to come to the Holy Communion, he read the "Exhortation" which has been appointed to be read under such circumstances. In that Exhortation some of the excuses which men are apt to make for not coming to the Lord's Table are stated and replied to. But the good clergyman, in the earnestness of his soul, enlarged upon the form before him. "You plead your unfitness," said he, "to come to the Holy Communion. Let me tell you, that if you are not fit to come to the Lord's Supper, you are not fit to come to church, you are not fit to live, you are not fit to die." There was in the congregation a young man, a native of the parish, who was at the time about twenty-one years of age, and who was so affected by these earnest words, that he at once resolved to place himself among the communicants on the following Sabbath. That young man was Howel Harris, who, on many accounts, may be regarded as foremost among the fathers and founders of Welsh Calvinistic Methodism. He began forthwith to prepare himself for the holy rite. On his way home, he called upon a neighbour with whom he had a quarrel, and made peace with him. During the week he kept himself from his usual sins, and from such vanities as he considered to be inconsistent with a religious life. The following Sabbath came, and he appeared at church, feeling thoroughly satisfied with himself and with the life which he had led for a whole week. He considered himself, in fact, to be a very good young man. But while kneeling before the altar, and repeating after the clergyman the following words of confession, "We acknowledge and bewail our manifold sins and wickedness, which we, from time to time, most grievously have committed, by thought, word, and deed, against Thy Divine Majesty, provoking most justly Thy wrath and indignation against us. We do earnestly repent, and are heartily sorry for these our misdoings; the remembrance of them is grievous unto us; the burden of them is intolerable," there suddenly flashed upon his mind the conviction that he was speaking falsehood in the presence of God. It was not grievous to him to remember his sins, nor did he feel them to be any burden at all. The sudden terror that came upon him had well-nigh compelled him to turn away, when there came to his aid the remembrance that he had sincerely resolved to amend his ways, and so, trusting in himself still, he for the first time in his life partook of the Lord's Supper.

The weeks that followed were weeks of earnest conflict. He endeavoured to keep his "heart and thoughts fixed on God;" but it was all in vain, as might have been expected, for he was attempting to make the fruit good while the tree was evil. On the 20th of April, a "Book on the Commandments, written by Bryan Duppa," was put into his hands. This he read; and the more he read, the more he saw the breadth of God's law and his own sinfulness before Him. He was constrained to flee from himself, and his own amended life and good works, to Christ to seek salvation. And he found it. When he came to the Lord's Supper on the following Whit-Sunday, the confession which in his mouth had been false seven weeks before was now true. The remembrance of his sins was indeed grievous unto him now, and the burden of them was intolerable; but he was enabled to believe on the Lord Jesus Christ, and in Him he found rest to his soul.

The following November his friends sent him to Oxford, "to cure him of his fanaticism." But it was of no avail. There he found pleasure in nothing but private prayer and the public means of grace. The immorality and ungodliness which he daily witnessed vexed his soul. The prospect of worldly advancement which a University education opened before him he did not regard as worth a thought, and earnestly did he pray God to deliver him from that unhappy place. At the close of the term he left for home, fully resolved not to return again to Oxford.[2]

In a short time after his return from the University he began to go about from house to house to warn and exhort his neighbours, not only in his native place, but likewise in the surrounding parishes.[3] He thus began to preach without the remotest idea that he was doing anything of the kind. He felt that his neighbours were in danger, and all that he did was to warn them of the alarming fact, and earnestly urge them without loss of time to seek salvation; and not satisfied with speaking thus to those whom he casually met, he called upon them that he might speak to them at their homes. He opened a day-school at the neighbouring village of Trefeca, and availed himself of that opportunity to speak to the children and young people who came together to be taught. At the time there was a man who went about the villages holding classes to teach psalm-singing, and Harris followed him about from place to place, that he might talk to the young people who assembled on these occasions about the salvation of their souls. By-and-by people began to assemble in great numbers at the houses which he visited, to hear him speak. Family gatherings became congregations, and these congregations became so large that there was not a place in the neighbourhood sufficiently commodious to contain them. His speaking was accompanied by great power. God gave testimony to the word of His grace. Many confessed their sins, earnestly prayed for forgiveness, made peace with each other, and forsook their wicked ways. Family worship was established in many houses, the churches of the neighbourhood were crowded, and great numbers sought admission to the Lord's Table. Thus began that mighty preaching that roused Wales from the sleep of ages, and thus was commenced the great Welsh Methodist revival.

But simultaneously with this, and quite independently of it, there was another beginning in the adjoining county of Cardigan. About forty miles, "as the crow flies" from Talgarth, in a north-westerly direction, and separated from it by ranges of wild trackless mountains, is the little village of Llangeitho. It lies in a somewhat narrow valley, on the banks of the little river Aeron. The officiating clergyman in the parish church of this place, at the time of which we write, was the Rev. Daniel Rowland, a young man of twenty-two years of age. He was the son of the former vicar of the parish, but his elder brother, the Rev. John Rowland, held the living now, and Daniel was his curate. He had been permitted to take Orders one year before the usual age, "in consideration of his superior scholarship." From the beginning he was a man of mark. He excelled in reading the Lessons, *and* in athletic sports. He spent a part of the Sunday morning in the former exercise, and a greater part of the afternoon of the day in the latter. He did both well; the great difference was that the latter had more of his heart. He did the one, for such was his duty; and joined the young men of the parish in the other, because he liked it. He had an idea, however, of becoming a popular preacher. There was a man in the neighbourhood who stole the people. This was the Rev. Philip Pugh, pastor of the Independent church at Llwynpiod, one of the very few dissenting ministers then in Wales who were able to gather together a considerable congregation. Rowland wanted to know the secret of the dissenter's popularity, and in thinking the matter over, he came to the conclusion that it was because he "thundered." Thought he, "I will thunder, too, and see the effect;" and he did so most awfully. He chose for his texts such passages as the following: "The wicked shall be turned into hell;" "And these shall go away into everlasting punishment;" "For the great day of His wrath is come, and who shall be able to stand?" His sermons were in character with such texts as these. He spoke of the sinner's miserable condition, of death, judgment, and everlasting torments, with such eloquence and power that the church soon became crowded with attentive and awe-struck listeners; and it has been said that above a hundred of the congregation were under deep impressions before the preacher himself began to think seriously at all.[4]

But his time came to be brought to a personal knowledge of the truths which he so effectually preached; and it happened thus. For more than twenty years before the occurrences which we have just narrated, there lived and laboured in the parish of Llanddowror, Carmarthenshire, an eminently able and devoted clergyman, the Rev. Griffith Jones, who has been designated by some "the Apostle of Wales," and by others "the Morning Star of the Methodist Revival." Both appellations are amply justified by the history of his laborious and eminently useful life. Mr. Jones was in the habit of administering the Lord's Supper monthly in his church, and assembled as many of his parishioners as were willing to attend on the Saturday preceding the Communion Sabbath, when, in addition to reading the Church Service, he catechised those who were present in the leading truths of the Christian religion. He was distressed by the ignorance manifested by his catechumens, and he traced that ignorance to their inability to read the Word of God. This led him to conceive the idea of establishing those "circulating charity schools," which proved such a blessing to Wales, and which have immortalised his name. Their sole object was to enable the people to read the Holy Scriptures. As far as it was practicable, pious men were employed as teachers, and the plan was for each master to remain at a particular place until he had taught a number of people to read, and then to shift his quarters to some other district. Hence they were called "*circulating* schools." There were 215 of these schools in operation the year before Mr. Jones's death—128 in South Wales, and 87 in the north; and it has been ascertained that as many as 150,212 men, women, and children, between the ages of six years and seventy, were in the course of twenty-four years taught by their means to read the Bible in the Welsh language.[5] In addition to the inability to read that was then so general in Wales, there was a great scarcity of reading material. Mr. Jones did much to supply this want by bringing out a number of good books, as well as by procuring several editions of the Bible in the language of the Principality. He was efficiently aided in these undertakings by the "Society for Promoting Christian Knowledge."

Mr. Jones was in the habit of making occasional excursions to various parts of the Principality to visit his schools, and to preach in their behalf in such churches as were open to him. Wherever he preached, great crowds came together to hear, for he was a mighty preacher as well as a great educationalist. On one of these occasions he came to Llanddewi Brefi, a place about five miles from Llangeitho. When he had commenced his sermon, he noticed standing opposite him in the crowd a young man of a proud and haughty bearing. His countenance appeared to him to wear a scorning aspect, though his dress indicated that he was a clergyman. He at once lifted up his heart to heaven in prayer in his behalf, entreating that that service might be the means of converting his heart to God, and that He might make him the instrument of saving many souls. That prayer was abundantly answered. The young man was no other than Daniel Rowland of Llangeitho, and he went home "a new creature."[6] If he had " thundered" before, he did so now with far more earnestness, and therefore with greater effect. That which he spoke now was not that which he had seen or heard only, but that which he had likewise felt in the depths of his own heart. His fame spread abroad, and he was invited to preach in other counties. He travelled through the country "thundering" until the multitudes trembled in his presence, and shouted and shrieked as if they felt themselves to be on the very verge of perdition.

But while this was the means of awakening the multitudes, there was something else necessary to save them. They were deeply wounded, but left without the balm that heals. Rowland made known to them their lost state, but said little or nothing of the saving mercy of our Lord and Redeemer Jesus Christ and the riches of His grace. That excellent Nonconformist minister to whom we have already alluded—the Rev. Philip Pugh—saw this deficiency in the ministry of his zealous young neighbour, and was kind enough to teach him the way of God more perfectly. "Preach the gospel to the people, my dear sir," said he; "apply the balm that is in Gilead to their wounded spirits, and show their need of faith in the crucified Redeemer." "I fear," said the young minister, "that I do not really possess that faith myself." "Preach it," was the reply,—"preach it until you feel it. It will come without fail. If you go on preaching the law after this fashion, you will kill half the population, for you thunder those awful curses in such a terrible manner that it is impossible for any man to stand before you." Mr. Pugh had sufficient liberality thus to advise an Episcopal clergyman, and the clergyman was sufficiently humble thankfully to receive the word of exhortation from a dissenter.

From this time there was a great and happy change in the tone of Rowland's ministry; now it was as full of gospel as it had been before of law. It became as remarkable for its sweetness as it had been for its terrors, and as effectual to comfort as it had been to alarm. When he proclaimed free forgiveness through the sufferings and death of the Saviour of the world, sinners ready to perish felt that there was hope even for them. In realising that hope, they rejoiced with joy unspeakable and full of glory, and great numbers expressed their ecstatic joy in shouts of praise. The deep wailings and despairing sighs and groans of a few weeks past were now replaced by glad shouts of "Hallelujah!" "Gogoniant!" "Diolch iddo byth!" We are more than half disposed to leave the last two exclamations untranslated, for in the mouth of the Welsh worshipper, when carried away with the mighty stream of his emotions, they mean very much more than the English reader can conceive by being told that the words which stand for them in his language are "Glory," "Thanks unto Him for ever." At this time there began at Llangeitho Church those "rejoicings" which have ever since, and especially on occasions of revival, more or less characterised the worship of Welsh Methodists.

Mention is made of one notable Sabbath morning at Llangeitho, when there came a great tide, carrying all before it. The clergyman was reading the Litany, and as he read on his own soul was filled with strong emotion. When he came to the words, "By Thine Agony and bloody Sweat; by Thy Cross and Passion; by Thy precious Death and Burial; by Thy glorious Resurrection and Ascension; and by the coming of the Holy Ghost," an overwhelming feeling passed through the great multitude. Many fell on the floor of the church, while others shouted through their tears the appointed response, "Good Lord, deliver us." It is but a very faint idea we can give the reader of the character of Daniel Rowland's preaching. We have before us a small (Welsh) volume of his published sermons. There are in it many passages of great power, and which could not, when spoken by him, otherwise than produce mighty effects. He is preaching from Romans viii. 28: "And we know that all things work together for good to them that love God."

"Seeming evils," he says, "are blessings. Their trials and afflictions work together for their good. The cross is the path to the crown. It is through much tribulation that we must enter the kingdom of God. 'Thou broughtest us into the net; Thou laidst affliction upon our loins. Thou hast caused men to ride over our heads; we went through fire and through water; but Thou broughtest us out into a wealthy place.' Conflict *is* the way to victory. Their falling into the net was their path to liberty. The boast of the foe was the dawn of their deliverance. Hark! The enemies say, 'They are *in* the net. Our feet are *upon* their necks. If *this* is the way to life, they shall be long enough before they reach it.' But what comes next? 'Thou broughtest us out into a wealthy place.'"[7] The preacher speaks like a foe. The glance of his eye, the whole expression of his countenance, and the tones of his voice are those of the bitter enemy. The people are conscious that there is pending a terrific conflict, upon the issue of which hangs their everlasting destiny, and they are beginning seriously to fear that the day is lost; when suddenly, and quite in a different tone, there comes the triumphant shout, "Thou broughtest us out into a wealthy place." It is echoed by a hundred shouts of praise from the great congregation, and it is some time before the people are sufficiently calm to allow the preacher to proceed. But this is only one wave. There comes another, and after that another yet, and so on to the end of the sermon. And sometimes the end was very long before it came. On one Sabbath morning Mr. Rowland was preaching, and the people hanging on his lips all unconscious of the flight of time, until a ray of light coming in through the western window of the church made them aware of the fact that the sun was about to set.[8] Such was the beginning of the Welsh Methodist revival at Llangeitho.

There was yet another beginning which does not seem to have had any connection with either of the wondrous events which we have just narrated. The Rev. Griffith Jones, already mentioned, besides all his other labours, devoted a part of his time to the instruction of youth. There was among his pupils a Mr. Howel Davies, a young man of good parts, and of a serious turn of mind. Mr. Jones's ministry was blessed to his conversion,[9] and he resolved to devote himself to the ministry of the gospel, and was accordingly ordained to the curacy of Llys-y-frân, in Pembrokeshire. On the Sabbath on which he was ordained, Mr. Jones desired the congregation at Llanddowror church to unite with him in earnest prayer for their young friend who was that day entering upon the work of the ministry. It soon appeared that these prayers were heard in heaven. Mr. Davies's ministry was with great power, and multitudes came together to hear him, and were blessed; but there were influential parishioners who could not endure that which was spoken, and by their means he was dismissed from Llys-y-frân.

After this he travelled the country preaching in churches or out of them as opportunity offered, and the Lord blessed his ministry to the salvation of a great many souls. When he administered the Lord's Supper, it often happened that the churches were too small to contain half the communicants. On those occasions great crowds stood outside waiting their turn, and the church had to be filled two or three times before all had partaken. The reader will not consider this at all strange, when we have added that those sanctuaries were comparatively small, and that Mr. Davies had at one time more than 2,000 communicants in the county of Pembroke.

Thus by means of these three young men, Howel Harris, Daniel Rowland, and Howel Davies, was the great work begun. In three different counties there sprang up simultaneously three distinct streams of the water of life, the confluence of which formed that mighty river which watered the whole of the Principality, and made it blossom as the garden of the Lord.

NOTES

1. His name was Pryce Davies.

2. Harris spent not a term but only a week at Oxford. Richard Bennett, *Howell Harris and the Dawn of Revival* (Bridgend, Evangelical Press of Wales, 1987), pp. 36-39.

3. Harris had in fact begun 'exhorting', that is, reading from a book and applying its message to the hearts of his hearers, before going to Oxford. *Ibid*, pp.31, 42-43.

4. In all probability it was *after* rather than before his conversion that Rowland 'thundered'. Eifion Evans, *Daniel Rowland*, pp.39-43; cf. p.57 in the present volume.

5. The number who actually learned to read cannot be ascertained quite as exactly as the text suggests. During Griffith Jones's life-time a total of 153,835 people were recorded as having attended his schools, but he himself acknowledged that two or three times as many as the numbers on the registers were taught at night. Perhaps totals of some 300,000 pupils and 200,000 actual readers would be nearer the mark, at a time when the population of Wales was around 400,000. Gwyn Davies, *Griffith Jones, Llanddowror: Athro Cenedl* (Pen-y-bont ar Ogwr, Gwasg Efengylaidd Cymru, 1984), pp.46-47.

6. A different version of the story is given in Eifion Evans, *Daniel Rowland*, pp.33-34.

7. Owen Jones, *Casgliad o Bregethau a Hymnau y Diweddar Barch. Daniel Rowland* (Dowlais, 1864), pp.61-62.

8. This story has an apocryphal ring about it. There is no mention of it in Eifion Evans's standard biography.

9. Howel Davies was converted through Howel Harris, not Griffith Jones, but he subsequently served as curate to Griffith Jones. Bennett, *Howell Harris*, pp. 128-9.

CHAPTER III

AMONG the earliest and most important results of the
ministry of these young men must be placed the
conversion of several who became efficient fellow-labourers
with them in the great work which they had undertaken.
One or two of these were so eminent, and took such a
prominent part in the Methodist movement, that they are
placed by common consent among the fathers and founders
of the Connexion. Howel Harris was in the habit of
attending the parish church at Talgarth on Sabbath morning.
At the close of the service he usually went out and stood on
a tombstone, or on the wall of the churchyard, to address
the dispersing congregation. On one of those occasions there
stood among his audience a young medical student from
Carmarthenshire, who was at the time pursuing his studies
at the neighbouring town of Hay.[1] The words to which he
then listened were blessed to his conversion, and he
eventually resolved to relinquish his medical studies and
to devote himself to the ministry of the gospel. This young
man became one of the mightiest instruments of the revival.
He afterwards became known as the Rev. William Williams
of Pantycelyn, eminent as a minister of the gospel, but more
eminent still as the sacred poet of Wales. Very often in those
early days was the smouldering fire which had been kindled
by the sermon fanned into a flame by a hymn of W.
Williams's which was sung at the close. It is not too much

to say that his Welsh hymns have never been approached by the productions of any other writer in the language; and now that every denomination has its own hymn-book, the great majority in each selection, including that of the Establishment, are the hymns of W. Williams, Pantycelyn. He also wrote some English hymns, several of which, such as "Guide me, O thou great Jehovah," and "O'er those gloomy hills of darkness," are found in very many selections in that language.[2]

Mr. Williams took Deacon's Orders in the Establishment in 1740, but his Church career was a short one. In his first curacy he gave so much offence that a representation was made to the Bishop, containing no less than nineteen charges against him.[3] One of these was, that he did not use the sign of the cross in baptism; another, that he omitted some portions of the service; and another, that he did not confine his ministrations to the church, but went out to the highways and hedges and preached wherever he could get the people to hear him. We have not been able to ascertain what were the other sixteen, but it is reasonable to infer that they looked in the same direction as the above three. When he came to the Bishop for his Priest's Orders he was peremptorily refused, and he therefore withdrew from the Establishment and gave himself to work among the Methodists.

A somewhat later accession was that of the Rev. Peter Williams, a native of Laugharne in the county of Carmarthen.[4] He was from his early childhood of a serious turn of mind, and was educated for the ministry. While he was a student at Carmarthen College,[5] the renowned George Whitefield came to preach to the town, and so full of prejudice was the tutor against the "fanatical preacher," that he gave strict orders that none of the students should go to hear him. Four young men ventured to disobey this injunction, and one of these was Peter Williams. The sermon so deeply affected him, that he lost all taste for his former amusements, and became so earnestly religious that he was thenceforth regarded by his tutor and fellow-students as a "Methodist." "And in their opinion," he writes, "that was sufficient to cover me with eternal disgrace." He afterwards took Orders in the Church, and served several curacies for exceedingly brief periods—for his earnest ministry gave such universal dissatisfaction, that he likewise was obliged to withdraw, and fully identify himself with those despised people whose spirit he had already so largely imbibed. These two young men, W. Williams and P. Williams, though they came a few years later on the scene than the three mentioned in the preceding chapter, are always associated with them as the reformers of Wales and the founders of Welsh Calvinistic Methodism.

They were all young men, and so were Whitefield and his colleagues, by whose instrumentality the Lord was, at the same time, carrying on a great work in England. The labourers in the Principality knew little of that which was done by their brethren on the other side of the Severn, but by some means reports of the former reached the ears of the latter, and, in 1738, Howel Harris, to his great delight, received the following encouraging letter from George Whitefield:—

"LONDON, *Dec.* 20*th*, 1738.

"MY DEAR BROTHER,—Though I am unknown to you in person, yet I have long been united to you in spirit; and have been rejoiced to hear how the good pleasure of the Lord prospered in your hands. Go on, my dear brother, go on, be strong in the Lord and in the power of His might, and the Spirit of Christ and of glory shall rest upon you, and effectually; which has and still is opening doors before you for preaching the everlasting Gospel. There have been, and will be, many adversaries; yet be not afraid, He that sent you will assist, comfort, and protect you, and make you more than conqueror, through His great love. I am a living monument of this truth; for the Divine strength has often been magnified in my weakness. I have tasted that the Lord is gracious, I have felt His power, and from my own experience can say, that in doing or suffering the will of Jesus Christ, there is great reward. Blessed be His holy Name, there seems to be a great pouring out of the Spirit at London; and we walk in the comfort of the Holy Ghost and are edified. You see, my dear Brother, the freedom I have taken in writing to you; if you would favour me with a line or two by way of answer, you would greatly rejoice both me and many others; why should we not tell one another what God has done for our souls? My dear Brother, I love you in the bowels of Jesus Christ, and wish you may be the spiritual father of thousands, and shine as the sun in the firmament, in the kingdom of your heavenly Father. My hearty love to Mr. Jones.[6] Oh how shall I joy to meet you at the judgment-seat of Christ! How you would honour me, if you would send a line to, dear Brother,

"Your affectionate though

"unworthy Brother in Christ

G. W."[7]

The following is Howel Harris's reply.

"GLAMORGAN, *Jan.* 8*th*, 1739.

"DEAR BROTHER,—I was most agreeably surprised, last night, by a letter from you of the 20th past, the character you bear, the spirit that I see and feel in your work, and the close union of my soul and spirit to yours, will not allow me to use any apology in my return to you. Though this is the first time of our correspondence, yet, I can assure you, I am no stranger to you. When I first heard of you and your labours and success, my soul was united to you, and engaged to send addresses to heaven on your behalf. When I read your Diary, I had some uncommon influence of the Divine presence shining on my poor soul almost continually. And my soul was in an uncommon manner drawn out on your account; but I little thought our good Lord and Master intended I should ever see your handwriting. I hope we shall be taught more and more to admire the wonderful goodness of God in His acts of free grace; sure no person is under such obligations to advance the glory of His free goodness and grace as this poor prodigal. But, alas, how little sense have I in my soul of all His wonderful blessings! Pray for me, that I may find my heart more drawn out in love and praise to Him. Oh, how ravishing is it to hear of such demonstrations of the divine love and favour to *London;* and, to make your joy greater still, I have some more good news to send you from *Wales.* There is a great revival in Cardiganshire, through one Mr. D. Rowland, a church clergyman; and he has been much owned and blessed in Carmarthenshire also. We have also a sweet prospect in Breconshire, and part of Monmouthshire; and in this county where I am now the revival prospers; there is also here a young dissenting minister of much use, who also is a man of universal charity. There is such another in Montgomeryshire. I have been twice there, and there seems to be some shining beams of the gospel of grace. There are two or three young curates in Glamorganshire (where now I am) that are well-wishers to religion; and we have one exceeding sweet and valuable man with us in Breconshire; but enemies are many and powerful; therefore I beg the help of your prayers, and the prayers of all your brethren, that God would stand up for His cause and interest against all His visible and invisible enemies.

"I hint this in general, as I could not testify my love any way more agreeable to your soul than to let you know how the interest of our good, gracious, and dear Saviour, Jesus Christ, prospers hereabouts. Oh! that I had more love in my soul, more humble zeal and spiritual boldness. Surely I should blush to think the name of such an ignorant, negligent, and unprofitable servant should reach your ears. I rejoice on the one side and fear on the other, by reason of the relics of self, pride, etc., which I find are not quite dead within. I would bless God that inclined you to write to me, and especially for making your letter so savoury to my fainting soul. Oh! that we could do more for so loving a Master, that His very enemies, by seeing our innocent behaviour and fruitfulness and love, etc., may be brought to glorify the Redeemer and to think well of His ways, etc. I am in a great hurry, as I am called away to discourse now quickly, yet I could not drop this opportunity without obliging you, and were you to come to Wales, I hope it would not be labour in vain; but I leave this to Him that knows best how to dispose of us. I hope the faithful account I have given you of the benefit I have received from you will excite you to send again a line to him that would be sincerely

  "Yours in Christ Jesus

     H. H."

Before the expiration of that year the two met for the first time at Cardiff in Glamorganshire. When the Welsh brethren were making preliminary arrangements for their first "Association," which in Wales means the same thing as a "General Assembly" in Scotland, it was resolved to invite the Rev. G. Whitefield to attend. He acceded to the invitation, and presided at the meetings of the Assembly. This first Association of Welsh Calvinistic Methodists was held at Watford, in the county of Glamorgan, in the year 1742.[8] Besides the chairman, there were present Daniel Rowland, Howel Harris, W. Williams, J. Powell, and other preachers and exhorters. They were met to devise means to bring the numerous converts which had been already made under some spiritual supervision, and to concert measures for the further extension of the great work; and it is worthy of remark that, all the leading spirits of this important assembly were young men varying from twenty-one to twenty-nine years of age.[9]

Of the tremendous power of their ministry it is difficult

now to form an adequate conception. Howel Harris was a veritable Boanerges.[10] We can judge from his portrait that he was a person of most commanding presence. The owner of those flashing eyes and firmly set mouth was not a man to be trifled with. It was not seldom that thousands in his presence experienced much the same sensations as the assembly of Israel at the foot of Sinai. Often were giants in iniquity, who had come for the express purpose of disturbing the services, made to quail before his fiery glance, or driven home trembling in every limb after listening for a few minutes to the thunder of his voice. A congregation of 2,000 people have been known to stand for upwards of two hours in a drenching rain to hear him preach. It is said that during the first few years of his ministry there was scarcely one instance of his preaching without being the means of bringing a number under conviction. For some time he confined his ministry to his own neighbourhood. He was afterwards invited to visit other counties, and soon he extended his travels into North Wales, everywhere lifting his voice like a trumpet against the prevailing irreligion and sin, and apprising the crowds that assembled to hear him of their impending doom. Everywhere he found the people like those of old who dwelt in the land of Zabulon and the land of Nephthalim, by the way of the sea, beyond Jordan, Galilee of the Gentiles, sitting in darkness and in the region and shadow of death; but it was a most unusual thing for him to leave a town, village, or hamlet without leaving behind him the nucleus of a religious community. His indomitable spirit triumphed over the rough usage to which he was exposed by his burning zeal for his Master's glory and the salvation of immortal souls. And his sufferings were neither light nor few. On several occasions, he, like another apostle, was pressed out of measure, above strength, insomuch that he despaired even of life when in the hands of an infuriated mob; but after barely escaping alive, with torn raiment and a bruised and bleeding body, he would again fearlessly face the storm. He went to fairs, wakes, and revels to preach the gospel, thus invading the kingdom of darkness, and attacking sin on its own territories. The gentry regarded him as a disturber of the peace, and threatened him with legal proceedings. The clergy looked upon him as a false prophet, and however badly off they might be for sermons, were never at a loss for a text when he was in the neighbourhood. The mob regarded him as a defenceless individual whom they could have the inexpressible delight of belabouring with impunity to their hearts' content—and they often did so without mercy. But it was useless to attempt by any such means to arrest him in his mighty career. Often while he was addressing an assembly in the open air did a magistrate appear on the scene, commanding the crowd to disperse, and enforcing his orders with the reading of the Riot Act. Harris would reply to the magnate by reading the sentence pronounced by the Judge of all upon his own guilty soul. When the rabble hooted him, his voice was heard above their loudest howls, telling them of judgment to come. When dragged about and beaten by a mob maddened by drink and by devils, he preached between the blows, and urged his savage assailants to hasten their escape from the stormy wind and tempest. Such is a faint picture of this extraordinary man. He believed and therefore spoke, and with such power and effect that many thousands in the Principality of Wales were turned to righteousness.

Rowland was by far the greater preacher. Harris never *made* a sermon. He made it a point to abstain from formal premeditation, but spoke as he was moved and enabled at the time. Rowland, on the contrary, carefully prepared, and his published sermons are full of matter, and of matter forcibly and eloquently arranged. He possessed extraordinary powers of mind, and was a speaker of unsurpassed eloquence; but after all, the secret of his tremendous power must be sought for in the depth and intensity of his own religious convictions. On Sabbath mornings he generally rose early, and as much as possible avoided conversation, even with his most intimate friends; but on some occasions, when his studies had been unsuccessful, it was difficult to get him out of his bed in time for the service. He was then "unwell, could not preach without any message from God to the people." Sometimes his servant had to help him in a half-fainting condition from his house to the pulpit, but once there he was at home; and it has been observed that it was on such occasions he usually preached with the greatest power. The people could see that he intensely felt all that he said. Once in his prayer before sermon, while dwelling on the sufferings of the Saviour for us, he seemed to have Him before his eye, and exclaimed, "Oh, those emptied veins! Oh, that pallid countenance!" and then, overwhelmed by emotion, he fainted away. After a while he recovered, and mighty indeed was the sermon that followed.

Howel Harris's ministry for many years was wholly itinerant, but Rowland, having a regular charge, confined his labours chiefly to Llangeitho, though he made occasional evangelistic tours to other districts, and from time to time visited every part of the Principality. But his ministry at Llangeitho alone exerted a mighty influence far and wide, for it soon began to attract hearers from the most distant parts of Wales. It was by no means an uncommon thing to see as many as thirty of the people of Bala, which is above sixty miles distant from Llangeitho, among his congregation on Sabbath morning. Those people started early on Saturday morning, each taking with him the provision necessary for the journey. There were well-known halting-places on the road,—on the banks of streams, from which they could moisten their morsel, and there they sat and refreshed themselves. They travelled far into the night, got a few hours' rest in such places as they could find, started again with the early dawn, and were right glad if they could reach Llangeitho in time for the morning service. On their pilgrimage homewards they had something to talk of—the sermons to which they had listened on the preceding day; and often was the resting-place by the brook a veritable Bethel, and echoed the sounds of joy and praise.

On one occasion forty-five people from Caernarfon went towards Llangeitho by sea as far as Aberystwyth, where they left the ship, intending to return in the same manner. But by Monday the wind had shifted, and they were obliged to walk the whole distance, which could not be much short of a hundred miles. On their journey homewards their large number created quite a sensation in the towns and villages through which they passed. At Aberdyfi they were recognised as "Methodists," and hooted well as they passed. At Tywyn, the population came out to meet them, and attempted to prevent them from passing through the place. At Barmouth, which they reached against night, in a pelting storm, some of them found accommodation in the town, while others were lodged in farm-houses farther on. One house in the town, at which they had been angrily refused, took fire; and was completely destroyed before the morning. Resuming their journey next day, they had to pass through Harlech, and here the people rose *en masse* to stone them. Some were struck in their heads and badly wounded; and one man was so injured by a blow on his foot that he was lame for weeks. This incident will give an idea of the burning zeal of the early Methodists, and of the inveterate hatred with which they were regarded by the great mass of the people.

A large number of the early converts being men of some talent, felt it to be their duty to preach unto others that gospel which they had found so precious themselves. They were for the most part men of little education, who scarcely knew anything of any book in existence, but the Welsh Bible; but they preached wherever they could find an opening, and were known and recognised, not as ministers, but as "exhorters." Numbers of these, from every part of Wales, congregated at Llangeitho on the monthly Sabbath. The effect of this periodical contact with the ministry of Rowland was most beneficial to themselves, and by their means his ministry told on the whole of the Principality. They caught the fire themselves, and, like Samson's foxes, spread it throughout the length and breadth of the land. The others whom we have named were young men of precisely the same spirit with Harris and Rowland. It is not strange, therefore, that their labours produced great results. In 1742, seven years from the beginning of the movement, we find that there were labouring in conjunction with the episcopally ordained clergy, who by this time had become ten in number, as many as forty exhorters. We have no more statistics of that date, but we find that by 1744, two years later, there had been formed, in South Wales alone, 140 "Societies," which in process of time came to be designated "Churches."

The following extract from the diary of Mr. Joseph Williams, of Kidderminster, appeared in the *Evangelical Magazine* for November 1814:—

"*June 28th,* 1746.—I have been this week at an Association at Trefeca, in Wales. We assembled for religious worship in a barn near Mr. Howel Harris's. There were present three clergymen, viz., Mr. Daniel Rowland, Mr. Howel Davies, and Mr. Williams, and about twenty exhorters, one of whom, Mr. Richard, preached and prayed in Welsh. It was somewhat painful to be present two hours in a religious service, of which I could understand nothing, while the preacher proceeded with the greatest fluency and marks of the most raised affections; but it was pleasing to observe in the countenances of the assembly how he bowed, or rather the Spirit of God, bowed their hearts as one man, and what heavenly smiles would in an instant overspread the faces of hundreds from time to time, while he was discoursing to them on these words, 'Father, I will that they also whom Thou hast given Me be with Me,' etc. (John xvii. 24). Mr. Howel Davies afterwards prayed, and then preached in English from Josh. i. 9, 'Have not I commanded thee? be strong,' etc. It was a sweet opportunity, though it scarcely seemed equally affecting to the audience, with what had gone before. Afterwards I dined with the clergymen and several of the exhorters; but oh! what a spirit of love to Christ and love to one another did they discover! I could not but think it had never been remarked with more propriety in primitive times, "See how these Christians love one another!" I learned from them that the Lord had remarkably raised up the Rev. Mr. Rowland in Cardiganshire, and Mr. Howel Harris in Breconshire, at one and the same time with Mr. Whitefield and the Wesleys, and all independent of each other, and had wonderfully owned their endeavours and spread their influence over the greatest part of Wales, and all in the space of eleven years from the first beginning of it, so that in the Principality of Wales about six or seven clergymen, forty exhorters, and one hundred and forty religious societies were now preaching and receiving the pure Gospel of Christ; that they had met with great opposition and much persecution, but all had contributed to the furtherance of the Gospel; so that now they seemed to bear down opposition by their numbers; and Mr. Rowland, who holds two livings, and preaches at two churches every Lord's Day, and at two chapels on weekdays, could tell me that he had 3,000 communicants; and Mr. Davies told me that he had 2,000 in Pembrokeshire, so mightily hath the Word of God grown and prevailed there! Shall not I rejoice in these triumphs of the cross of Christ? But I shall see greater things than these."

NOTES

[1] He was a student at the Nonconformist academy of Llwyn-llwyd, situated between Three Cocks and Hay, but may actually have been pursuing his studies at a branch of this academy at Chancefield, near Talgarth. G.M. Roberts, *Y Pêr Ganiedydd*, I, pp.24-34.

[2] The first verse of 'Guide me, O thou great Jehovah' was in fact translated by Peter Williams from William Williams's original Welsh hymn. Idem, *Bywyd a Gwaith Peter Williams* (Caerdydd: Gwasg Prifysgol Cymru, 1943), pp.184-5.

[3] There were seven, not nineteen, charges against Williams, all of which were strongly rebutted by him. Idem, *Y Pêr Ganiedydd*, I, pp.58-64.

[4] Peter Williams was born not in Laugharne but in the adjacent parish of Llansadyrnin. Idem, *Peter Williams*, p.12.

[5] He was a student not at the College but at the Grammar School. *Ibid*, pp.14-16.

[6] Griffith Jones, Llanddowror.

[7] Slightly different versions of these letters are to be found in Arnold A. Dallimore, *George Whitefield*, I (London: Banner of Truth Trust, 1970), pp.233-5.

[8] The first Welsh Association was in fact held at Y Dugoedydd, Cil-y-cwm, near Llandovery, on 8 January 1742. The Watford Association was the first meeting at which both Welsh and English Methodists were represented, and was held on 5 January 1743, not 1742. Gomer M. Roberts, ed., *Hanes Methodistiaeth Galfinaidd Cymru. I: Y Deffroad Mawr* (Caernarfon: Llyfrfa'r Methodistiaid Calfinaidd, 1973), pp.172, 179, 442.

[9] John Powell, a Methodist clergyman in Monmouthshire, was slightly older than the others named; he was born in 1708. *The Dictionary of Welsh Biography* (London: Honourable Society of Cymmrodorion, 1959), p.774.

[10] 'Boanerges'—'sons of thunder'—is the title usually ascribed not to Harris but to Daniel Rowland. See pp.55, 57, and Williams Pantycelyn's elegy to Rowland.

CHAPTER IV

THE men whom God in His Providence raised to
inaugurate this great movement had no idea that the
steps which they felt it their duty to take would result in
the rise of a new denomination. They belonged to the
Establishment and had neither the intention nor the wish
to separate themselves from it. Their fellow-countrymen
were ignorant of the first principles of Christianity, and they
sought to enlighten them. They were indifferent to religion,
and they sought to rouse them from their deadly apathy.
They saw that a great work required to be done, felt
themselves impelled to attempt it, and entered upon it with
a fiery enthusiasm. They began by preaching to their
immediate neighbours, and the success of their efforts at
home encouraged them, while their sense of the wants of
their country impelled them to extend their labours to other
districts. Those who had the charge of religion had suffered
it to degenerate into superstition—a mere round of religious
rites heedlessly and hastily performed in the intervals of
self-indulgence, and exerting no influence at all over the
every-day life of the people. Those whose duty it was to
rebuke sin were themselves carried away by its mighty
flood. There were exceptions, but those were few and for
the most part feeble. It was to correct those evils that the
"Fathers of Methodism" addressed themselves with self-
sacrificing zeal and untiring perseverance. In going beyond

their own parishes, and intruding upon districts assigned to the care of others, they acted irregularly; but their apology is found in the fact that those others, almost without exception, neglected their solemn charge. They loved order, but they loved Christ and immortal souls more, and they sacrificed the lesser to the greater. They suffered not the laws of the Church to deter them from pursuing that course which was dictated to their consciences by the law of love.

Their ministry told upon thousands, and it was soon found necessary, for the benefit of those numerous converts, to form some kind of organisation. Accordingly, a "Society" was formed in each locality where a few disciples could be brought together, and each Society was placed under the care of an exhorter. A number of those Societies were grouped together into districts, and each district was placed under the care of an "overseer." But they regarded themselves, and the whole body that they thus formed and controlled, as belonging to the Church,[1] and were therefore careful in all the measures they took to avoid as far as possible giving offence to Church susceptibilities. In deference to this feeling, those who preached without episcopal ordination were not designated preachers but "exhorters." The communities of Christians that were gathered together in the various localities were not designated Churches, but "Societies." Those who were placed in charge of them were not "ministers," nor yet "pastors," but "overseers;" and the men who discharged the duties devolving upon the *deacons* of the present day were "*private* exhorters," and sometimes "stewards of Societies." The quarterly gatherings of the representatives of the whole body were not Synods, but "Associations." Eleven years[2] had passed away after the beginning of the movement before any place of worship was erected; and when it was found necessary to make a move in that direction, our cautious fathers seem to have been at a loss to determine by what name to call the building. To call it a chapel would clash with the Church, for there were numerous chapels belonging to the

Establishment; and to call it a "meeting-house" would savour of dissent, for the few dissenting places of worship that were then existing in Wales were called "meeting-houses." To avoid danger on either side, it was necessary to devise for it a name that was unknown to any existing ecclesiastical vocabulary. Accordingly, among the minutes of an Association held at Porth-y-rhyd, October 3rd, 1744, we have the following resolution: "Agreed that *a House for Religious Purposes* be erected at Llansawel."[3] This resolution was not carried into effect, for the first place of worship was not erected until three years after it was passed, and that not at Llansawel, but at Builth, in the county of Brecon.[4]

They continued for many years to communicate in the Church, but it appears from a resolution, passed at the first Association of the body, held at Watford, January 5th and 6th, 1742,[5] that some of the brethren felt serious scruples on that subject. It was then "resolved, That those brethren who feel an objection to receive the Communion in the Church, on account of the ungodliness of the ministers and of the other communicants, and object likewise to communicate with dissenters on account of their lukewarmness, be requested to continue to communicate in the Church until the Lord opens for them a clear way to leave its communion." At a subsequent Association held at the same place, October 3rd, 1744,[6] a charge was brought against one of the brethren who was an overseer, Thomas Williams by name, that he had spoken against Church vestments, and especially against the gown and cassock; but upon his explaining that he had never spoken against those things "in themselves," only against "the idolatrous regard in which they were held by some people," he was excused. They were persecuted, as we shall hereafter show, in the most merciless manner, only because they persisted in adhering to the Church. The Act of Toleration had been long in force, and gave ample protection to Nonconformists; but they endured persecution, they suffered fines and imprisonment, and all manner of bodily abuse, rather than avail themselves of the protection afforded by that Act,—for they were not willing to declare themselves "dissenters." At an Association held at Blaen-y-glyn, July 3rd, 1745, letters were read from Brother John Richard and Brother Richard Tibbott, in which they asked whether it would not be better for them to place themselves beyond the power of their persecutors by taking licences to preach, inasmuch as they were in imminent danger of being taken away by force and sent to the army if they ventured to public places to preach the Gospel. After some discussion, it was resolved, "That to take a licence to preach at the present time, or, on the other hand, to forsake the work, would be a dishonour to God; that it is the duty of those who are beyond the reach of danger (ordained clergymen, it is presumed) to go to the most public places, while others should go to less public localities, employing at the same time all legitimate means to secure their own safety, inasmuch as it is believed that this is a temporary trial, and one not to be regarded in the light of a 'persecution.'" It was likewise resolved, "That if the persecution became general, and the preaching of the gospel entirely forbidden, it would be necessary to appeal to the Government, and if that fails to the Bishops; and if our liberty be completely taken away from us, it will then be clear that we must secede." It would be easy to cite much more to the same effect, but the above will suffice to illustrate the extreme tenacity with which the early Methodists clung to the Establishment.

At the same time they found it necessary to organise. "Societies" were placed under the charge of "private exhorters and stewards." Over the different districts some of the "public exhorters" were placed in charge, and in that case they were "overseers." Over those overseers every district had its moderator, while over all there was the general moderator of the body. All this seems a little like a hierarchy, but it was nothing of the kind. Moderators were simply chairmen of meetings. The general moderator had no more authority than the rest of his brethren; all that the office involved was the chairmanship of the general meetings. The first chosen to this office was the Rev. George Whitefield. He accordingly presided at the Watford Association, and at the few other meetings of the kind which he was able to attend; but Mr. Howel Harris was chosen as his deputy, and was for a long time the acting moderator of the Connexion. The following is the first distribution of districts, etc.:—[7]

1. Radnor and Montgomery—moderator, William Williams; overseer, Richard Tibbott.

2. Carmarthenshire and part of Cardigan—moderator, Daniel Rowland; overseers, John Richard, James Williams, William John, and David Williams.

3. Breconshire—moderator, Thomas Lewis; overseers, Thomas James and James Beaumont.

4. Pembrokeshire and the lower part of Cardigan—moderator, Howel Davies; overseers, William Richard, Thomas Meyler, and John Harris.

5. Monmouth and Glamorgan—moderator, John Powell; overseers, Morgan John, Thomas Williams, Morgan John Lewis, and Thomas Price, to whom was afterwards added John Belcher.

It will be seen that the above arrangement embraces only one of the counties of North Wales, namely, Montgomeryshire. This county was convenient to Howel Harris's base of operations, and was therefore visited frequently by him in the first years of his ministry; but it was not until a later period that the work extended to the other districts of the north.

The overseers were required to furnish a periodical report to the Association of the districts or sub-districts, as the case might be, under their charge; embracing the numerical strength of each Society, and, as far as they could ascertain, the spiritual state of its individual members. The following is an example:—

"DEAR BRETHREN IN THE LORD,—This is to inform you what a wide door has been opened unto me by the Almighty God in the Societies named underneath, and what successful progress the Gospel makes among them. I verily believe that they excel every other part which is known to me in the Principality of Wales in love to God and His gospel, in their carefulness to walk in accordance with its precepts, as well as in their unity with each other: not being persecuted or disturbed by any, excepting a little persecution that happened lately at Lampeter, in the county of Cardigan. While the members of the Society were together singing psalms and praying to God, a Justice of the Peace, with his servants, came upon them to disturb them, and the man who was praying at the time was taken prisoner; but through the providence of God the persecution has somewhat moderated, and the prisoner has been set at liberty, but the Justices continue their threatenings.

"Caeo Society contains 60 members, 27 of whom enjoy liberty, the others are under the law.

"Talley Society contains 68 members, 24 of whom have obtained deliverance through Christ, the others are under the law. William John, exhorter; Thomas Griffith, steward.

"Llangathen Society contains 14 members, 5 of whom are free in Christ, and the others under the law. Morris John is exhorter.

"Llanfynydd Society contains 54 members, 23 of whom are free in Christ, and the others under the law. Morris John, is exhorter here also.

"Llansawel Society contains 47 members, 18 of whom are free in Christ, and the others under the law. Joseph John, exhorter, and John David, steward.

"Cil-y-cwm Society contains 26 members; 9 free, and the others under the law. John Thomas, exhorter, and Isaac David, steward.

"Lampeter Society contains 28 members; 13 free, and the others under the law.

"David Williams, an exhorter at Llanfynydd, has left me and gone to keep a school. Thomas John has not been settled in any place.

"This from your fellow-traveller and unworthy brother in Christ,

"JAMES WILLIAMS."

Sometimes these reports descended to even more minute details. Take the following examples:—

"Builth Society—Thomas James, overseer; Thomas Bowen, exhorter.

"Thomas James, a full and abiding testimony.

"Thomas Bowen, enjoying much liberty.

"Evan Evans, having obtained a testimony, but weak in grace.

"Sarah Williams justified, and coming out of the furnace.

"Sarah Jones, a full testimony, but under heavy bondage.

"Ann Baisdel, a sweet experience, but yet weak.

"Mary Bowen, seeking the Lord Jesus in earnest." Etc. etc.

The following is from the report of another overseer, William Richard, who had the charge of Pembrokeshire and part of Cardigan:—

"Dyffryn Saeth Society—

"Thomas David, believing, but subject to doubts, through the power of temptation; he desires and longs for greater liberty.

"David Morgan has tasted much of the love of God, believes daily, and his experience is very clear.

"David Rees, believing, but under many clouds; has passed through many temptations, but prevails more and more.

"Jenkin John, under temptation for a season; dark and dry in his spirit.

"Jane John enjoys peace with God and goes forward happily, leaning on her Beloved.

"Sarah Thomas, enjoying a clear testimony of her salvation through Christ, but in many a battle with sin.

"Ann David, under the law.

"Ann Jenkin, under conviction.

"Eliza Thomas, under convictions, but very dark and very dry." Etc. etc.

Some may be led to infer, from there being such a great number of exhorters at the time, that many of them were self-appointed,—men who had taken it into their heads to preach, and preached accordingly. But it was not so. No one was permitted to hold forth in public until he had been authorised to do so by the Association, and that authorisation was never given but after the most careful inquiry into the character and qualifications of each candidate.

At the Watford Association it was resolved, "That no one is to be regarded as an exhorter among us until he has been first proved and accepted, and that no one go beyond the limits assigned to him without previous consultation." The following resolution was passed at a later Association:— "When any one offers himself as an exhorter, he must first of all exhort at the meetings of the church to which he belongs.

"1. That he may have the approbation of one or more experienced Christians who have often heard him.

"2. To ascertain the opinions of three or four public or private exhorters and ministers respecting him.

"3. He must undergo a searching examination as to his grace, his calling, his qualifications, his gifts, and his doctrine."

For a while they were obliged to exhort in and about their own homes, that full proof might be had of their ministry before they were permitted to travel to distant places.

The authorisation was not obtained as a matter of course whenever applied for, and the examination was something more than a mere matter of form. We quote a few resolutions passed with reference to the subject at various Associations:—

"That the following brethren be restrained until the next Association, viz., James Tomkins, David Prys, Richard Thomas, John David, John Watkin, and Thomas Prys."

At the following Association it appears that John David and David Prys were permitted to remain for some time longer under probation, but the case of the others was finally disposed of, for it was resolved, "That James Tomkins, Richard Thomas, John Watkin, and Thomas Prys be entirely restrained, as it is considered that they have not been sent of God."

After brethren had been authorised to exhort, they were kept under strict supervision. The overseers were required to keep their eyes on their private character and public ministry, and report to the Association. The following is extracted from the report of Thomas James, one of the overseers of the Breconshire district:—

"Builth—Thomas Bowen, exhorter. He preaches the gospel in his life and conversation, and is greatly blessed.

"Llangamarch—Rhys Morgan, exhorter. A kind, humble, and faithful man.

"Merthyr[8]—William Williams, exhorter. A kind and humble Christian, and of clear sentiments."

Sometimes "reports" were received which were not of such a pleasing character as the above. There was one William Prys who was charged with spreading doctrines of an Antinomian tendency. Among other strange things, he asserted that he had not sinned for some time, and that there *was* no sin either in his understanding, his will, or his conscience, and because he clung stubbornly to these views, he was expelled, and the Societies were warned to beware of his heresies, and the brethren to avoid his society. "After long discussion and prayer," says the report, "and with great solemnity, we turned him out, while our hearts were overwhelmed with love to his soul and jealousy for the glory of God, and full of fear and anxiety for the safety of the flock."

There was another brother whose conduct had not been blameless, and the following is the resolution passed in his case:—"Howell Griffith having been overtaken in a fault, but having manifested satisfactory evidences of repentance, it was agreed that he should be restored on trial, on condition that he henceforth avoid that which has been the occasion of his fall."

But purity of doctrine and blamelessness of life were not all that was required in exhorters. They must be faithful and diligent in the discharge of their duties, otherwise they would be brought under discipline. At an Association held at Porth-y-rhyd, it was resolved, "That Brother Harris, in the name of the assembled brethren, administer a reproof to John Williams for his negligence in watching over the Society under his charge, and that he give him to understand that he shall be expelled after another month of trial, unless he show evidences of obedience and faithfulness."

All the moderators and overseers were expected to attend every quarterly Association, or to send a message explaining their absence, otherwise they should hear from the brethren. At one Association it was resolved, "That letters be written to Howel Davies and John Harris, because they have not sent to say why they are absent; and that Thomas Meyler be written to because he neglects attending the Associations."

But how were these brethren to live? When they attended meetings and went about the country preaching the gospel, their own worldly affairs were neglected, while those for whose benefit they ministered had scarcely any notion at all of contributing towards their support. The following is an extract written to one of the Associations by a very excellent man, John Richard, overseer:—

"I have been in great distress during the last quarter, so that I have not been able to visit the Societies more than twice in the three months, in consequence of my own illness and that of my wife, and so far I am in too straitened circumstances to be able to go about; and yet, through mercy, I am free in my spirit to go, if that will be to the glory of God. The Lord has not left me in want of anything since I threw myself into the arms of His providence. If He were to ask me now, 'Hast thou wanted anything?' I could answer with the disciples, 'Nothing, Lord.'"

After the reading of the above letter it was resolved, "That Brother John Richard be requested to go about as usual until the next Association, and that in the meantime Mr. Harris visit the Societies under his charge, with a view to induce them to *bear fruit to him.*"

The following resolution was passed at Trefeca,[9] October 18th, 1744:—"That the brethren earnestly exhort the people to walk worthily, and to *bear fruit,* as there is a general complaint of great deficiency in this matter."

There was in those days a very excellent and able man, Richard Tibbott by name, whose whole time the Societies required, but whose temporal necessities they do not seem to have been in a position to supply; hence we find his case coming up frequently at the Associations, and presenting a considerable amount of difficulty. At the Watford Association, already referred to, it was resolved, "That Richard Tibbott be appointed general visitor of the districts."

At a subsequent Association it was resolved, "That Richard Tibbott open a school in Pembrokeshire."

Later, it was resolved, "That Richard Tibbott continue to work (with his hands) until he can get a Welsh school."[10]

April 18th,[11] 1744, it was resolved, "That Brother Richard Tibbott be requested to give himself entirely to visiting all the Societies in Montgomeryshire once every week." This was glorious, provided that the Societies in Montgomeryshire furnished the good brother with means to supply his bodily wants; but unhappily they did not, and consequently in the following October Association it was resolved, "That Brother Richard Tibbott go to Brother John Richard to learn the trade of a bookbinder."

So it was at the time, and so it continued for many years afterwards. Able men were willing and anxious to devote all their time and energies to the service of the cause, but the Societies were either unable or indisposed to give them the means of living, and they were therefore obliged to turn for subsistence to other sources. This good man, after itinerating for twenty-five years, settled down as Independent minister at Llanbryn-mair in Montgomeryshire, but at the same time he retained as long as he lived his connexion with the Methodists.

NOTES

1   That is, the Church of England.

2   Twelve years; see note 4 below.

3   A similar resolution had been passed at the Monthly Association held at Abergorlech on 4 September. *Journal of the Historical Society of the Presbyterian Church of Wales*, XLIX (1964), pp.26, 84.

4   This statement is incorrect. The first chapel was probably that erected at Llansawel (Carmarthenshire) early in 1747. Another was built at Cil-y-cwm sometime between July 1746 and July 1747. The chapel at Builth, opened in 1748, was the third belonging to the Welsh Calvinistic Methodists. G.M. Roberts, *Y Deffroad Mawr*, pp.200-1.

5   For the correct date, see note 8, p.74.

6   The date was not 3 October but 27 September. *Jnl Hist. Soc. Presb. Church of Wales*, XLIX (1964), p.27.

7   During the rest of this chapter there are numerous references to resolutions passed and to reports submitted by overseers at early Association meetings. The resolutions as presented here have been translated into English from the Welsh version contained in John Hughes, *Methodistiaeth Cymru*. The original English version is extant, however: it is to be found in National Library of Wales, Trevecka MS 2945, and has been published in *Jnl Hist. Soc. Presb. Church of Wales*,

XLVIII (1963), pp.29-48, 69-80; XLIX (1964), pp.21-28, 84-90; L (1965), pp.27-32. Details of later Association meetings are published in the last-named and subsequent volumes. The early reports are comprised in National Library of Wales, Trevecka MSS 2947-98, 3000-85 (many were also copied into Trevecka MS 2945 above), and published in *Jnl Hist. Soc. Presb. Church of Wales* LI (1966), pp.63-83; LII (1967), pp.8-28, 44-61, 84-89; LIII (1968), pp.19-24, 45-52, 83-88; LIV (1969), pp.22-32, 52-62.

8 Merthyr Cynog, between Builth and Brecon.

9 The resolution was passed not at Trefeca but at Nantmel, Radnorshire. *Jnl Hist. Soc. Presb. Church of Wales*, XLIX (1964), p.85.

10 'A Welsh school' would have been one of Griffith Jones's circulating schools, which served as excellent training-grounds for men of Methodist sympathies. Gwyn Davies, *Griffith Jones*, pp.54, 80.

11 13th, not 18th, April (Nantmel Association). *Jnl Hist. Soc. Presb. Church of Wales*, XLVIII (1963), p.73. The Methodist societies of south-west Wales have received detailed attention in Eryn M. White, *Praidd Bach y Bugail Mawr* (Llandysul: Gomer, 1995).

CHAPTER V

OPPOSITION AND PERSECUTIONS

Harris mobbed at Newport and other places—Peter Williams at
Kidwelly—At Wrexham—In the dog kennel—At Trefeca—
At Penrhos—The grey Mare—Rowland mobbed at Llanilar—
Mike and Dick—A persistent Church Choir—Patent Rattle—
A small Gunpowder Plot— Lewis Evan and the Magistrate—
Imprisoned—Morgan Griffith arrested—Sent on board a
man-of-war—A Sermon *en route*—Furlough—Again sent
away—Dies.

WE have already intimated that those earnest men were
not permitted to pursue their work in peace, and we
shall devote a few of the following pages to give the reader
some idea of the strong opposition they encountered, and
the varied forms of persecution which they were called to
endure. We have materials enough to fill a volume on this
subject alone, but shall content ourselves with citing a
comparatively few instances, not exactly in the order in
which they occurred, but all relating to the earliest days of
Welsh Methodism. We have already alluded to the
sufferings of Howel Harris. It appears that he had to endure
more personal abuse than any of his brethren, and probably
the mob took more liberty with him, because, unlike the
other leading men in South Wales, he was not an ordained
clergyman. On one occasion, having barely escaped with
his life from the hands of a mob in Monmouthshire, he made
in the direction of his home. About two o'clock in the
morning, and almost fainting from loss of blood, he was able
to reach a farm-house called Tor-y-gaer, on the slope of the
Black Mountain, just above Crickhowell, occupied by a Mr.

Walter Rumsey. He knocked at the door and feebly asked for admittance. Mrs. Rumsey heard and recognised the voice and at once let him in. He presented a sad picture. His clothes were torn, his face covered with blood, his body bruised, and his head cut in no less than thirteen places. Mr. and Mrs. Rumsey were zealous friends of the cause for the sake of which he had thus severely suffered, and all that the tenderest love could devise was done in his behalf, but he was obliged to remain under their hospitable roof for a week before his strength was sufficiently recovered to enable him to leave.

We shall give a few extracts in his own words in an Autobiography published in 1791:—

"My life being now in danger in several places by the mob, especially in February 1739, when they found I could not be prosecuted as a rioter, because it did not appear I disturbed the peace, yet in Montgomeryshire, a knight, a clergyman, and two justices, whilst I was discoursing, came, attended by a constable, with the mob, and took cognisance of me, and such as met together to hear my exhortation in a place unlicensed; then they began to charge me with a breach of the Conventicle Act.[1] I told the magistrate that I was a Conformist, and for that reason not subject to the penalties of that Statute. Then they said that they would consult the best lawyers in order to know if there was a law to be enforced against me, and if there was, that I might expect to suffer its utmost extremity. My persecutors thus continued to threaten me until Session came on, at which time a lawyer was consulted, and the case was dropped.

"After my dismission I went to Merionethshire, where I trust the Lord blessed the seed sown to some. In my return from thence I came by Dinas Mawddwy, and discoursed there, and at the request of a friend I went on to Machynlleth; but at my first entrance there, I found none were disposed to receive me. However, I proposed to preach the gospel to such as met in the street, being placed in an opening window or door in an upper room, but I was obliged to desist by the noise of the multitude, who continued hallooing, threatening, swearing, and flinging stones or anything they could lay their hands on; and especially by an attorney's coming up to me with such rage and fury in his looks, and his mouth so full of the language of hell as if his name was *Legion,* and with him a gentleman and a clergyman in the same spirit and language to head the mob. One of them discharged a pistol at me. I received no hurt, but was obliged to go among them into the street, not expecting that I should escape alive, seeing every circumstance threatened me with death. But my hour was not yet come; though they used me ill, yet I was miraculously preserved; and at last one of the mob was disposed to fetch my horse, and as soon as I mounted they observed which way I went and crossed my road, and began again to throw sticks and stones at me, till the Lord delivered me out of their hands.[2]

"In the summer of 1740, as I went through Glamorgan-shire, I met with Mr. Seward at Cowbridge. From thence he came on with me to Cardiff, and then we went on comfortably together to Monmouthshire and preached at the several towns of Newport, Caerleon, Usk, and Monmouth, when Satan was permitted to rage against us in a most horrible manner. At Newport the mob rushed on us with the utmost rage and fury. They tore both my coat-sleeves, one quite off, and took away my peruke,[3] I being now in the rain. *O, sweet bareheadedness—under the reproach of Christ!* Having little silence I discoursed on, but soon they hallooed again and pelted me with apples and dirt, flinging stones in the utmost rage about me. I had one blow on my forehead, which caused a rising, with little blood. Many friends would have me give over in the tumult, but I could not be free to do that till the storm would be over and God be glorified over Satan. When we came to Caerleon everything seemed calm and quiet, whilst Brother Seward prayed and discoursed sweetly by the Market-house; but when I began to discourse after him, then they began to roar most horribly, pelting us with dung and dirt, throwing eggs, plum-stones, and other hard substances even in our faces and hallooed so loudly as to drown my voice entirely. Brother Seward had a furious blow on his right eye, which caused him much anguish; and as it affected his left he was obliged to be led by the hand blindfold for some days, till at last he became totally blind of it. When we came to Monmouth, we had much the same treatment as at Newport and Caerleon. It happened to be the horse-races there, and both high and low were assembled against us. As I began to discourse on a table over against the Town-hall windows, where the Duke of B_____ and Lord N_____, and a great number of gentlemen and ladies were at dinner, they ordered a drum to be beat by our sides; although the Lord enabled me to bear my testimony against their balls, assemblies, horse-races, whoredom, and drunkenness, the drum continued to beat, and the mob pelting with apples, pears, stones, dirt, and a dead dog. During this storm Brother Seward was much afraid of hurt, yet he endured it with much calmness of spirit, saying, 'Better endure this than hell.' Thus all their opposition could not hinder our progress, but in the strength of the Lord we went on from conquering to conquer...[4]

"In the beginning of the year 1741 I went to North Wales, and as I proceeded the enemy was provoked at my attempt thus to propagate the Gospel in his territories, and resolved to make a stand against me, and endeavoured as much as he should be permitted to take away my life. Having been importuned to visit Bala in Merionethshire, and to proceed to the north, though I had been there once or twice before, after prayer and consultation I entrusted God with my life, relying on His faithfulness, and went on. Accidentally, as I was near Bala, I overtook the minister that belonged to that place, who cautioned me to desist at my peril. I meekly replied I was fully persuaded it was my duty—that I had no other intention but to publish the glad tidings of salvation, and would not wilfully offend any person. However, he gave me very ill language, and came towards me with a great club to strike me. I told him, when I was reviled I was taught not to revile again, and rode on quietly. But when I entered the town I found a numerous assembly waiting for me, and it was said that all the county mob were met together purposely to abuse and hinder me. At the request of my friends I quitted the streets, and went into a house to discourse.

"During all this I was happy in my soul, and full of power and courage, my voice being lifted up like a trumpet, so that people could hear in spite of all the disturbance that was made at the door and window, which was broken to pieces by the mob, and thus I discoursed on for some time. But when the mob, who had been preparing themselves for the work by excessive drinking—it was supposed that the minister had given them the drink—came among the people, a friend desired me to leave off though I was yet full of power in my spirit; yet, preferring my friend's advice before the call in my own soul, I ceased to speak, but I immediately felt the power withdrawn from me, and then I understood that I had done wrong. However, I retired to an upper room, but the mob, instead of withdrawing, appeared to be more enraged. Some surrounded the house, while others climbed to the top of it, threatening me with instant death as soon as I should come out. As night drew on, I thought it my duty to go out among them, committing myself to the hands of God; but as soon as I went out of the house one seized me by the handkerchief; by it giving way I was prevented from falling to the ground. Another hit me on the face, whilst others flung stones and dirt at me. I then thought it was my lot to die Stephen's death in the midst of them. I spoke to them and prayed for them, but whilst I did this one desired me to go away, telling me that I tempted the Lord by staying there, and no sooner had I turned my back on my enemies to go away than I was somehow left to myself, and sank under the waves, though I was not afraid of death, knowing it was an entrance to eternal rest; having no fear of hell or doubt of God's favour through the blood of Christ my Saviour; yet being rather unwilling to die by the hands of these villains, gave me some uneasiness. They still inhumanly continued to beat me with sticks and staffs, and to pelt me with stones, etc., until I fell under their merciless feet, where they continued to beat me until the Lord touched the heart of one of them with pity, or fear of being prosecuted for killing me. He swore that they should beat me no more, and rescued me out of their hands whilst they were employed in giving my friends the like treatment; although they were able to make defensive resistance, yet they imitated Christ the Lord, their Master, in bearing all patiently, as I desired them to do. So at last we came to our lodging, and dressed our wounds, and there also I exhorted my fellow-sufferers, and we rejoiced together that we were counted worthy to suffer for Christ's sake."[5]

Writing to a friend in the year 1748, respecting a recent journey in North Wales, he says, "I was seven nights in succession during this journey without undressing, and travelled a hundred miles from the morning of one day to the evening of the next, without having any rest, preaching at midnight or in the early morning on the mountains. This I was obliged to do to avoid persecution. The week before my visit a man near Wrexham had been fined £20 by Sir W. W. Wynn, and several of the hearers had had to pay five shillings each, and one ten shillings, a sum which he had been obliged to pay once before. This is the third time that the brethren have been treated in this manner; and on the last occasion there was only one brother present praying with a family."[6] In this case the zealous magistrate overshot the mark. Representations were made in high quarters by the Countess of Huntingdon, and Sir W_____ was obliged to return the fines, the number assembled being too few to bring the case under the Conventicle Act. A few months afterwards this merciless persecutor was killed by a fall from his horse.

Peter Williams was likewise oftentimes roughly handled. At Kidwelly, within four miles of his home, he attempted to hold a service in the open air on a Sabbath afternoon. A number of roughs assembled together, and as soon as he began to pray, they pulled him down and savagely beat him. When he mounted his horse they led the animal to the neighbouring marsh and compelled it to leap across the dykes which abound there, promising themselves the mighty fun of seeing the preacher tumbling over. But he was too good a horseman to afford them that kind of amusement. They afterwards dragged him into the public-house, swearing that they would make him drunk. This again proved fruitless labour, for instead of drinking the beer which they continued to put into his hands, he poured it into his boots. He remained there a prisoner in the hands of the mob, until some of his own servants, whom Mrs. Williams, alarmed at his lengthened absence, had sent in quest of him, came to his rescue. Preaching in the neighbour of Wrexham, he was arrested by the orders of Sir Watkin,[7] and brought into his presence. We have no account of the examination which he underwent, but at the close of it he was committed to the dog-kennel, where he had to remain for the night. In the morning he was set at liberty, and bent his steps towards the friendly roof of Moses Lewis, a farmer in the neighbourhood. Here he was followed by the constables who had arrested him on the preceding day, not, it is supposed, by the order of the magistrate, but wishing to do a little business on their own account. His host seeing them approach the house, and suspecting their purpose, took possession of his watch. He was obliged to submit to be searched by these worthies, and they appropriated to themselves all the money which they could find upon him, which amounted to three shillings and sixpence. Our readers will not be shocked when we say that he took snuff. The constables took possession of his snuff-box, but at his earnest entreaty were kind enough to return it. Possibly they would not have returned it unopened if they had only known that besides a quantity of the sweet-scented dust, it contained half a guinea. At Trefriw, near Llan-rwst, he was set upon by a great crowd, which was headed by two "gentlemen," dragged into a public-house, where he was kept prisoner from six o'clock in the evening until two next morning, a butt to the gibes and badinage[8] of the rabble, and subjected to the most disgraceful outrages. At length the two "gentlemen" called for their horses and departed, having first paid the score, including the cost of food and lodgings for their victim. By-and-by the roughs left, and the preacher, finding a clear coast, hastened to make his escape, "sorry in his heart that he had not been permitted to preach."

A rather ludicrous incident happened in connection with an attempt to disturb his preaching at a place called Penrhos in Anglesey. A crowd of rioters had assembled and were making for the place where Mr. Williams was preaching. Among them was an elderly man riding a grey mare and armed with a bludgeon, as eager for the fray as any of the tumultuous throng. When they came near the congregation, some one quite accidentally touched the grey mare in the vicinity of the crupper,[9] and she resented the insult with a tremendous fling, which produced no little amusement. Another tried the experiment, with the same result, and it all at once struck them that it would be quite as good fun to tickle the mare as to beat the preacher. To this they applied themselves in good earnest. The infuriated animal scampered off, plunging and kicking, followed by the crowd, each eager to get one chance more to touch the crupper, in spite of the angry protests of the rider, who had as much as he could do to keep his seat in the saddle, and the preacher and the few who had come together to hear him were left in peace.

Daniel Rowland was mobbed on some occasions, but not so frequently as some of his brethren. When attempting to preach at Llanilar, in his own county, a great crowd, under the leadership of Squire Jones, of Aber-mad, a mansion in the vicinity, assaulted him so fiercely with stones, brickbats, and other missiles that he was obliged to desist and escape for his life, exclaiming, "I bear in my body the marks of the Lord Jesus."

He soon made another attempt, and on this occasion the "Squire" did not put in an appearance, but not willing that the service should pass undisturbed, he treated two of his servants, a stalwart Welshman named Dick James, and an Irishman named Mike Daniel, to a liberal quantity of *the* drink, and sent them to the place of meeting, with orders to give the preacher a sound thrashing. When they came to the spot they agreed to listen for a while before beginning their assault. It struck Dick that the preacher was saying something very solemn, looking very grave, and crying withal, which had the effect of shaking him in his purpose. After a few minutes says Mike, "Let's at him now." "No," says Dick. "Then I will go my own self and hit him," says Mike. "If you do," says Dick, "I'll hit you, and such a blow that you shan't want another." The service concluded in peace, and Dick and Mike returned to their master. "Did you beat him well ?" asked the Squire. "Not at all at all, Masthur," replied Mike. "Why?" "Sure enough it was all Dick's fault: he threatened to bate me instead of the preacher," was Mike's reply. "How is this, Dick?" inquired the master. "Indeed, sir," replied Dick, "when I came to his sight he looked so serious and wept so uncommonly, that I could not think of hitting him while he cried." "Ah, well," said the Squire, "I see that you frightened him. He will not be in haste to venture to this neighbourhood again."

At Nefyn in Caernarvonshire, a very original device was had recourse to, to prevent him from preaching. The church choir were instructed to sing the 119th Psalm from beginning to end; and they sang on for hours without intermission. Possibly their music was none of the best, but it was less painful to endure than stones and mud, and yet it answered precisely the same purpose—for it effectually prevented the preaching.

There was a good deal of ingenuity exercised in those

days in devising means and methods to annoy the preachers and their friends. When Peter Williams was with some friends passing through a little town in Anglesey, most of the population followed them, hooting and pelting them with stones and other missiles. Some had bags loosely filled with stones, and tied to the ends of stakes, which they rattled away with all their might *to frighten the horses.*

At a place in Denbighshire, on the road leading from Gwytherin to Llansannan, there was a Gunpowder Plot on a small scale. An excellent man, named Lewis Evans, had engaged to preach on a Sabbath afternoon on a small mound in a field near the roadside. A person happened to come to the place some time before the hour for beginning the service, and walking up and down he observed a singular-looking bunch of straw coming up out of the ground. On examination he found it filled with gunpowder, a small train of which he traced to the top of the mound where the preacher was expected to take his stand. Here he found a hole two feet in diameter filled with powder, and carefully covered over with turf. He was no Methodist himself, nor a friend to the Methodists, but he thought that he would like to disappoint the ingenious plotters. He accordingly scraped the powder from the hole, replacing the turf, separated the train which led from the straw in several places, and put himself in a convenient position to watch the event. While the service was proceeding, he observed a man, who was servant to a solicitor in the neighbourhood, and dressed like a waggoner, approaching the straw and setting it on fire. There was a flash, but it was only "in the pan." The seeming waggoner was greatly disappointed, a feeling which very possibly was shared by his master, while the preacher and his friends escaped what might have been a very serious injury.

The above Lewis Evans was one of the mightiest workers in the Methodist movement, and one of the few of their number who suffered a lengthened imprisonment. On one occasion when he was preaching at Bala, a magistrate residing in the neighbourhood sent officers to arrest and bring him into his presence. He was ushered into the parlour, when the following dialogue took place between the magistrate and himself:—

Magistrate. "Art thou the man who has been preaching at Bala?"

Preacher. "Yes, sir; it is I who have been giving a word of exhortation to the people."

M. "Where art thou from?"

P. "From the parish of Llanllugan, Montgomeryshire."

M. "What is thine employment when thou art at home?"

P. "A weaver, sir."

M. "Hadst thou not enough work at home?"

P. "Yes, sir, abundance."

M. "What for then didst thou come this way?"

P. "To give a word of exhortation to my fellow-sinners."

M. "Thou art not wanted here. We have clergymen brought up at Oxford at great cost for the work of preaching."

P. "There is enough work for them and me, for the people in great multitudes go to ruin in spite of us all."

M. "I shall send thee to prison for thy pains."

P. "My better has been in prison before me. The Lord Jesus Himself was put in prison after He had come to the world to save sinners. The Lord Jesus—"

M. "Stop! Dost thou intend to preach in my parlour?"

P. "I do not think that your parlour is too good to speak in of the Lord Jesus Christ."

Eventually the preacher was committed to Dolgellau jail, where he lay for six months. Some of his friends, feeling that they ought to interfere in his behalf, inquired into the case, found that the magistrate had overstepped his authority, and commenced legal proceedings against him. It appears that the great man himself made the same discovery, and began to fear that a storm was brewing. He therefore hastened to Dolgellau to have an interview with his prisoner.

"Well, Lewis," said he, "here thou art still."

Preacher. "Yes, sir; here I am."

Magistrate. "And here thou art likely to be for ever."

P. "No, sir; neither you nor I shall be here for ever."

M. "If thou wert but to give me a little money I could get thee out."

P. "Indeed, sir? I think that you ought to get me out for nothing, for you had most to do in putting me in.

M. "Tell me, are there many of you?"

P. "O yes, sir, a great number, and there will be many more of us by-and-by."

M. "May you all be hanged by the same tree!"

P. "You shall have been turned to dust, sir, long before that happens."

The preacher was set at liberty "for nothing," the magistrate, as it appears, bearing the expenses, and the legal proceedings against the latter were stayed; but he was given to understand that a sharp eye would be kept on his movements, and that he should not be permitted to play such a freak again at so little cost.

Another exhorter of the period was Morgan Griffith, commonly known as Morgan the Sievemaker, who lived near Pwllheli in Caernarvonshire. He understood music, taught classes, and was leader of the choir in his parish church. While discharging this service it occurred to him that the kind of singing in which he was engaged was not praise unto God; that he and his companions of the choir were not singing in their hearts to the Lord, and that their performance therefore was mockery and not praise. This thought haunted him continually, and it so affected him that he durst not say at the giving out of the psalm, "Let us sing to the praise and glory of God." He applied himself earnestly to read the Bible and to hear the Word preached when opportunity offered, and at length found rest to his troubled conscience through the blood of Christ. About the year 1744 he began publicly to exhort his neighbours to flee from the wrath to come. But he lived in the neighbourhood of one of the most furious persecutors of the Methodists, a tyrant out and out, namely, the Rev. John Owen, rector of Llannor and chancellor of Bangor. Poor Morgan Griffith was not long before he had to enter upon a course of suffering. On his return home from a place where he had been preaching, he was arrested and taken to Pwllheli, where he was lodged in prison to await his examination. He was at the time a widower, with two children, one of whom was a boy of eight years of age, and the other a girl of six. A maternal uncle of the poor motherless children took them to Pwllheli to present them in court, hoping, simple man that he was, that the sight of them and their helpless condition would melt the magistrates' hearts. But he was mistaken. The harmless little ones were the means of greatly aggravating their father's case. A book was put in the hands of the boy, and, to the disgust of the bench, he was found to be able to read. The same experiment was tried on the girl, and with the same result. This was intolerable. It was evident that the man was a disorderly person, and that he was bringing up his children to the same ways with himself, and therefore he must by some means be got rid of. There were other Methodists examined at the same time. No law existed by which they could be committed to prison, and merely to fine them for their breach of the Conventicle Act would not answer the magistrates' purpose. But the Royal Navy was at the time in need of sailors, and the whole batch were sent on board a ship of war. They were taken first to Caernarfon, and afterwards to Conwy. At the latter place it was for some reason a holiday, and a large number of people assembled before the place where the prisoners rested, anxious to catch a glimpse of them. Morgan Griffith stood up and addressed the crowd, telling them that he and his companions in suffering were there, not for murder or robbery or any other crime against the laws of the country, but for reading the Scriptures, praying together, and exhorting one another in the interests of their souls; and with great earnestness he entreated them to consider their ways and to turn to the Lord. "As for us," he added, "our consciences are at peace, and we rejoice that we are counted worthy to suffer reproach for the sake of Christ." Two young men among the audience were impressed by this discourse, and became zealous helpers in the cause of the gospel.

After remaining for some time on board ship, Morgan Griffith and one of his companions were permitted to return to their homes on furlough. It was generally believed that they would have been allowed to remain at home unmolested if they had only refrained from the doings which had given offence to the authorities. But refrain they could not; the Word was in their hearts as a burning fire shut up in their bones, and they were weary with forbearing and could not stay. On one of the first Sabbaths after their return, Morgan Griffith preached in the neighbourhood, and his friend introduced the service. They were consequently sent away before the expiration of their furlough, and word was sent with them to the commander of the ship, that they were disorderly people, creating a disturbance in the country, and that Morgan Griffith was the worse of the two. The latter was told by the officers that they had had complaints against him from Government that he was a ringleader of seditious men, and that he must put away his religious sentiments and practices, and become a "quiet Churchman," otherwise he should be shot. Time was given him to make up his mind on the momentous subject. At the expiration of that period he was asked what he had determined to do, and this was his heroic reply: "I must obey God rather than man. I give myself to the care of Him who is able to keep that which is committed to Him, and am determined that neither reproach nor suffering shall induce me to dishonour my Master." He was consequently placed at the end of the ship, and a file of men were ordered to fire on him. The poor exhorter had no idea but that he must die, but his tormentors only intended it for a lark, and the guns were only charged with powder. Possibly the officers considered it a good joke, but it was, to say the least, a very cruel one, and one that might have ended in a catastrophe which would have made it an expensive one to themselves. From that day he was treated with greater respect; but that respect came too late, for he soon afterwards sickened and died, abundantly enjoying in his last moments that peace which passeth understanding. He had to die far away from the helpless orphans from whom he had been so ruthlessly torn; but it is comforting to know that a kind Providence took care of the little ones, and that they never wanted any good thing.

NOTES

[1] The Conventicle Act of 1664 was aimed at restricting the spread of Nonconformity. It declared illegal all meetings attended by more than five persons (apart from members of the household) for purposes of worship other than that prescribed in the Book of Common Prayer.

[2] Howel Harris, *A Brief Account of the Life of Howel Harris Esq., Extracted from Papers Written by Himself* [by Benjamin La Trobe] (Trevecka, 1791); republished as *Howel Harris: His Own Story* (Chepstow: Bridge Publishing, 1984), pp.27-29.

[3] Wig.

[4] *Howel Harris: His Own Story*, pp.42-44. The attack at Caerleon occurred on 9 September 1740. While preaching at Hay the following month, Harris and Seward were again assaulted; the latter was struck by a stone from close range and subsequently died (on 22 October). He was the first Methodist martyr. Dallimore, *George Whitefield*, I, pp.583-4.

[5] *Howel Harris: His Own Story*, pp.47-49.

[6] *Brief Account of the Life of Howel Harris*, p.196.

[7] 'Sir Watkin' was the 'Sir W. W. Wynn' (Sir Watkin Williams Wynn of Wynnstay, Rhiwabon) named on p.93.

[8] Mocking.

[9] In a general sense, the crupper was the rump of the horse; technically, it was the leather strap buckled to the saddle and passing under the horse's tail which kept the saddle from slipping forwards.

CHAPTER VI

More Persecution and Oppression—William Pritchard—Hugh Thomas hiding in Caves—Edward Parry—Margaret Hughes—Owen Thomas Rowland—Thomas Lloyd sold up—Sale at Wrexham—Richard Hughes and the Agent.

PREACHERS and exhorters were not the only sufferers in those troublous times. Those who received them into their houses, as well as those who were in the habit of attending on their ministrations, were equally exposed to the displeasure of the great and the fury of the rabble. There was living at Glasfryn Fawr, near Pwllheli, a farmer who was somewhat wealthy, and better educated than most of his neighbours, of the name of William Pritchard. He was a religious man before his neighbourhood had been visited by any of the Methodist preachers, and his conversion had been brought about in a remarkable manner. On one Sunday evening, having remained later than usual at a public-house, where he had been drinking with some of his wild companions, he missed his way home. He wandered for a while in entire ignorance of his own whereabouts, but at length seeing a light he made towards it, and had no sooner reached the place than he understood where he was, and at once he moved on in the direction of his own residence. But he soon lost himself again, and again found himself by the cottage from which the light emanated. He looked in and saw the occupant reading the Bible, and after some time he beheld him fall on his knees to pray. William Pritchard, who could hear every word that was uttered, stayed to the end of the prayer, and then found his way home without any further difficulty. Some of the words to which he had listened clung to his mind, made him feel unhappy, and he could find no rest until he had been made willing to give himself to the Lord. There was a small Independent church at Pwllheli, and of this he became a member. It was at his house that Howel Harris preached his first sermon in that part of the country. He admired the zeal of the Methodists, and encouraged and helped them in every way, but he thus brought numberless troubles upon himself. It seems that he was in the habit of occasionally attending the church in which Chancellor Owen officiated, and when returning from the service on one Sunday, he was asked how he liked the sermon. He answered that he did not like it at all, and expressed it as his opinion that the doctrines it contained were not in accordance with the Word of God. These words were carried to the ears of the Chancellor, and the result was that William Pritchard was cited before the Ecclesiastical Court of Bangor to answer for the slander. With much difficulty and expense the case was removed from that court to the county assizes, where it was decided in favour of the defendant. But the vengeful Chancellor succeeded in inducing W. Pritchard's landlord to turn him out of his farm, and finding no other place in the neighbourhood, he was obliged to remove to the Isle of Anglesey. Here he settled in a farm called Plas-pen-mynydd; but the report that he was a man having embraced a strange kind of religion, and followed some unheard-of practices, had reached the place before him, and he was subjected by his new neighbours to numberless annoyances. Cattle were turned in his hay and corn crops, his implements of husbandry were broken to pieces, and his property damaged in every possible way. But he still continued to seek his neighbours' spiritual benefit. He had a cottage near his house licensed for preaching, and made every effort to get the little building supplied with the ministry of the gospel. The injury done to his property he suffered patiently until one Sunday evening, when matters reached an unbearable point. He was from home at the time, but the report had gone abroad that he had been seen returning on Saturday evening, and in company with a preacher. Mrs. Pritchard was within with an infant of three months old and a young maid-servant, the other servants having gone to church, when a great crowd assembled in front of the house, and seeing Mrs. Pritchard, shouted to her, "We are come to kill thy Roundhead and his preacher." "If Roundhead you call him," she replied, "he is not at home now." "It is a lie!" they all answered; but they did not think it proper to put it to the proof by searching the house, but broke all the windows, and then entering the cow-houses and stables, they broke stalls, mangers, racks, and every other breakable thing which they could find. After this they went into the barn, and mixed together all the winnowed barley and oats which they found lying there. When Mr. Pritchard came home, and saw the wreck which had been made of his property, he resolved that he would suffer such doings in silence no more. He was well aware that a Roundhead had but a poor chance of justice from the magistrates of his own country, and therefore put the case in the hands of an English lawyer who was known as a friend of religious liberty. He gave this gentleman a list of the leaders in the work of ruin about his house, and an action for damages was brought against these at the Shrewsbury assizes, and they were obliged to pay in full for the mischief they had done. But it was resolved that he should not remain in the neighbourhood, and he had therefore to quit his farm. It was but a short time that he was allowed to remain at his next farm, but when driven from this last, he was happy enough to meet with a landlord who believed in liberty of conscience. The enemy gained nothing by causing this good man to be driven about thus from place to place. The things that happened unto William Pritchard fell out rather unto the furtherance of the Gospel, for wherever he went he was immediately followed by the Methodists.

At the time when Morgan Griffith was sent on board a

man-of-war, there was a friend of his named Hugh Thomas, against whom a warrant was issued, but who managed to escape being arrested. A religious friend of his who had been doing harvest work for two successive summers at a farm called Cae-glas,[1] near the foot of Snowdon, advised him to flee thither, assuring him that the family at Cae-glas would not refuse to give him shelter. "The first year I was there," said he, "I asked permission to hold family worship in the house, and the people did not know what I meant. They looked stupid and confused; but I did it every day, and was tolerated. The following year the Bible was brought to me the first day, and I was asked to conduct family worship regularly. I think that those people would be disposed to give you protection." Towards Cae-glas, therefore, Hugh Thomas bent his steps. The place was about thirty miles from his home, and he was obliged to start by night lest he should be discovered. We give the sequel in his own words:—

"When I had reached the place, and had told the family my troubles, they showed every disposition to afford me shelter; but it was easy to see that they were afraid, lest they should, in harbouring me, bring evil upon themselves. In this perplexity it was resolved that a bed should be fitted up for me in a cave which was far up on the side of Snowdon where I should remain day and night, and where the shepherd should bring me food daily in going up the mountain to look after the sheep. Here I remained concealed for several weeks: after which I was permitted to sleep in the house, escaping to the cave every morning before the dawn, and not returning until after dark. At length the vigilance of the search for me having somewhat relaxed, I was allowed to dispense with my hiding-place and to remain in the house day and night.

"Meanwhile my wife did not know what had become of me, and I had no means to know how she fared; and my heart being well-nigh broken with a sore longing for seeing her, I resolved to go home. I left Cae-glas a little before night, in the hope of reaching my house while it was yet dark. As I was drawing near my own neighbourhood I was more afraid lest any should see me and report my arrival. I succeeded, however, in reaching home before daylight. I spent the whole of the first day after my arrival in bed, but when night came I was afraid to remain any longer in my own house, thinking that very possibly it might have become known to some people that I was there. I therefore, with the assistance of a friend, made a hole in a high bank which was covered with furze, and this I made my refuge. Whenever I entered this cave I pulled a quantity of furze after me against its mouth to conceal it. My poor wife had not the means to support me here in idleness; I therefore employed my time in making small nets for family uses, which she took about the neighbourhood to sell, or to give in exchange for morsels of food. I went on thus for some time before I ventured to sleep in my own house; and even then I took care to return to my hole every morning before daylight. At length the news came that Morgan Griffith's companions were allowed to return to their homes. I then ventured to show myself, and was permitted to remain in peace."

Poor Hugh Thomas felt that his own case contrasted unfavourably with that of his friend Morgan Griffith. "He faced the storm," said he, "but as for me, my heart is sore now because I fled like Jonah." It did not occur to him, perhaps, that he had been given the honour of adding one to the number of those worthies of whom it is written, that to escape the fury of savage persecutors, "they wandered in deserts, and in mountains, and in dens and caves of the earth."

At a farm called Cefn-byr, in the parish of Llansannan, Denbighshire, there lived a man named Edward Parry, who having been brought to know and to love the gospel, offered an open door to its ministry. Services were held at his house, which were attended by a number of his neighbours. This gave offence to several, and especially to the clergyman of the parish. The proprietor of Cefn-byr was made acquainted with the conduct of his tenant, and the result was, that the latter was given to understand that if he did not refrain from harbouring those strangers who tramped the country taking upon them to preach, he should be turned out of his farm. This was told him by his master, and his reply was, "Your land, sir, is only temporal, while religion is eternal." He refused to yield, and was expelled from his home and obliged to leave the neighbourhood, to the great sorrow of the little flock who usually assembled to worship at his house, and who felt that his departure involved their utter deprivation of those services which were to them the only social means of grace. But it was not so. A widow named Margaret Hughes, who held a farm in the vicinity, ventured, with Edward Parry's fate before her eyes, to open her house to receive the Methodist services. Complaints were made to her landlord by the accuser of Edward Parry, and she was served with a notice to quit her farm. At the expiration of the notice, however, no one came to take possession, and she was therefore induced to remain, in the hope that her landlord had relented. Probably he would have let the poor widow alone if he had been let alone himself; but the indefatigable informer of the parish would not let him rest until she had been ejected. She was accordingly turned out, with all her goods and chattels, in the month of August, and having no home to go to, she was obliged take up her abode under a temporary shelter thrown up in the corner of a common in the vicinity, where she had to remain till the close of the year. It was a wretched home, which could not protect her or her little household from either wind or rain; but she bore it bravely for the sake of Christ. And even here she did what she could. Her poor habitation was made a house of God, and the services which had been excluded with her from the comfortable home from which she had been so mercilessly expelled were continued under her roof of twigs and branches. As the winter advanced, a gentleman in the neighbourhood took compassion upon her, and allowed her to dwell in a house of which he was the owner, until the following spring.

This was not all that Margaret Hughes had to suffer for the sake of the gospel. On one Sabbath-day she went to Denbigh to hear a sermon at the house of one Thomas Lloyd. While the service was proceeding, a great crowd came up to the house, rushed in, and began to abuse the few worshippers, so that they were obliged to escape for their lives. They were pursued in the direction of Nantglyn, and Margaret Hughes was overtaken, pulled off her horse, and most brutally treated. Her clothes were partially torn off her body, and it is not known to what other lengths the ruffians would have proceeded if a gentleman had not happened to pass at the time and rescued her out of their hands. This kind gentleman charged her to make complaint to a neighbouring magistrate, adding, that if he did not do his duty, he would see him punished himself. Some of the actors in that dastardly outrage belonged to the wealthy class, and were possibly called "gentlemen;" and it is some satisfaction to know that the proceedings of that day turned out to be far more expensive to them than they had anticipated.

Owen Thomas Rowland was a blacksmith living at Llechgynfarwy in Anglesey. In his youth he was remarkable for his ungodliness, but he was induced by a friend to accompany him to hear a sermon by one of the Methodists. Owen did not at all enjoy the early part of the service, and made an attempt to go away, but the press was so great that he was obliged to remain where he was to the end; and from that day he was another man. He soon became as remarkable for his religious zeal as he had been for his wickedness. But those who had let him alone in his ungodliness would not tolerate his earnest religion, for he was not satisfied with quietly and peaceably seeking the salvation of his own soul, but he must likewise, to the great annoyance of some of his respectable neighbours, exert himself might and main for the salvation of others. The clergyman of the parish and a lady in the neighbourhood engaged a poet to write a satire on the Methodists, in which Owen Thomas Rowland was made conspicuously to figure. The following is a free translation of one of the stanzas:

> "The Blacksmith in pointing his nails,
>   Thinks in his heart no less
> Than that he has more learning and wisdom by far
>   Than a host of the bishops possess."

A copy of these doggerel verses was left at every house in the parish, and great was the excitement which they produced. But the blacksmith was not a man to be sung away from his religion, and therefore recourse was had to more stringent means. He held a little land under Lord Boston, and he was summoned into the presence of his Lordship's agent, and was given to understand by that great man that he must either break off his connection with the Methodists or give up his little farm. He chose the latter alternative; but depriving him of his few fields answered but little purpose, for he could not be turned out of his smithy, and he continued to work, to sing, to pray, and to exhort his neighbours as before. But he was a man that must be got rid of, and since there were no means by which he could be *turned* out of his workshop, there was nothing for it but to *starve* him out. Orders were accordingly sent to all the farmers on the estate that they were not to employ Owen Thomas Rowland on pain of losing their farms. By this tyrannical measure he was driven to the greatest straits, and, to escape utter starvation, was obliged to leave the country.

Thomas Lloyd of Denbigh was the owner of the house in which he lived, and because he made it a house of God, he incurred the displeasure of his persecuting neighbours. They could not turn him out of his habitation, but they seized all his furniture, leaving him nothing but the bare walls, and sold it publicly in the market-place. The same thing was done with the furniture of a house near Wrexham, where religious services were held. Every stick was taken to the town and publicly sold, and the whole of the proceeds was spent in drink. It was sport to some of the magnates of those days to plunge innocent families in the deepest distress, and to make their little property afford to the ruffianly tools of their despotism the means necessary for a "jollification."

Possibly all this was done under colour of law, and nothing was more easy. Complaint was made to a magistrate that a certain person held a "conventicle;" the offender was heavily fined, and the rest followed as a matter of course. We could greatly multiply instances of this nature, but it would be a mere repetition to do so. Let it suffice to say, that this kind of oppression was allowed to go on for many years over a large portion of the Principality. If it is martyrdom to suffer, and to suffer much, for the sake of the Gospel of Christ, the glorious host of martyrs will be greatly increased from the ranks of the Methodists of the last century.

But it was useless to attempt by any such means to arrest the mighty stream. The Methodists were like Israel in Egypt,—the more they were oppressed the more they multiplied; and they multiplied by means of the oppression. Those who were driven from their farms because they allowed preaching in their houses, found farms in other localities where earnest religion was unknown before, and were soon followed there by the preachers. Though driven from their homes for the crime of making them houses of God, as soon as they found other houses they did it again. Richard Hughes, a small farmer in Anglesey, was a fair sample of hundreds of his brethren. He was summoned, with a number of his Methodistical neighbours, into the presence of his landlord's agent and that of the clergyman of the parish. The former held in his hand a paper containing a list of the obnoxious tenants, and all those unhappy people were given to understand that they must either give up their

Methodism or quit their farms. One of their number ventured to plead that the law gave full liberty to every man to worship God according to the dictates of his own conscience; but the only reply he obtained was, that such were the landlord's orders, and that these must be carried out. Some of them gave way under the hard pressure, but Richard Hughes was so overwhelmed with a sense of the honour bestowed upon him in being thus called to suffer for conscience' sake, that he clapped his hands and shouted, "Blessed be God!" "Hosanna to the Son of David!" This unexpected outburst frightened the agent so much that he let the paper to which we have referred drop on the floor. The clergyman stood it bravely, and attempted to prevent the noisy Methodist from making such an uproar, but it was of no avail. The more the reverend gentleman remonstrated, the louder did Richard shout "Hosanna to the Son of David!" At length he went out, saying as he went, "Farewell, dear brethren; whoever is willing to sell an everlasting kingdom and a glorious crown for a poor farm at a high rent, it is not I; no, by the help of the Brother born for adversity—no, *never!*" And there were many and many in those days who, in similar circumstances, said again and again, *"No, never."*

NOTES

[1] The farm was Cwm-glas, not Cae-glas. John Hughes, *Methodistiaeth Cymru*, II, (Wrexham: Hughes, 1854), p.134.

CHAPTER VII

The Instigators of the Persecution—False Representations—
Sensible Gentry—Mr. Lewis, Mr. Bulkeley, and the strange
Preacher—A Sermon at Llysdulas Hall and its Results—Mr.
Bulkeley and Chancellor Wynne—Hugh Williams the
Blacksmith and Hugh Williams, Esquire—Mrs. Holland
Griffiths—Young Holland Griffiths's opinion—Griffith Siôn
and his Master.

MANY of the Welsh magistrates and gentry were
sufficiently inclined of their own accord to persecute
the Methodists, but it must be said, that even when they
were themselves disposed to let them alone, they were
frequently moved to take severe measures against them by
the representations and persuasions of others; and it is
painful to add, that those others were, for the most part, the
clergy of the Established Church. There are not many
instances of services having been disturbed and preachers
abused and beaten by the mob, or of people haled before
the magistrates and fined, or turned out of their farms on
account of their Methodism, which could not be traced to
the influence and efforts of some clergymen. The invariable
excuse for persecuting them was, that they were "against
the Church." But it is not true that they were against the
Church. Wherever the truth was earnestly preached in the
parish church, they gladly availed themselves of its services,
and the men whom for many years they acknowledged as
their leaders were nearly all episcopally ordained
clergymen. But many of the clergy of the time were men of
immoral lives, and there were many more who were
regarded by earnest people as anything but able ministers
of the New Testament; for although not chargeable with

113

conduct which might be regarded as unworthy of gentlemen, they yet lacked the earnestness and the life which, in their opinion, should characterise ministers of the gospel. From these they consequently turned away, and met in dwelling-houses and in barns to pray together, and to exhort, admonish, and encourage one another. The clergyman therefore felt insulted when he found his parishioners neglecting his ministrations and showing a preference for those of the blacksmith, the weaver, or the shoemaker. The measures which he would take to put down that which he looked upon as an opposition depended upon his own character. He would head a rabble to mob a preacher and scatter his hearers; or persuade a magistrate to take legal proceedings against the conventiclers; or make representations to the landlords of those people, with a view to induce them to turn them out of their farms or habitations: he would do either of those things, or the whole three, according to the sort of man he was himself. A drunken clergyman would not mind doing the first, and it was done by not a few, and the second and third were done by a great many.

False representations were made of those men and of the services which they held. Church services were only held by daylight, but those Methodists frequently met in the evenings, and conducted their services by candlelight. It was reported by their enemies that they put out the candles after a while, and that then followed the "dark prayer," which came to be the general designation for Methodist services; and there were base things said of their proceedings in the dark by men who ought to have known, and who *did* know, better.

But there were some magistrates and landed proprietors who had sense enough not to take those slanderous reports on credit, but who examined the matter for themselves; and there were others who, for a time, sorely oppressed the Methodists, but who forbore, and even encouraged and helped them after they had become better acquainted with their character. Mr. Marmaduke Gwynne, of Garth Hall, who was a magistrate of the county of Brecon, had heard such evil reports of Howel Harris that he resolved to avail himself of the first opportunity that offered itself to have him arrested and sent to jail. Finding that Harris was to preach at a short distance from Garth Hall, he went to the place fully intending to carry out this resolve, and taking the Riot Act in his pocket for the sake of dispersing the congregation. As he was leaving his house, he said to Mrs. Gwynne, "I will hear what the man says before I lay a hand upon him." So he did; and the result was, that at the close of the sermon he went up to the preacher, shook hands warmly with him, apologised for the mistake into which he had been led by false and malicious reports, and took him home with him to supper. From that day Mr. Gwynne became the protector and friend of the poor persecuted Methodists, and eventually one of his daughters was married to the Rev. Charles Wesley.

An aged preacher was going about exhorting in the neighbourhood of Amlwch in Anglesey, in the year 1740, and was very roughly handled by the populace. A magistrate in the vicinity, Mr. Lewis of Llysdulas, heard of the poor preacher's troubles, and sent for him to his house, where he invited a brother magistrate, Mr. Bulkeley of Bryndu, to meet him. The whole family were collected together into the hall, and Mr. Lewis, addressing the stranger, said, "We are here like the family of Cornelius, assembled to listen to your sermon, and you must preach to us now just as you are in the habit of preaching about the country." The preacher obeyed, and at the close of the sermon the gentlemen remarked to each other, "If this kind of thing is all the crime of this poor man, we must protect him and silence his persecutors." So they did; and an end was put for the time to that kind of persecution at Amlwch and its vicinity.

There was a dignitary of the Church known as

Chancellor Wynne living at Bodewryd in the same county, who was greatly vexed in his spirit by Methodistical services which were held at a house called Carreg-lefn, not far from his residence. The house was the property of the above Mr. Bulkeley, and the Chancellor sought to induce him to put an end to the annoyance. A servant was despatched to Bryn-du with a letter to Mr. Bulkeley, asking him to pull the house down if he could not put an end to the services in any other way. Mr. Bulkeley replied that he was very sorry that he could not accede to the Reverend Chancellor's request, and begged to be allowed to commend to his attention the fifth chapter of the Book of Acts, and especially the advice of Gamaliel to the Sanhedrin of the Jews. He received no more letters from the Chancellor. At Pentir-isaf, Caernarvonshire, there lived a blacksmith named Hugh Williams, who, after spending his early years in ungodliness, was deeply impressed by listening to one of the Methodist preachers, and from that hour became a zealous and devoted disciple of Christ. His landlord happened to be of the same name with himself, only he was called Hugh Williams, Esquire. The blacksmith was a special favourite with the Squire, for he found him to be an honest, trustworthy, and industrious man. The change in the former was for a while unnoticed by the latter, but an Association was held at Beaumaris, and Hugh could not resist the temptation to attend it. The Squire soon found that Hugh had been absent from his smithy, and, what was more important, he found where he had been. Next day he was sent for to the master's house, but before he had reached the place, he saw him coming to meet him in a terrible rage, and brandishing his staff in such a way as led poor Hugh to the conclusion that the first thing he was going to have was a beating, whatever might come next. He escaped, however, without blows, but his master bitterly reproached him for his ingratitude after all the kindness that he had shown him since he was a boy. Had not he been always kind to him? and here he was now changing his religion and joining these Roundheads, without as much as acquainting him with his intention to do so, or asking his permission.

"By your leave, master," said Hugh, "I have a word or two to say."

"What have you to say?" replied the master. "Have not I spoken the truth? If you have anything to say, say it. Let me hear what it is."

"I acknowledge, sir," said Hugh, "that all you have said is true. You have been very kind to me from my childhood to this day, for which I feel very grateful to you.

"Well," said the master, "and what next?"

"I need not tell you, sir," said Hugh, "that the way in which I have lived since I have grown up is well known to you. There was not a fair held within reach, nor a revel, nor any other wicked and sinful gathering but that I was present, and yet you never intimated to me that I was doing wrong; but now that I am seeking the good of my soul, you are offended with me, call me by ill names, and threaten to turn me out of my home. Oh, master! I have only one soul; and the time that is left me to provide for its welfare is very short; and I am resolved, if need be, to suffer being turned out of my habitation rather than do wrong to my immortal soul."

This appeal was too much for the Squire. He threw up his hands in amazement, and exclaimed, "Go! and in the name of God I shall never molest you." He was as good as his word; Hugh was allowed to remain in his smithy, and was as great a favourite as ever as long as his master lived. At Mr. Williams's death his estate fell to his brother, a clergyman, and then the blacksmith was obliged to leave.

After long seeking in vain for a place to live in, he heard that a Mrs. Griffiths had a house and smithy and a little land, which would just suit him, to let at Llanidan in the Isle of Anglesey. Thither he bent his steps, and having obtained an interview with the lady, preferred his request. One of her tenants was already under notice to quit his farm on account of his Methodism, and Hugh being aware of this fact, said, "I must tell you the truth, madam; I belong to the people who preach in dwelling-houses." "Which sect?" inquired the lady. "I belong," said Hugh, "to the Methodists." Upon this her son, Mr. Holland Griffiths, appeared on the scene, and his mother remarked to him, "I was about to let Tŷ-gwyn to this man. He seems to me to be an honest man enough, but he tells me that he belongs to the people who preach in houses."

"Pooh!" said the son, "what does that signify? If I were not ashamed to do so, I would go to hear them myself."

"You would, Holland?" asked the mother in astonishment.

"I would, indeed," was the son's reply. "They are a great deal better people than most who find fault with them."

"Then if it is so," said the mother, "Hugh Thomas must be allowed to remain in his farm after all, and this man shall have Tŷ-gwyn." And so it came to pass.

Griffith Siôn of Ynysypandy, Merionethshire, was a zealous Methodist, who kept his house open for religious services, and occasionally preached himself. But the meetings at Griffith's house were frequently disturbed by the clergyman of the parish, who came in making a great uproar, scolding by name those of his parishioners whom he found present, and occasionally making havoc among the plates and dishes on the kitchen shelves. On one occasion he entered during a prayer-meeting. A young man was at the moment engaged in prayer, and the parson recognising his voice, shouted aloud, "Is it you, Jack?" and forcing his way to the worshipper, roughly grasped his arm. Griffith Siôn was a man of great physical strength, but remarkable for his good temper. This, however, was more than he could bear. He laid hold of the reverend gentleman's arm with a mighty grip, dragged him out of the house, and flung him on the dunghill opposite the door. The clergyman did not care to encounter that sort of thing any more, and, accordingly changed his tactics. He drew up a memorial in which Griffith Siôn was represented as disturbing the peace of the parish and opposing the Church and the laws of the land. To this document he procured the signatures of some of his parishioners, and it was sent to the poor Methodist's landlord, Mr. Price of Rhiwlas, near Bala, where it promised to produce the desired result, for Griffith Siôn immediately received notice to quit his farm. The latter, understanding full well from whence the storm came, had a memorial in his favour drawn up and signed by a number of his neighbours, and with this he resolved to go to Rhiwlas and see Mr. Price for himself. He earnestly begged to be allowed to retain his little farm, but his master replied, "You shall not, Griffith, for I find that you disturb the neighbourhood, and prevent people from going to church."

"In truth, master," said Griffith, "I am not doing any such things."

"It is useless your denying," said the master; "and you shall not on any account live on my estate, for do you not hold the dark prayer, and bring men and women together to do mischief?"

"We are doing nothing of the kind, sir," was Griffith's reply.

"What then? You are in the habit of meeting in the evenings?"

"Yes, sir; we do sometimes meet after the work of the day is over."

"And what is it that you do in those meetings?"

"I will tell you, sir," said Griffith. "We read the Bible and sing psalms. We exhort one another to be honest and truthful, and to pay all rents and taxes. We pray for the Church, the King, and our country. This, indeed, sir, is what we do, besides exhorting each other to cease from sin and to seek the favour of God and everlasting life; and since we do no injury to any man, I hope, sir, you will allow me to remain in my farm."

"Well, Griffith," said the master, "if you promise me that you will give up those meetings you shall remain."

"Master," said Griffith in a determined tone, " I cannot do that. If you were to give me the half of your estate I could not make that promise. *No, never.*"

Mr. Price, who had been for some time melting, was now completely vanquished, and bursting into tears said, "Go home, Griffith, go home. You shall *keep* your farm; and when you come to Bala to attend your Association, remember to bring your horse to Rhiwlas." From that day Griffith Siôn was a great favourite with his master. On one occasion when he wanted to see him on business, Mr. Price was attending a magistrates' meeting at Bala, but finding that his tenant was waiting outside, he went out to speak with him. On his return he was asked by one of his brother magistrates who his visitor was, and he answered that he was a preacher. "Is he a great preacher?" one of the bench asked. "I do not know about that," replied Mr. Price, "but I know one thing about him,—*he is a godly man.*"

CHAPTER VIII

Checks to Persecution—Miracles or what ?—End of some of
Howel Harris's persecutors—The unfulfilled Vow—
Chancellor Owen and his Clerk—Sir W. W. Wynn—The great
Prayer-Meeting—Deliverance—Penrhyndeudraeth—A Plot
to pull down the Chapel—How it failed—A Feast, and how
it finished.

THE more *favourable* light in which the Methodists
gradually came to be regarded by some of the leading
gentry of the Principality checked, as we have seen, in a
great measure, the persecutions to which they had been
exposed. But there were other causes which mightily
contributed to the same effect. Certain occurrences took
place from time to time, and in various localities, which are
so strange that many will refuse to credit them, while they
will be regarded by some as the interventions of Divine
Providence in behalf of persecuted Christians, and by others
as nothing more than strange coincidences. We have not the
least objection in the world to being numbered among
"those who have unlimited faith in the miraculous," if by
that phrase is meant a firm belief in the power of God to
perform a miracle when that is necessary, in the present day
as well as in the ages that are long past. But our present
duty is not to discuss the subject of miracles, nor to defend
our own particular views on that important subject, but to
relate facts, leaving it to our readers to draw their own
conclusions, only premising that those which we lay before
them are vouched for by people whose evidence upon any
other subject no one would have hesitated to receive.

The man who threw the first stone into the house in
which Howel Harris preached at Bala, when he suffered that

brutal treatment which we have already described, fell off his horse as he was returning from a fair a short time afterwards, injured his spine, and soon died. There was one who made a desperate effort to push the preacher over a rock into a pool six yards deep, and not long after he fell over that very rock himself, and was killed on the spot. Another who was most active among the mob fell off his horse, fractured his skull, and instantly died. Thus three of the most violent persecutors on that memorable occasion had, before many days had elapsed, died violent deaths.

There was a tenant of a Mrs. Lloyd of Gesail, near Penmorfa, Caernarvonshire, who opened his house for religious services, and had been allowed to do so unmolested for some time. At length there came a clergyman, who had already distinguished himself for his anti-Methodist zeal, with his wife, to pay a visit to Mrs. Lloyd. One morning while he was staying at Gesail, he went out to call on a brother clergyman who resided in the neighbourhood. In the course of their conversation the local clergyman remarked to his visitor that there was a tenant of Mrs. Lloyd who had Methodist services held in his house although he lived very near the mansion, and that he was afraid that no one had been kind enough to inform the lady of the man's misconduct. "Then," said his visitor, "I shall not eat my dinner to-day before I have informed her." But he was never permitted to do so. When he reached the house he was found unable to speak. He never uttered a word again, and died in a few days. We have spoken of Chancellor Owen of Llannor as a fierce and merciless persecutor. He had a clerk who was likewise a rhymer, and this worthy was employed by him to compose a satirical poem against the Methodists, which was printed and industriously circulated about the country. At a festive gathering which occurred soon afterwards, the Chancellor introduced his clerk to the company as the author of the song which they all so greatly admired, and a collection was made on the spot for the gifted rhymer, which amounted to fifty guineas. Soon afterwards the master conceived a most bitter and unaccountable enmity against the servant, and one Sunday as they were leaving the service he rushed upon him in the churchyard and commenced beating him with all his might, charging him with having made an attempt to murder him by *throwing the church bell on his back.* The astonished clerk turned upon his master, and there was a furious fight. The former was of course dismissed from his office, soon managed to get through his fifty guineas, and spent the remainder of his days in poverty and wretchedness.

Sir W. W. Wynn was the owner of an estate at Llanuwchllyn, near Bala, and Methodism had made considerable progress among his tenantry at that place. We have already mentioned his having been obliged to return some fines which he had illegally imposed on some of the Methodists in the neighbourhood of Wrexham, and it appears that this had roused his ire to such an extent that he expressed the resolve that not a single member of the "sect" should be allowed to reside anywhere on his estates. Tidings of this reached the ears of the little flock at Llanuwchllyn, and great was their distress at the prospect which it held before them. They knew their master too well to entertain the least hope that any man would be able to shake the resolution which was to them so fraught with disaster, and in their trouble they resolved to lay their sad case together before their heavenly Father. A special prayer-meeting was held to ask Almighty God to open for them a way of deliverance, and especially to entreat Him for strength to be faithful to His truth whatever might happen to themselves; and they had not to separate without evidences which satisfied them that He was willing that they should thus approach Him, and that He would with the temptation also make a way of escape, that they might be able to bear it. In a few days the news reached them that the great object of their dread had fallen from his horse on the hunting-field and had been killed on the spot.

Some years after the event which we have just related, an

effort was made by a little band which had been gathered together at Penrhyndeudraeth, in the same county, to build a place for worship. When they had finished it up to the roof, they found the greatest difficulty in procuring slates to cover it in, for all the proprietors in the neighbourhood had agreed not to let them have any on their property. The Ffestiniog quarries were within a few miles, but were closed to them, and not a slate could they have on any terms, and the building, therefore, remained for some time unroofed. At length they were enabled to get over their difficulty by the kindness of another Sir Watkin, who was a man of a very different spirit from his persecuting sire. He gave them permission to search for slates on his property, which was lying at some miles' distance. It was very rough and uncouth material that they succeeded in finding, and so rugged and mountainous was the spot where it was found, that the chapel people had to convey it to its destination on the backs of horses; but they pushed on though all their difficulties, and the little chapel was completed. The persecutors were annoyed, but not disconcerted. If the Methodists had succeeded in completing their chapel, it would not cost much labour to pull it down, and this they resolved to do. A day was fixed for this act of Vandalism, but on the evening of the preceding day, the man who was to take the lead in the bad business suddenly died, and the rest, having lost their leader, had not strength of heart enough to proceed, and the chapel was left in peace. But there was a wealthy woman in the place, a relative of the deceased man, who was by no means willing to let the Methodists have their way. Little would they be the better of their chapel unless they could hold services in it. It had been built for preaching, and she would take care that no one should preach in it in peace *as long as she lived.* Such was the resolution that she expressed, and she did her utmost to give it effect. A sermon was announced at the chapel, and the report of it reached the lady's ears. She accordingly hired a number of strong men, who were likewise men of Belial, to go to the place, disperse the congregation, and send the preacher about his business; and it was arranged that, after having done all this, they were to go to her house to dinner. The morning came, and the preacher and a few people assembled together to hear the Word, but scarcely had the proceedings commenced when there came upon them the lady's hired host, who soon broke up the meeting and chased the preacher away. Having done this, they retired to the house of her who had employed them to enjoy the promised feast. There were great preparations, in which, as it seems, the mistress herself took an active part; but before it was complete a disaster took place which made the house anything but a house of feasting. By some mismanagement on the part of the lady herself, or some of her assistants, the contents of a large boiling pot were poured over her person, and she was scalded so severely that she almost immediately died.

"But are we to rush to the conclusion that these and similar events were the interpositions of Providence? Is a man able to know good or evil, love or hatred, by all that is before him? Do not the same things happen to the evil and the good? Have not preachers died in the pulpit? And have not good Christians expired in the very act of prayer? When one reflects on the innumerable things which continually happen, such coincidences are perhaps fewer and less remarkable than a fair calculation of chances would warrant us to expect." Perhaps it is so. We have not had much experience in the calculation of chances, and have not much faith in the process; but events of the kind which we have narrated affect our story, not according to the light in which they are regarded in the present day, but according as they were looked upon at the time in which they happened. We are getting quite familiar with modes of expression and of thought which the Welsh people of those days had never heard of. Whatever we may think of those occurrences, the poor persecuted Methodists of that time had no doubt but that they were the interventions of their God in their behalf;

and their enemies and persecutors had, to say the least, grave suspicions that such was the case, and, therefore, thought it safer to let them alone.

CHAPTER IX

THE indomitable zeal of the Methodists, their hearty
consecration to the work of their Master, and the mighty
influences which attended their ministry, at length
completely did away with that which the occurrences which
we have narrated in the preceding chapter only served to
check. Not only were their preachers remarkable for their
zeal and devotedness, but also the private members, both
men and women, were characterised by the same spirit.
There were a great many small farmers, farm-labourers,
artisans, and women in the humblest walks of life, who saw
no sacrifice too great to make for their Lord, and who made
every other consideration subservient to His cause and the
salvation of their neighbours.

There was a Thomas Hughes living near Llangollen, who
was a poor man, but a zealous and devoted Christian. His
wife was of the same spirit with himself, and she had a brother
who was older than herself by many years, and who was the
owner of considerable property. This gentleman regarded her
religion with much disfavour, and made several attempts to
dissuade her and her husband from attending the Methodist
meetings. He thought that he had a powerful auxiliary in the
"almighty guinea," but had the disappointment to find all
his efforts, even with that assistance, proving of no avail. He
told his sister, that if she and her husband gave up their

Methodism he would leave her the whole of his wealth, but that otherwise she should not have a shilling. "Never mind, brother," was her reply; "if you only gave me three halfpence I would give two of them towards the cause of Christ, and keep only the third for myself." In great anger he declared that she should never have a penny after him; and such, no doubt, was his intention; but his poor sister was not called upon to make the sacrifice, for he died suddenly and intestate, and she inherited all the wealth she had been so willing to forego for the sake of the gospel.

Another Thomas Hughes lived at Mochdre, in Denbighshire, who was in very humble circumstances, but a man of great Christian energy and zeal. He was an exhorter of small talent and slender knowledge; but his sense of the darkness and danger in which his neighbours lay constrained him to labour, in season and out of season, to see if he could by any means save some of them. He occasionally went to Conwy to exhort, where he stood forth in the street, or under the old walls of the town, or anywhere that he could get a few people to stand and listen. But the clergyman of the place and others would often disturb him in these efforts to do good; and at length, seeing that he persisted in intruding himself and his doctrines into the town, the reverend gentleman gave orders that he should be arrested and brought before him. There were many of the established clergy of those days who had but very little religion; but we would fain hope that there were not many who had as little common sense as the then vicar of Conwy. When the poor exhorter was brought into his presence, the following dialogue took place:—

Clergyman. "You ought to be a learned man to go about to preach, and able to answer deep questions."

Exhorter. "What questions, sir?"

Cler. "Here they are,—those which were asked me by the Lord Bishop. Let's see whether you will be able to answer them: Where was St. Paul born?"

Ex. "In Tarsus."

Cler. "Hem; I see that you know something, too. Well, can you tell me who took charge of the Virgin Mary after our blessed Redeemer was crucified?"

Ex. "John."

Cler. "Well. Once again: Who wrote the Book of Revelation? Answer that if you can."

Ex. "John the Apostle."

Cler. "Ho; you seem to know a good deal after all."

Ex. "Perhaps, sir, you will allow me to ask you one or two questions?"

Cler. "O yes, only they must be religious questions."

Ex. "What is holiness? and how may a sinner be justified before God?"

Cler. "Ho! we have no business to bother ourselves with such things; and you have no business to put such questions to a man in my position. Go out of my sight this minute." And to the men who had brought him, "Take care that you do not bring such men into my presence any more."

After this interview Thomas Hughes was allowed to pursue his labours at Conwy in peace, and this encouraged him to extend them to other quarters. There was a place called Tywyn Ferry lying about midway between Conwy and Llandudno, the inhabitants of which were steeped in ignorance and sin, and our exhorter resolved to make an attempt upon it. He got a report circulated in the neighbourhood that a sermon would be preached at a place where crowds of the people usually assembled to play, on the next following Sunday afternoon. The report, as it appears, said nothing at all as to who the preacher was to be, or where he was to come from. When the time arrived, he went to the place accompanied by a religious friend, and he found there a great number of people, some pursuing their games, and others looking out for the preacher. The appearance of things was by no means promising, for there were several heaps of stones put up in readiness for the stranger's reception as soon as he made his appearance; but Thomas Hughes being unknown in the neighbourhood, and as unclerical in his garb as any among the crowd, no one for a moment suspected that he was the man; and he laid himself down on the grass among the rest and entered into conversation with them. After a time, and when their patience was beginning to fail, he stood up and said, "Well, lads, there is no sign at all of a preacher coming; very likely the man has heard that we were going to stone him, and that he won't come after all. Let one of us go on the top of that heap of stones and exhort, and the rest sing; would not that be first-rate play?"

"Capital," said a bully, who was the recognised leader of the crowd. "Go you now on the heap and preach to us."

"Yes I will," said Thomas Hughes; "but what shall I do for a book?"

"I have a book," said the friend who had accompanied him to the place, handing him a Bible.

"Very well," said the exhorter. "I am willing to try; but mind you, you must be civil, and not laugh if I make some blunders."

"I'll make them civil," said the bully. "Listen here, lads, whoever dares to laugh, *I'll* put one of these stones into his head."

"Stop you," said Hughes, "the first thing to do is to pray, is it not?"

"Ay, ay," said the bully, "and I'll be clerk. I'll stand before you and you shall use my shoulder for a pulpit."

Prayer was offered, and that in right earnest, and which elicited at its close several favourable remarks such as "Pretty well indeed!" "'Pon my word, as good as a parson!"

The preacher proceeded to read his text, when the bully shouted, "Hold on, you fool! let's sing first." And they sang a Welsh hymn after a fashion. Then came the sermon, which was listened to most attentively, and one at least of the hearers, and he the bully and extempore clerk, left the place a changed man.

There was a poor woman named Lowri Williams, who with her husband was living at a fulling-mill, called Pandy Chwilog, near Pwllheli. The husband was not a decidedly religious man, but he encouraged Methodistical services by attending them with his wife, and for that reason they were turned out of their home. But Providence led them to another "Pandy" in the parish of Maentwrog, Merionethshire. This was called Pandy'r-ddwyryd, which being interpreted, means the fulling-mill on two streams.[1] Here they were at a great distance from the religious means which the wife so greatly loved. The two nearest places at which they were held were Brynengan on one side and Bala on the other, and the former of these was at a distance of fifteen and the latter eighteen miles. By dint of much labour Lowri Williams succeeded in getting preachers now and again from great distances to hold services at her own house. Their ministry and her godly conversation were blessed to the conversion of a number of people. A Society was formed in the place, numbering eight members, who continued for a time to be called "The Noah's ark family." This was a small beginning, but the increase was truly marvellous. The earnest prayers and persevering zeal of this humble woman were the means of establishing in the north-western portion of Merionethshire no less than eighteen churches, and those before she was called to her rest had so increased as to number together about a thousand communicants. It is not strange, therefore, that to this day she is designated "Lowri Williams the apostle." There were places in a neighbouring wood where she spent much time alone, wrestling with God, and it is said that there were red paths leading from her house to those Peniels, where many a time she had prevailed and carried away with her a blessing for her own soul and for her perishing neighbours. She would not let any living man alone. As sure as any one talked with Lowri Williams he would have to listen to something about his own soul and about Him who came to seek and to save that which was lost; and often were her words a blessing to those to whom they were spoken. On one occasion a young man who was on his way to one of the merry-makings which were then so frequent in Wales, called at her house to inquire for the safe place to cross a neighbouring stream. She accompanied him out and gave the necessary directions. Just as she was turning back she asked him, "Now, my young man, are you in the habit of inquiring the way to everlasting life sometimes on the Sabbath?" "No, never," was the reply; "I do not care at all about such things." "Then," said she, "come here to my house at such a time, and there will be a man showing the way to heaven." "Not I, indeed," said the young man, and away he went to his amusement. But Lowri Williams had spoken, and her words did not usually fall to the ground. She had prayed, and her prayers were not often left unanswered. The words cleaved to the young man's conscience, and he found himself constrained to go to her house at the appointed time to hear about the way to heaven. From that time he became himself a traveller in that way, and God made him an eminently useful one. Griffith Ellis, for that was the young man's name, joined the company of eight in the little church, and so made them one too many to he called "The Noah's ark family" any longer. He proved a great blessing to his district, and travelled frequently and far to procure preachers to proclaim the everlasting gospel to his perishing neighbours. His lofty piety and holy conversation made him the terror of all the sinners in his neighbourhood, and even the clergyman of his parish, much as he loved cock-fighting, would never venture to meet him with a cock under his arm. It mattered nothing whom else he would come across; he would walk along bearing his game bird without the least shame or fear, but if he caught a glimpse of Griffith Ellis coming to meet him, one of two things would surely happen,—either the reverend gentleman would turn round and walk hastily away, or the captive bird would be set at liberty. The times of which we write produced a great number of such men as Griffith Ellis scattered over the whole surface of the Principality, and it is the weight of their character that completely crushed persecution. Their eminently pure, unselfish, and godly life caused a whisper in the consciences of the people, which made itself known as the voice of God, and which said, "Touch not Mine anointed, and do My prophets no harm."

There are many instances in which the earnest and persevering efforts of a very few eventually resulted in the establishment of strong and flourishing churches. Let us give a few examples.

Tonyrefail is a lonely hamlet of the parish of Llantrisant, in Glamorganshire, and situated in a deep glen some five or six miles from the little town which gives the parish its name. On a mountain, which rises from the village towards the south, and which is known as Peterstone Mountain, there was an annual gathering, which in Wales went by the name of "Mabsant" which, being interpreted, means "The son of a saint."[2] From the name we infer that in its origin it was a religious gathering, and that its object was to celebrate the anniversary of the patron saint of the parish church; but it had become the source of sin and immorality. It extended over several days, and great numbers came together from the surrounding districts to eat, drink, dance and play; but they seldom separated without a considerable amount of fighting; and the great day of the feast was Sunday. An eminent clergyman, who was as remarkable for his preaching power as for his Methodism, had been presented to a living about eight miles to the south of this scene of riot. This was the Reverend David Jones of Llan-gan, of whom by-and-by we shall have much more to say. Mr. Jones conceived the idea of going to the Peterstone "Mabsant" to preach the gospel; and so effectual was his ministry that an end was put to the dancing and the games, and the annual festival became an annual sermon, which was continued for many years on the same day and the same spot. There lived at a comfortable little mansion known as "Collennau" (The Hazels), near Tonyrefail, a gentleman of the name of Mr. Evan Pritchard, whose love for rural pleasures had induced him to refuse a University education with a view to the ministry in the Church. On one occasion he and Mrs. Pritchard resolved to go to Peterstone to hear the renowned clergyman. They were both prejudiced against him on account of his Methodism; but that prejudice was not sufficient to restrain their curiosity to see and hear him. He preached from Rev. vi. 17: "'For the great day of His wrath is come; and who shall be able to stand?" A thrill of fear passed though the lady's soul at the announcement of the text, and that feeling greatly increased during the sermon which followed; and Mr. Pritchard himself was likewise deeply affected. After the service they went on towards Cowbridge to visit Mrs. Pritchard's mother. They were gloomy enough as they rode along; but the lady found a crumb of comfort, which she sought to impart to her husband, in the hope that, after all, there was not such a verse in the Bible as the clergyman had taken for his text, and that it was only his Methodistical device to frighten people. Anyhow, she had been frightened enough, and attended a ball at Cowbridge, in the hope that it would be the means of dissipating her painful feelings. But it proved to be a miserable ball. The louder the merriment, the unhappier she became; and very unhappy she and her husband continued to be until a few weeks afterwards they heard another sermon, which, by the blessing of God, was the means of leading them to seek rest in the Lord Jesus. After this religious services were held at Collennau; and those being blessed to the conversion of several of the neighbours, a little church was formed in the house. After some time, in consequence of the severe illness of Mr. Pritchard,—an illness from which he never recovered,—the services were removed to a house in the village, where, for a while, the cause wore a very prosperous aspect; but in the course of time the death of some and the removal of others from the neighbourhood, reduced the church to eight members, all of whom were females. Under such discouraging circumstances, it would not have been strange if the little community had dissolved itself; but the sisters clung together, and held their weekly "Societies" among themselves, at which Mrs. Pritchard discharged the duties of an elder, while Jane Morris led the singing, and Mary James, who excelled in the gift of prayer, opened and closed the meetings. On the Sabbaths, and whenever besides it was practicable, some minister or exhorter was obtained to preach. By-and-by the church began again to grow, several men joined it, and among them one David Evans, an exceedingly gifted young man, who proved of great service to the cause, and who in process of time married one of the young sisters. Mr. and Mrs. Evans had a numerous family; and one of the youngest of their sons is now living, and has been for many years one of the most talented and popular among the ministers of the Calvinistic Methodist Connexion. The Reverend William Evans of Tonyrefail is now verging on eighty-nine years of age, having preached for upwards of sixty-six years; and he preaches still, in the neighbourhood of his home, almost every Lord's Day. On the 7th of June, 1871, we had the pleasure of hearing him preach in the open air to a very large congregation, within a few yards of the spot where Howel Harris first breathed the spiritual life. He had a complete mastery over his subject and his audience; his spirit seemed to burn with the love of Christ and of souls; while his silvery voice made the welkin ring. The faithfulness of the eight sisters bore abundant fruit, for there has been for very many years, and is now, at Tonyrefail, for the neighbourhood, a numerous church.

We give a still more remarkable instance of great results arising from the faithfulness of a small number. The Rev. W. Davies of Neath had been invited to preach at a small chapel at a considerable distance from his home, where, on his arrival, he found three unmarried sisters, somewhat advanced in life, occupying together an adjoining house, and in very humble circumstances. In this house he was entertained, and humble enough was his fare. A few people came together to hear the sermon, and Mr. Davies preached with great pleasure to himself and to his audience. After the service he inquired of the sister who attended on him what was the number of the church. "There are only we three," was the reply. "We are trying between us to keep up the cause. One of us cleans and opens the chapel; another attends to the preachers' horses; while I have the honour of attending on the preachers themselves. We hold a Society in the chapel once a week, and leave the door open to any who may wish to join us." When Mr. Davies was about to leave, she tendered him sixpence for his services. At first he declined to receive it; but she pressed him, saying, that it had been dedicated from their small means unto the Lord, and that they were very sorry that their deep poverty made it impossible for them to devote more to the same purpose. After some years Mr. Davies visited the place again, and found the church increased to 180 members. Religion was with those people the one great business of life, to which every other consideration must be made subservient; and they made very light of every obstacle that was thrown in their way to the enjoyment of its privileges or the discharge of its duties.

Robert Lloyd was a journeyman shoemaker living at Rhuthun, in Denbighshire, and was very popular in the town in consequence of the kindness of his disposition and the extent of his intelligence. He seems to have been the oracle of the place, and it was a very common occurrence, when a difference of opinion upon any subject arose between men who were much higher in station than himself, for the disputants to refer the matter to "Robert the Shoemaker." He could read English well, and was able to give the last news of the war that was then raging between England and France. This made him a general favourite, but there was one drawback, and that was that he was a Methodist. His master greatly valued him as a skilful and conscientious workman, but he was bitterly opposed to his religion. There was a small church then formed at a place some three or four miles from the town, and of this little community Robert was a member. They met weekly for spiritual conversation, and, in consequence of the great distances at which some of their number resided, it was found necessary to hold those meetings at mid-day; and on those days Robert's master usually gave him some work of great urgency, on purpose to prevent him from going to the service. He was too religious either to disobey his master or to lose the opportunity to meet his brethren to worship God, and he would, therefore, on those occasions, rise at one or two o'clock in the morning, and never fail to finish his allotted task in time for the service. But his mother was as opposed to his religion as his master, and it sometimes happened, when he went home from his work, that he could find neither his coat nor his hat, both having been hid by the old lady, to prevent her son from going to the meeting of "The Roundheads." But Robert could not be hindered by his mother's device any more than by his master's. When the search for his hat and coat would prove fruitless, as it often did, the only difference it made was, that the young shoemaker would then appear among his brethren in his paper cap and shirt-sleeves. On one occasion, when on his way to Bontuchel to hear a sermon, he was met by one of his neighbours, a man of wealth and position, who remonstrated with him on the folly of attending such meetings, adding, that it was a pity that such a respectable and intelligent young man as he was should demean himself by mixing with such a poor lot as the Methodists, and urging him to withdraw from them altogether, and to live like a man among his neighbours. A discussion ensued, which resulted in the gentleman's going with Robert to hear the sermon, and a very effectual sermon to him it proved to be. He returned to his home in great distress, and on that night he could not help relating to a friend who slept with him some of the dreadful things the preacher had said. On the following night, when they were retiring together to rest, the friend said to him with great earnestness, "Upon my soul, if you mention anything of that which you talked about last night, I'll pay your skin to-morrow.[3] I was so desperately frightened by what you said after the preacher, that I could not sleep the whole of the night." But the sermon had reached the hearts of both, and they soon became the companions of Robert Lloyd in his journeys to the services, and zealous members of the same community.

For many years there was in North Wales a great dearth of preachers. In the South, as we have seen, ten episcopally ordained clergymen had at an early period joined the Methodist movement, several of whom made frequent journeys into distant localities to preach the gospel, and there soon arose a large number of "Exhorters," many of whom were men of great preaching power. But in the North it was very different for a long time. It was chiefly through the evangelistic labours of preachers from the South that the churches in the northern province of the Principality had been formed; and though the members of these churches regularly met together for mutual prayer and edification, it was to the South they had for a number of years to look for preachers, and many and long were the journeys made by those zealous brethren and sisters for that purpose. They derived spiritual edification themselves from the converse of each other, but they ardently thirsted for the salvation of their neighbours, and they saw no labours too arduous to undertake, and no sacrifice too great to make, in order to secure the preaching of the gospel in their respective localities. They had unbounded faith in the power of the ministry, which they had found so efficient towards themselves. They were firmly persuaded, if they could only secure a visit from a preacher of the gospel, that the Spirit of

God would accompany his ministry, and that some of their neighbours would be saved; and it was very rarely that they were disappointed. When the cry, "Come over and help us!" went from them towards the South, there went forth another cry to heaven from the depths of their heart. It was, "Come, O breath, from the four winds!" When the preacher came, he went forth like Ezekiel in the Spirit of the Lord, and the hand of the Lord was upon him, and therefore it is not strange that there should have been a noise and a shaking, and that many who had been so far dead in trespasses and sins were made partakers of the life of God.

At Caergwrle, in Flintshire, there lived a good man named Thomas Edwards, but who was known among his neighbours as Thomas the Turner. Being a bachelor, and an industrious man, it seems that he had been able to save some money, and this he laid out in the building of a small chapel. The only assistance he had towards the erection was the sum of five shillings from one Ithel Hill. He made several journeys to Llangeitho, a distance of more than a hundred miles, to procure preachers for his little sanctuary. When they had come, it was very rarely that he had the pleasure of listening to their ministry, for the rabble would gather around the door and make a great disturbance, and it was as much as he could do to prevent them from rushing in to abuse the preacher. He was able to manage the outside mob pretty tolerably, for he was a man of great physical power; and this satisfied him, while he hoped that the preacher, by the blessing of God, would be able to do something greater and better inside. But he had a way to compensate himself for these deprivations. The preacher was on a tour, and only took Caergwrle in his way, preaching two or three times a day as he went along. Thomas would follow him from place to place as long as his money held out, and when that was exhausted he would return home and work away at his trade, while waiting for the blissful time when another preacher would pass.

But all were not like Thomas the Turner. When he had five-and-twenty shillings in his pocket it was all his own, and he felt in his conscience, when his wealth had so increased, that it was full time for him to start south to look for a preacher, and if he found it all gone by the time he returned, he had only to go to his lathe for more. Those who were not so favourably circumstanced usually made a subscription to enable one of their number to go to Llangeitho against[4] the great monthly gathering, where there would be an abundance of preachers and exhorters, in order to invite some of them to take a tour through portions of the north. This was the custom at Berthen-gron in Flintshire. The subscription usually amounted to about twenty shillings, and Catherine Owen, the wife of John Owen, who was himself a humble exhorter, was generally the chosen messenger of the Church. With that small sum in her pocket this woman would start on her pilgrimage of upwards of a hundred miles of rough roads and bleak mountains. She made that journey seven times, and on several occasions returned jubilant, having not only heard Rowland, and enjoyed the delightful feasts of Llangeitho, but having likewise secured promises of visits to the north from as many as fifteen preachers.

Such were the men and women of those days: such their zeal for the cause of Christ, their self-sacrifice and entire consecration to His interests. The result was only such as might have been expected. The Word of the Lord grew and multiplied, and in almost every district throughout Wales great multitudes were converted to the faith.

NOTES

[1] The translation is both incorrect and misleading. The Dwyryd in this instance is the name of the river flowing through the Vale of Maentwrog.

[2] This translation, while strictly literal, is inadequate.

'Mabsant' would be better translated as either 'saintly man' or 'dear saint'. [I am grateful to Richard Crowe of the University of Wales Welsh Dictionary staff for supplying information on the derivation of this term.]

[3] 'Pay your skin' is a literal translation of John Hughes's original text. The proper English equivalent would be 'give you a hiding'

[4] In preparation for, in anticipation of.

CHAPTER X

WE have now to turn from this scene of earnest labour
and triumphant success to another, which we cannot
contemplate but with painful feelings. Up to the year 1750
the career of the Calvinistic Methodist body had been one
of success. Persecution had in a great measure ceased, and
outward opposition had been prevailed over; but about that
time there arose a contention within the body itself which
threatened it with utter ruin. Harris and Rowland were
regarded as the leading men of the Connexion, but which
of the two was the leading *man* was a point which was not
determined, and a point about which few, if anybody, cared.
Between those two men a serious dispute arose, which had
the disastrous result of dividing the Connexion for many
years. It was not a dispute on the question, "Who shall be
greatest?" as some have groundlessly insinuated, nor was
it on a personal matter at all, but on a question of doctrine,
and not of doctrine either, properly speaking, but about the
words in which a doctrine, which each of them believed with
all his heart, ought to be expressed.[1] There is no truth which
those brethren held with a firmer and deeper conviction
than that of the proper Deity of our blessed Redeemer; but
the terms in which that great truth was taught by Rowland

142

and others were too indefinite and colourless to satisfy Howel Harris; while he, on the other hand, employed terms and expressions which to his brethren sounded harsh, if not irreverent. A few passages from Harris's Diary will help the reader to form an idea of the nature of the misunderstanding between those apostolic men, which began as early as 1745, and came to an open rupture in the year 1751:—

"In the year 1743, the glory of the Divinity of Jesus Christ was more deeply impressed on my soul than ever. The more I meditate on that text, 'Great is the mystery of godliness; God was manifest in the flesh,' the more the glory thereof shineth on my soul. I had also much help to see more of the glory and wonders of the Divinity of Christ by reading a tract called 'A Sling and a Stone.' I now was brought to see more and more wonders in His infinite incarnation, life, blood, death, and resurrection."[2]

In 1746 he writes, "As my spirit increased more and more in beholding the glory of that God-Man, whom I now beheld clearly the wonder of all worlds, the terror of devils, the delight of angels, and the real and only hope of poor sinners, then I began to find great opposition to my preaching His Godhead and death, especially in Wales. This opposition gained ground, and I began to be openly opposed, and also by many who called themselves my spiritual children. But the year following (1747) the enmity grew stronger against the preaching of God's humiliation and death; still I bore all in the hope of seeing this storm ceasing, as I had seen many others. I now also beheld very evidently a tendency in the ministry to please men, and to appear wise and popular in the world, and a great many of my nearest friends both in England and Wales losing their former simplicity, although the number of teachers increased daily. I found also that the spirits of many grew whole, great, and proud, and would not take the word of reproof or exhortation, although they called me their father, and [I] really was so, as I began the work in this last revival,

especially in Wales, though I have spent a great part of my time in England, to spread abroad the fame of the dear Saviour... As the Lord Himself sent me round the country at my first setting out, and gave me a desire to please Him only, and helped me to speak plain truths, so at this time a necessity was laid upon me to preach that great truth which He revealed to my own soul, viz., the wonderful condescension and mystery of God in our nature reconciling the world to Himself, not imputing their sins; that He was God in the womb of Mary, when He assumed our nature, laying in Himself the foundation of our salvation and deliverance, and was the supreme God in His poor birth and swaddling-clothes, and in all His sufferings; that He was the great I AM, the ALPHA and OMEGA, and that there is none other God but He! There are three Persons, but one God, and those who worship another god besides Him do so worship an idol, for in Him dwelleth all the fulness of the Godhead bodily. And when the time came to make an atonement for our sins; when He, the great sacrifice, was raised on the altar of the cross, all nature, earth and hell, was in an uproar or confusion. The sun was darkened, the earth trembled, the dead awoke and were raised, that all might inquire what is the cause and meaning of all this—
"TIS THE MIGHTY MAKER DIES!'—*Dr. Watts.*

"I went on thus some years through Wales bearing my testimony to those truths in the face of carnal professors, *Arian* and *Socinian,* who all railed against me. Although it proved to be an occasion of much murmuring, contention, and division, yet I am in a lively hope that the Lord will bless His own truths in His proper time; it may be when I am gone."[3]

The great truth of which Howel Harris speaks as having been revealed to his soul, is now held in the Welsh Calvinistic Methodist body as the main foundation on which the whole fabric of Christianity rests; but there is not one amongst us who would express it in the same words as he did, nor one whose feelings would not be shocked by hearing it so expressed. It strikes us that he began to preach with a very incomplete knowledge of Christian doctrine. The burden of his ministry for years was, "Escape to the refuge!" The world was perishing in sin. His soul within him longed to save it from its terrific doom, and he devoted himself with fiery zeal and tremendous energy to that great object. Gradually the distinctive doctrines of the gospel began to dawn upon his mind, and foremost of all the great fundamental truth of the Divinity of our Redeemer, and he regarded it as having been revealed to his own soul. Most probably he was under the impression that his brethren were still as ignorant of it as he had been so far himself. This is by no means an uncommon thing. Wales has in our days been visited from time to time by zealous evangelists and revivalists from beyond the Severn; and we have heard some of those good brethren insisting with great vehemence on very rudimentary truths, which, to themselves, were evidently recent discoveries, but which to most of their hearers were old, familiar, and much-valued friends.[4]

The probability is that Howel Harris, after these great truths "were revealed to his own soul," began to preach them in a manner that implied that they were unknown to his brethren, and it is certain that he expressed them in terms that were, to the wisest and best among them, offensive. Rowland and others could have taught him the way of God more perfectly had he been willing to be instructed; but it is evident that he suspected them of not being quite sound in the faith. They did not preach that God had died; they were even unwilling that he should say so, and that went far with him to prove that they did not really believe that He who died was a Divine Person.

The contentions of those years have not been preserved on record, but there are allusions to them here and there in Howel Harris's Autobiography. In 1746 he writes: "Yet we proceeded in Wales, not withstanding the great jars and disputes that arose amongst us."[5] There are allusions to the same painful state of things made by others; but there is no history of those disputes that could throw complete light upon them.[6] During the first years of the movement, the fathers were engaged at their Associations in organising means and measures for the consolidation of the churches and the spread of the cause, and of those we have ample records; but when misunderstandings arose, the Associations became the scenes of disputes and contentions, and of these we have no minutes at all.

It was at an Association held at Llanidloes, in the year 1751,[7] that the disagreement, which had been raging with more or less violence for several years, culminated in a separation. At that time it could be said of Harris and Rowland, as it had been said before of two other apostles, "And the contention was so sharp between them, that they departed asunder one from the other." It does not appear that the great mass of the people knew much of the subject in dispute between them; but they of necessity took sides, and did so, most probably, according to their personal preferences. Most of the preachers went with Rowland; but the people clung to one or the other according to the esteem in which each was held by them. The body was divided into two parties, known respectively as "Harris's People" and "Rowland's People;" and for a number of years a most unhappy spirit prevailed between those two sections. Let us give an instance:—Edward Parry of Brynbugad, Denbighshire, was one of the exhorters who adhered to Howel Harris. At the time of the disruption he gave up preaching himself; but he received "Harris's People" to preach and hold services at his house. His father lived in the adjoining house; and he, being on the other side, opened his door for sermons and services by "Rowland's People"; and so strong was the bad feeling between those two parties, that not any of the one ever attended the services of the other. This is an extreme case; but there are instances of the same kind all over the country. The consequences were most disastrous. Many of the exhorters ceased from their exhortation. Many of the members returned to the Establishment, and others joined Dissenting communities; while the churches everywhere, torn by internal dissensions, were brought to the very brink of ruin. It seemed for some years as if the work which had begun so mightily and prospered so greatly was coming to naught.

Howel Harris was an extraordinary man, and he did many extraordinary things. The step which he took at this time astonished a great many of his friends, and is now regarded by some as the grand mistake of his life. He gave up the work of an itinerant evangelist and confined himself almost exclusively to his own home, preaching daily to those who would come together to hear him. Great numbers coming from a distance, and wishing to remain near enough to Trefeca to enjoy his constant ministrations, led to another strange step. He built a large house, into which was gathered a numerous family from all parts of Wales, and which in some respects was like a monastic institution. We give a few extracts from his "Biography," which was "collected by his successors," and published at Trefeca, with his Autobiography as "The second part," in the year 1791.[8] Those "successors," like Harris himself, wrote in English, and, therefore, we are not in any danger of doing them injustice by translation:—

"After seventeen years of hard labour in the Lord's work through Wales and great part of England, Mr. Harris settled at Trefeca, where he spent the greatest part of his time in his own house; though he made several journeys from thence in the following years. A few of those who received a blessing through his ministry in former years began to gather to him there; and as he preached to them two or three times a day, they earnestly desired to stay there with him. The ardent desire of these sincere people he could not withstand, and thus in April 1752 he laid the foundation of the present building at Trefeca, though he had at that time neither friends nor money. He set about it purely in faith, relying on the Lord and His promise; having an impression in his mind for some years past that he should build a house for God. And he set about it in full persuasion that the same God, who had sent him at first in an uncommon manner to awaken the country, also laid this undertaking upon him. He himself writes thus concerning it:—'I was impelled to build by the same Spirit which sent me about to preach, and at a time [when] I was far from being provided with money and friends; for the latter had deserted me, and instead of the former I had demands upon me, and about forty workmen to pay and maintain; and yet I made use of no means to get one shilling, but an humble pleading of and confiding on the promise, on which I trust my all, as both for temporal and spiritual things.'

"But soon after he began to build, some people came to offer their work, and to help him, that they might have a more convenient opportunity to be under his care and profit by his ministry daily. Thus the family began to be gathered together this year. Mr. Harris had at this time a severe fit of sickness; but yet, though very weak, he would preach to the people till he was seemingly ready to die from fatigue, being not able to move himself from the chair he used to sit in and speak from, but we were obliged to carry him in it into his room. At other times, when he recovered a little, he would call the family to his bedroom, and would exhort them from his bed for a long while; the Divine blessing attending it to their souls. He continued some months in this fit of sickness, expecting to go home to his dear LORD and SAVIOUR; as he himself expresses it, 'I was all this time in continual hopes of going home to my dear SAVIOUR, and expecting it with solicitation.' And yet all this while he continued to discourse daily to the people, as one already in the suburbs of heaven.

"In the year 1753, a part of the building being finished,

a great number of people flocked to him from all parts, many of them under conviction, merely to hear the Word, and others partly from curiosity, the report of Mr. Harris's preaching daily at Trefeca having spread throughout all Wales. Satan also began to rage and set the whole country as it were in an uproar, inventing all manner of lies, etc., that originated in their various ideas of the aim of the multitude crowding to that place. However, the people continued to come there from all parts of Wales, some staying for a time, others returning home, partly because their circumstances did not admit of their staying at present,—partly complaining, some of the fare, others that the preaching and discipline were too hard, and that Mr. Harris was an intolerable reprover, etc.; yet, for all this, many settled there this year, especially single persons, both men and women, giving themselves to the Lord and His work, because they believed it was a part of the Lord's work, and suited to the rules laid down in the Bible.

"At the end of this year and the beginning of the year 1754, there was a settled family at Trefeca of about a hundred persons, besides those coming and going, as we hinted before; and Mr. Harris took upon him the sole care of their spiritual and temporal concerns, having nothing outwardly adequate to provide for such a family, nor any manufactory set up, but only a couple of small rented farms and a little quantity of wool bought for the women to spin, to get their maintenance by. It is a difficult thing to imagine what straits Mr. Harris went through at this time concerning the outward care of the people only, besides the care of their souls, preaching publicly and exhorting privately daily, watching many nights to pray and wrestle with the Lord, and as soon as the family arose in the morning, preaching again, exhorting them for hours together without having had any rest in bed, but yet with fresh power and spirit from the Lord. Of this we are living eye-witnesses.

"As to outward matters the Lord has been with him in a

surprising manner. Frequently, when a call for payment came to him, he had no prospect in the world how to discharge the debt but applying to the Lord in prayer and pleading His promise, and that he did not bear these burdens for himself, but for Him, and therefore relying upon Him that he would certainly help and carry him through. And very often the Lord answered him in an unexpected manner, by sending some person or other with as much money as he wanted, either as an acknowledgement for the benefit received from his work or as a loan. Thus the Lord never forsook him, as he writes:—'Being often in straits concerning temporal things, wanting twenty, or fifty, or even a hundred pounds, and having nowhere to turn to for assistance but to the promise, the Lord not relieving till the last pinch, and then appearing from a quarter that none could ever imagine, some bringing and some sending me £10, or £20, and even £100, though living at the distance of seventy or eighty miles, being compelled so to do only by the Word sounding in their conscience night and day, and no man in the world knowing or imagining anything of it. Thus the Lord appeared for me many times. This seems strange to many, and well it may, yet it is real truth.'

"In the year 1755 several families came to Trefeca, especially from North Wales, some to live in the family, and others to farms in the neighbourhood, that they might have a more convenient opportunity of attending Mr. Harris's preaching. Many of them had substance; others were poor, and having many children, were obliged to be assisted. Mr. Harris wrote thus about that time:—'No sooner was a great part of the building finished, but there appeared presently here and there a family, which I neither thought of nor sent for, nor could expect. Therefore it appears evident to me that not man, but the Lord, hath done great things for us. Many people continued to come here, notwithstanding crosses and trials, to a place represented by all in the blackest manner, being drawn only by love to the truth, and the force of the

Lord's voice they found to their hearts through my ministry, freely leaving their country and all that was dear to them, working and living hard, and leaving it wholly to me to order them, both in their work and fare. There are now above one hundred persons, old and young, that board, work, and sleep in the house, amongst which are ten families; and ten families live out in farms in the neighbourhood.'

"At the end of this year there were about one hundred and twenty persons in the family, besides those families in the neighbourhood that belonged to it. Mr. Harris preached publicly two or three times daily to the family, besides keeping private meetings with one part or other of them an hour every day of the week. They gave themselves thus to the Lord, and to His servants by the will of God, as the Holy Ghost directs us to do (2 Cor. viii. 5). From the beginning of this work the Lord had moved and fitted two or three 'exhorters' as assistants to Mr. Harris, to exhort both at home and abroad; and by this time the Lord had raised others as helpers, both in the ministry and government of the family."[9]

Some of the "exhorters" above alluded to were not very successful in their labours "abroad." They went out to preach at fairs and merry-makings, as their leader had once done, but soon found, to their dismay, that not one among them was a Howel Harris.

About the end of 1759 Howel Harris did another strange thing. We shall let his "successors" and himself tell the story in their own words:—"Towards the end of this year, when the nation was alarmed with an invasion intended from France, Mr. Harris showed much concern about the welfare of the kingdom in general, and our rights and privileges, both public and private. About that time some of the gentlemen of the county offered him a commission in the Breconshire militia, and he then answered that he would not agree with the offer but upon condition that they would give him liberty to preach the gospel wherever he should go; and told them further, that his chief motive and concern in that affair was the danger he saw to the liberty of the gospel and of our privileges being taken from us; and having been for many years in danger of his life for preaching the Word of God in many places, he was now willing to lay down his life, if occasion required, to defend it; but that if he should serve as a soldier for King George, he must have liberty to preach the gospel of King Jesus. The officers assenting to these motives, and insisting upon his accepting the office, he replied again that he must pray to the Lord for knowledge of His mind and will, and have the consent of his large family, to which also they made no objection.

"Thus, after waiting on the Lord in prayer, he was fully persuaded in his mind that the same Spirit of God who sent him at first to preach the Word in an uncommon manner would send him now in the like extraordinary way to defend it, and to offer his life for the truth he preached and the liberty we enjoy in this kingdom. He laid the matter thus before the family, imploring the assistance of their prayers how to act in this critical affair, and also asked whether any of them had an inclination to go for the Lord's sake with him, to offer their lives in defence of the Gospel. The matter was then further considered, and laid before the Lord in prayer by the whole family, and all consented that Mr. Harris should go, believing it to be the will of God. Many also of the men were willing to go with him and to lay down their lives for the precious Word of God, if occasion required, and the rest of the family willingly resigned him and the men who intended to accompany him.

"Mr. Harris, having settled all at Trefeca, and delivered the affairs of the family into the hands of trustees, went intending to serve the Lord and his king even unto death, together with twenty-four men of the family, twelve of them as volunteers at Mr. Harris's own cost,—arms, clothing, and maintenance for three years. They embodied with the Breconshire Militia in the beginning of the year 1760. Mr.

Harris received an ensign's commission at his entrance into the battalion, but afterwards was made a captain. Before we proceed we must insert a few lines that he himself wrote at this time on the value of the Word of God, the Bible:—

"I am resolutely and coolly determined to go freely and conscientiously, and die in the field of battle in defence of the precious Word of God, the Bible, against Popery. Who can sufficiently set forth the value of a Book wherein God speaks, and that to all ranks, degrees, ages, and languages of men? Who can set it forth in its own real and majestic glory? O the infinite and unfathomable depth of glory and Divine wisdom and love that are in it! The glory of the sun is nothing in comparison to the glory of this valuable treasure, which is indeed the image of God Himself drawn by Himself. A Book which He has made the standard, touchstone, and rule to try even His own work by; whereby all spirits, doctrine, ministry, and church discipline, all faith, love, truth, and obedience are proved! A Book that God has referred all men to, from the monarch to the peasant,—the universal Teacher of all men! Here is the seed whence the Church and her faith are begotten, and herein is she purified and nursed. Here is the believer's armoury. Herein is the true ineffable light of the world. Herein the unerring Father and Teacher of all speaks, both to young and old, high and low, rich and poor. Here man's pride is humbled, his wounds searched, the SAVIOUR revealed, and declared to be made ours... O the ineffable Treasure! No wonder so many thousands triumphed in dying for the precious Bible! Now I go freely, without compulsion, to show the regard I have for the privileges we enjoy under our best of kings,—our ineffable privileges, especially the precious gospel of our Saviour, contained in the whole Book of God, which now is openly read throughout the kingdom; every person being suffered to exhort his neighbour without molestation. Now I commit my family to the Lord, and am going with a part of it, who freely offered their lives on this occasion, to defend our nation and privileges, and to show publicly that we are dead to all things below, or at least, that we can part with all for our dear Lord and Saviour, even with life itself, and that we seek a city above, Heb. xiii. 14.'

"The first route which Mr. Harris and the militia had, was, in the spring of the year 1760, to Yarmouth, a seaport town in Norfolk. It pleased the Lord, as soon as they arrived at Yarmouth, to open a door for him to preach there and at other places, in his regimentals, every evening to many hearers, who seemingly attended to the Word, and a blessing rested upon some souls there.

"The following winter they returned to Brecon by another road, which gave him an opportunity to preach in other towns; and as they made Brecon their head-quarters for that winter, he had an opportunity to be a part of his time, now and then, at Trefeca with his family. The following summer they took another route, to the west of England, so that he had a new field for preaching the Gospel. Then they settled for a while at Bideford and Torrington, where he met with a kind reception and many hearers. In the summer of 1762 he went to several other populous towns in the west, as Barnstaple, Plymouth, etc., where he continued to preach the Gospel at every opportunity.

"After being thus three years in the militia, the war over, and a treaty of peace concluded, he and his little company returned to Trefeca, after showing his faith and love to the Lord Jesus, and also his love and loyalty to his king and country. He spent the remainder of his life at Trefeca with his large family, except only some few rounds he took, now and then, to preach both in England and Wales.

"In the year 1764 he agreed with the vicar to have a monthly Sacrament at our parish church, which had only been administered four times a year before. On Sunday, February the 6th,[10] 1764, we received the first monthly sacrament, and he wrote thus:—

"'This was a great day indeed,—the first day we had the

Communion according to our wish and request; and this privilege has been given us in answer to our prayer, and is a further open proof of our Saviour's love to us. We were happy in the morning in exhorting, and went happily together to the public service, and, I trust, in one spirit to the Lord's Table.'

"The 19th of this month our people sat for the first time in the gallery of the parish church, to sing, and ever since continue to do so every Sunday… And as the late revival in religion began in the Established Church, we think it not necessary or prudent to separate ourselves from it; but our duty to abide in it, and to go to our parish church every Sunday, to join in the prayers, to hear the reading of God's Word, and to use the ordinances. We find that our Saviour meets us there by making them a blessing to our souls."[11]

NOTES

[1] This statement does not convey the whole truth of the matter. There were indeed doctrinal differences, not least Harris's tendencies towards Patripassianism (as described in the text) and his over-emphasis on the 'blood-theology' of the Moravians. Added to these, however, were more personal issues. One was Harris's attachment to Madam Sidney Griffith, the wife of an Anglesey squire, who laid claim to prophetic utterances; it was not only Harris's wife who deemed their relationship to be unwise. But perhaps still more basic was the clash of temperaments and attitudes, Harris tending to be overly subjective and impulsive whereas Rowland was inclined to be more reasoned and deliberate (cf. pp.65-67, 69, 147-8 in the text). The potential for conflict was increased by the capacity of both men for obstinacy when they considered themselves to be in the right, and the question of authority within the Methodist movement provided abundant scope for such obstinacy to reveal itself. Eifion Evans, *Daniel Rowland*, pp.269-80.

[2] *Howel Harris: His Own Story*, p.54.

[3] *Ibid.*, pp.57-59, 68-69.

[4] Cf. p.175.

[5] *Howel Harris: His Own Story*, p.58.

[6] For recent attempts to analyse the disputes, see Eifion Evans, *Daniel Rowland*, pp.269-80; G.M. Roberts, *Y Deffroad Mawr*, pp.314-55; G.T. Roberts, *Dadleuon Methodistiaeth Gynnar* (Abertawe: Gwasg John Penry, 1970); Geraint Tudur, 'Llwybr Llithrig y Diwygwyr', in E. Stanley John, ed., *Y Gair a'r Genedl: Cyfrol Deymged i R. Tudur Jones* (Abertawe: Ty John Penry, 1986), pp.144-55.

[7] 1750, not 1751. Eifion Evans, *Daniel Rowland*, p.278.

[8] It is in fact the 'Biography' which constitutes 'The second part' of the volume, the first part being in Harris's own words.

[9] *Howel Harris: His Own Story*, pp.71-76.

[10] The original has 'February the 5th'.

[11] *Howel Harris: His Own Story*, pp.79-85.

CHAPTER XI

WHATEVER may be thought now of the institution at
Trefeca, it is certain that there were many among the
best people of those days who did not regard it with
disfavour. The Reverend Henry Venn, author of *The
Complete Duty of Man,* and one of the most eminent of the
early Methodistical clergymen, visited the place in 1769, and
we give his impressions of it in his own words:—"Happy
Trefeca! Howel Harris is the father of that settlement, and
the founder. After labouring for fifteen years, more violently
than any of the servants of Christ, in this revival, he was so
hurt in body as to be confined to his own house for seven
years. Upon the beginning of this confinement, first one and
then another, whom the Lord had converted under his word,
to the number of near a hundred, came and desired to live
with him, and that they would work and get their bread.
By this means, near one hundred and twenty—men, women,
and children, from very distant parts of Wales—came and
fixed their tents at Trefeca. We were there three days, and
heard their experience, which they spoke in Welsh to Mr.
Harris, and he interpreted to us. Of all the people I ever saw,
this Society seems to be the most advanced in grace. They

speak as men and women who feel themselves every moment worthy of eternal punishment, and infinitely base; and yet at the same time have such certainty of salvation through the second Man, the Lord from heaven, as is indeed delightful to behold. My heart received a blessing from them and their pastor which will abide with me."[1]

The Countess of Huntingdon had been long acquainted with Howel Harris and other leading Welsh reformers. Her Ladyship, in 1748, had accompanied several of these men on a tour through parts of Wales, of which we have the following account in her *"Life and Times:"*—

"About the month of May 1748, Lady Huntingdon and her daughters, accompanied by Lady Anne and Lady Frances Hastings, left Bath on a tour through Wales. It is a matter of regret that so little information can now be obtained of her Ladyship's journey into a part of the kingdom where she was destined in after years to reap a harvest so abundant.

"From the scanty materials, however, which remain, an imperfect and irregular journal, in the handwriting of Lady Frances Hastings, we are informed that Lady Huntingdon was met at Bristol by Mr. Howel Harris, Mr. Griffith Jones, Mr. Daniel Rowland, and Mr. Howel Davies, all of whom accompanied her into the Principality. They appear to have travelled slowly, taking short stages every day. For fifteen days successively two of the ministers that accompanied her Ladyship preached in some town or village through which they passed, by which means the seed of Divine truth was widely scattered over a large extent of the country. In Cardiganshire her Ladyship was visited by the Rev. Philip Pugh, a Dissenting minister, eminent for his piety, diligence, and success. On their arrival at Trefeca, they were joined by several of the awakened clergymen, particularly Mr. William Williams, Mr. Thomas Lewis, Mr Penry Baillie, Mr John Powell, and Mr. Thomas Jones; also by some of the exhorters, or lay preachers, and some pious and laborious

Dissenting ministers, amongst whom Mr. John Watkins, Mr. Lewis Jones of Glamorganshire, and Mr. Lewis Rees from North Wales, were the most notable. Her Ladyship remained a few days at Trefeca, which exactly twenty years after became her chief residence and scene of action. Whilst there, they had preaching four or five times a day to immense crowds who had collected from all the adjacent country. 'The divine influence of the Spirit of God,' says Lady Frances, 'was very evidently afforded with His Word, and many were added unto the Lord's people.'" [2]

Howel Harris was likewise for many years one of her Ladyship's regular supplies in London, Brighton, and other places. In the year 1767, Lady Huntingdon conceived the idea of establishing a college or "seminary," as it was called at the time, for the purpose of preparing earnest and devoted young men for the ministry of the gospel. It was not intended to confine the benefits of this school of prophets to any particular denomination; on the contrary, the young men who were trained in it were at liberty to take orders in the Establishment or to join themselves to any other section of the Christian Church, according as they were led by the providence of God or by their own inclinations. Her Ladyship consulted a great many of her ministerial and other friends with reference to this important project, and as is usual in such cases, was encouraged to persevere in her intention by some, and dissuaded from it by others. Among the latter was the Rev. J. Berridge, whose characteristic letter in reply to her Ladyship we take the liberty to insert:—

"The soil you have chosen is proper. Welsh mountains afford a brisk air for a student, and the rules are excellent; but I doubt the success of the project, and fear it will occasion you more trouble than all your other undertakings besides. Are we commanded to make labourers, or to pray the Lord to send labourers? Will not Jesus choose and teach and send forth His ministering servants now, as He did the disciples aforetime, and glean them up when and where and how He pleaseth? The world say 'No,' because they are strangers to a Divine commission and a Divine teaching. And what if these asses blunder about their Master's meaning for a time, and mistake it often, as they did formerly? No great harm will ensue, provided they are kept from paper and ink, and from white wall and charcoal. Do you like to see cadelambs[3] in a house, and suckling with a finger, or to view them skipping after the dam in their own proper pasture? We read of a school of prophets in Scripture, but we do not read that it was God's appointment. Elijah visited this school, which was at Bethel, and seems to have been fond of it, yet the Lord commands him to fetch a successor, not from the school, but, as the Romans fetched a dictator, from the plough. Are we told of a single *preaching* prophet that was taken out of this school? Or do we find any public employment given the scholars, except once sending a light heeled young man, when light heels were needful, with a horn of oil to anoint Jehu? (2 Kings ix.) That old prophet, who told a sad lie to another prophet, was of this school, and might be the master of this college, for he was a grey-headed man (1 Kings xiii. 11). While my heart is thus prattling to you very simply, like a child, it stands in no fear of offending you; and if your project be right, the Master will keep you steadfast, and you will only smile at my prattling. Indeed, I am the most dubious man in the world about my own judgment, and will stickle[4] for nothing excepting to live to and trust in my Lord."[5]

Her Ladyship fixed upon Trefeca for her College, and we suppose that her reason for making that choice was, that the students might have the advantage of Howel Harris's earnest ministrations. The building was prepared by him. He repaired and enlarged Trefeca House, "an ancient structure, supposed to have been part of an old castle erected in the reign of Henry the Second. The date over the entrance, now almost effaced, is 1176. This building was opened as a college for religious and literary instruction, and the chapel dedicated to the preaching of the everlasting gospel on the 24th of August 1768, the anniversary of Lady Huntingdon's birthday, by the Rev. George Whitefield, who preached from Exodus xx. 24, 'In all places where I record My Name, I will come unto thee and bless thee;' and, on the following Sabbath-day, he addressed a congregation of some thousands in the court before the College. His text on this occasion was,—'Other foundation can no man lay than that is laid, which is Jesus Christ.' When speaking of the dedication of the College, Mr. Whitefield says, 'What we have seen and felt at the College is unspeakable.'"[6]

The Rev. J. Fletcher of Madeley was chosen President of the College; and Mr. Easterbrook, afterwards the Vicar of the Temple and Ordinary of Newgate, "a deeply pious and useful man, an able preacher, and a bold defender of the truths of Christianity," the first Master. The latter does not appear to have remained at Trefeca more than a few months; and a Mr. Jones, who had been one of the Masters at Kingswood School, applied to Mr. Fletcher for the appointment. A short extract from the reply of the President to this gentleman will give the reader some idea of the character of the College and of its promoters:—

"The first and grand point to be kept in view at Lady Huntingdon's College is to maintain and grow in the spirit of faith and power that breathes through the Acts of the Apostles, and was exemplified in the lives of the primitive Christians. The first and grand qualification required in a person called to be at the head of such a College is, then, a degree of faith and power from above, with an active devotedness to God and His cause. The Master who is there at present seems, on account of his youth, to be deficient in point of Christian experience; nor is he a proper master of the Greek, nor even of the harder classics, so that he can hardly maintain his superiority over those who read Cicero and Horace.[7] Whether this inconveniency, Sir, would be avoided, suppose you were to succeed him, I cannot judge by your letter. He is also unacquainted with Divinity and the Sciences, of which it is proper he should give the student some idea; and how far you may excel him in these points, Sir, is not in my power to determine. He hath twenty-five guineas a year, with his board, room, and washing. I daresay the generous foundress would not hesitate to raise the salary of a master of superior merit, though she hopes none would undertake that province for the sake of money. The variety of classes demands great assiduity and diligence in the master. I would not, therefore, advise any one to engage without a proper trial... I think that, if upon consulting with the Lord in prayer, and with Mr. Maxfield in conversation, you find your heart free to embrace so peculiar an opportunity of being useful to your generation, it might be best to come and see how you like the business, and how it agrees with you; and should not matters prove agreeable on either side, I daresay Lady Huntingdon will pay your expenses to Talgarth and back again."[8]

In August 1769 the anniversary of the opening of the College was held, and this was a great occasion. "On Friday the 18th, Mr. Daniel Rowland, Mr. Fletcher, and Mr. W. Williams, arrived at the College, and, on the following morning, Mr. Rowland preached in the chapel to a crowded congregation, on the words, 'Lord, are there few that be saved?' In the afternoon the Lord's Supper was administered, when Mr. Fletcher addressed the communicants and spectators in a very close and pointed manner. Power from on high accompanied the Word, and rendered it effectual to the conversion of many. Mr. Williams then gave out the hymn, 'Come, let us join our cheerful songs,' etc., which was sung with the most lively feelings of devotion. Abundance of people being gathered together, Mr. Howel Harris stood in the court and gave a solemn warning to a large congregation from these awful words: 'The time is come that judgment must begin at the house of God.'

"On the 19th Mr. Shirley and several exhorters and lay-preachers arrived at Trefeca. The next day being Sunday, a very numerous congregation assembled in the court, the chapel being much too small to contain the half of the people. Public service commenced at ten o'clock. Mr. Fletcher read prayers, and Mr. Shirley preached on 'Acquaint thyself now with him, and be at peace.' At one, the sacrament was administered in the chapel. Mr. Rowland and Mr. Fletcher alternately addressed the communicants during the distribution of the elements, and Mr. Williams closed the solemnity with a suitable address to the awakened and unawakened. In the afternoon, Mr. Fletcher stood in the court and applied the words of the apostle—'I am not ashamed of the gospel of Christ,'—to an immense congregation, many of whom appeared to receive the Word with gladness. When the sermon was concluded, a hymn was sung, and Mr. Rowland explained and enforced, in the Welsh language, those solemn words, 'It is appointed unto men once to die.'

"From this time to the day of the anniversary, people flocked from all parts to Trefeca. Mr. Howel Harris, and several of the Welsh exhorters, assisted the clergymen assembled at the College, so that there was preaching twice every day. On Wednesday the 23rd, Mr. Wesley, accompanied by Mr. Howel Davies and Mr. Peter Williams of Carmarthen, arrived at Trefeca. Mr. Wesley preached on that day; and in the evening, at Mr. Harris's desire, gave a short exhortation to his family.

"At an early hour on the morning of Thursday the 24th, the Lord's Supper was administered by Mr. Wesley and Mr. Shirley, first to the clergymen assembled at the College, then to students; after which the Countess of Huntingdon, the Countess Buchan, Lady Anne Erskine, Miss Orton, and other members of her family, received. An amazing concourse of people being collected from all parts, the public service commenced at ten o'clock. Mr. Howel Davies and Mr. Daniel

Rowland read the prayers, with appropriate lessons selected for the occasion; after which Mr. Fletcher preached an exceedingly lively sermon in the court, the chapel being far too small to contain the congregation. When he had finished, the Rev. W. Williams preached in Welsh till about two o'clock. At two they all dined with Lady Huntingdon, and baskets of bread and meat were distributed amongst the people in the court, many of whom had come from a great distance. Public service commenced again at three o'clock, when Mr. Wesley preached in the court, then Mr. Fletcher. About five the congregation was dismissed. Between seven and eight the love-feast began, during which Mr. Shirley, Mr. Davies, and Mr. Rowland gave short exhortations; and Mr. Peter Williams and Mr. Howel Harris engaged in prayer."[9]

Of these manifold and prolonged services Lady Huntingdon writes:—"Truly our God was in the midst of us, and many felt Him eminently nigh. The gracious influence of His Spirit seemed to rest on every soul. Many with whom I have conversed experience a spring-tide of sensible comfort, and strong joy, and vehement longings after more communion with Him, especially in the means of grace. Though necessarily much hurried with outward things, my mind was preserved in peace. I enjoyed a divine composure, a heavenly serenity of soul; while my communion was with the Father and the Son. Words fail to describe the holy triumph with which the great congregation sang—

'Captain of Thine enlisted host,
Display thy glorious banner high'

It was a season of refreshing from the presence of the Lord,—a time never to be forgotten."[10]

Daniel Rowland, William Williams, Howel Davies, and Peter Williams, as we see, took an active part in these services. Here are Howel Harris and his dear old friends together again, after an estrangement of eighteen years.[11]

The sore had been completely healed, for these good brethren had by this time discovered that there were no substantial reasons after all for their separation.

Some time after the anniversary services which we have just described, the Rev. Joseph Benson was, by the recommendation of Mr. Fletcher and Mr. Wesley, appointed head-master of the College; but he only continued in that position for nine months. The great Calvinistic controversy began in 1770, and he was dismissed in consequence of the part which he took in relation to the celebrated "Minutes" of the Wesleyan Conference of that year.[12] His dismissal was soon followed by the resignation of Mr. Fletcher as President. From this time there was a complete separation between Mr. Wesley and his people on the one hand, and the Calvinistic Methodists on the other. There was an effort made to effect a reconciliation, which at first promised to be successful; but it completely failed, and there ensued a long and bitter controversy. The two eminent brothers, Richard and Rowland Hill, Augustus Toplady, and John Berridge, entered the arena on the Calvinistic side, against the brothers John and Charles Wesley, Mr. Fletcher, and two or three more, on the other. The titles of some of the pamphlets which were then written prove that the writers had not engaged in the controversy in the best and mildest spirit; and there were passages in those books themselves which were more remarkable for their vigour than for Christian charity, and which the authors on either side would have been glad to be able to withdraw when the heat of the battle had passed. This controversy did not at all affect Wales, inasmuch as all the Welsh Methodists adhered to the Calvinistic side; and therefore it does not appertain to us further to enlarge upon its history. The College continued at Trefeca until after the death of the Countess of Huntingdon in 1791, when it was removed to Cheshunt. Up to that time anniversaries continued to be held in August each year, and to draw together great crowds of people. The

Rev. Augustus Toplady, in a letter to his friend Mr. Hussey, gives an interesting account of one of those meetings which he attended in 1774. We give an extract:—

"The night I left town, the Worcester coach, in which I went, broke down, but not one of us received the least injury. I have a still greater deliverance to acquaint you with, even such as, I trust, will never be blotted out from my thankful remembrance. On the anniversary day in Wales, the congregation was so large that the chapel would not have contained a fourth part of the people, who were supposed to amount to three thousand. No fewer than thirteen hundred horses were turned into one large field adjoining the College, besides what were stationed in the neighbouring villages. The carriages also were unusually numerous. A scaffold was erected at one end of the College court, on which a bookstand was placed by way of pulpit; and from thence six or seven of us preached successively to one of the most attentive and most lively congregations I ever beheld. When it came to my turn to preach I advanced to the front, and had not gone more than half through my prayer before sermon when the scaffold suddenly fell in. As I stood very near the highermost step, and the step did not fall with the rest, Providence enabled me to keep on my feet, through the assistance of Mr. Winkworth, who laid fast hold on my arm. About forty ministers were on the scaffold and steps when the former broke down. Dear Mr. Shirley fell undermost of all, but received no other hurt than a very slight bruise on one of his thighs. A good woman, who, for conveniency of hearing had placed herself under the scaffold, received a trifling contusion on her face. No other mischief was done. The congregation, though greatly alarmed, had the prudence not to throw themselves into outward disorder, which, I believe, was chiefly owing to the powerful sense of God's presence, which was eminently felt by most of the assembly.

"Such was the wonderful goodness of the Lord to me,

that I was not in the least disconcerted on this dangerous occasion, which I mention to the praise of that grace and providence, without which a much smaller incident would inevitably have shocked every nerve I have. About half a minute after the interruption had commenced, I had the satisfaction to inform the people that no damage had ensued, and, removing for security to a lower step, I thanked the Lord with the rejoicing multitude for having so undeniably given His angels charge concerning us. Prayer ended, I was enabled to preach, and great grace seemed to be upon us all."[13]

The same eminent man gives an insight into the character of the conversation which the assembled friends held together around the hearth at the close of each day. The following we give as examples:—

"'The Spirit of God can convert men without the Bible, but the Bible cannot convert without the Spirit.'—*Mr. Shirley in conversation at Trefeca this day, August 29, 1776.*"[14]

"'The sanctifying principle of grace in the heart may be compared to a candle in a lantern, which transmits its light through the lantern, though in and of itself the lantern still continues what it was before, a dark body.'—*Lady Huntingdon in conversation at Trefeca, August 29, 1776.*"[15]

"'If comfort fails, God's faithfulness does not. What though your pitcher is broke? The fountain is still as full as ever.'—*Rev. Peter Williams at Trefeca, August 1776.*"[16]

It was such talk that those good people had among each other when they "unbent" after the labours of the day.

Howel Harris had more than three years before this time been called to his rest. He died triumphantly on the 21st of July, 1773, and his funeral was a "great mourning" of the Methodists. Lady Huntingdon says that "there were present no less than twenty thousand persons," and that there were "some special seasons of Divine influence both upon converted and unconverted." His withdrawal to Trefeca was a strange proceeding, and in some respects an unhappy one, and yet it proved in the result to be the best for the benefit of the Connexion, and, as we take it, of the Principality. Had he, after the final disruption at Llanidloes, continued to itinerate, and to plant and organise churches all over the country, as he had done before, there would have been inevitably two distinct, and, for a long while, antagonistic, denominations. As it was, there were for a time two sections, known as "Harris's People" and "Rowland's People," who, as we have seen, were not remarkable for their love to each other. His continued itinerancy would have perpetuated and most probably intensified the evil; but he withdrew to Trefeca and left the field to his brethren. He was followed there by perhaps altogether a couple of hundred people from all parts of Wales. Those, we may naturally conclude, were drawn to him, some by personal attachment, and some by sympathy with his manner of setting forth the truth. They were no doubt the most zealous of those who were regarded as "Harris's People." Their withdrawal, therefore, from the various congregations was the withdrawal of an element of discord, and the withdrawal from the whole of Wales of the people who had sufficient zeal and ability to keep up another denomination. Some of those who remained behind returned to the Establishment, and others joined the Independents; but the great mass adhered to the Connexion, and by-and-by forgot all past disagreements. The "family" at Trefeca soon ceased to be replenished from the country, and therefore of necessity became smaller and smaller as its members one by one passed away, and long before the whole of them had been taken home, the remnant had become part and parcel of the Connexion from which they had withdrawn themselves.

Some years later there arose another contention, which, although it did not affect the Connexion to anything like the same extent as that which had occasioned the withdrawal of Howel Harris, resulted in the expulsion of one of the earliest and most eloquent of its preachers. We have already spoken of the labours of the Rev. Peter Williams, and of the persecutions he endured in going about to preach the Gospel. This excellent man conceived the idea of publishing a Welsh edition of the Bible, with marginal references, and explanatory and practical observations at the close of each chapter. He applied himself to this task, and in the year 1770 a quarto edition of 8600 copies was brought out. Nine years later another edition of 6400 was published.[17] Nothing of the kind had ever been attempted in Welsh before, and though several have since followed in the same track, this Book has hitherto kept the lead by far of all others in popularity. Several editions have been published since the author's death—four or five at least within our own memory, one a handsome folio published in London by Fisher above forty years ago, and another, handsomer still, published quite recently by "The London Printing and Publishing Company, Limited." In fact, Peter Williams's is *the* Family Bible of the Welsh people. The Welsh bride in the humblest walks of life does not feel that her little room has been completely furnished until she has, lying on her chest of drawers, a well-bound copy of "Peter Williams's Bible."

But the appearance of the first edition of this great work was the beginning of contention between the author and his brethren, because he had, in his "observations" on the first chapter of the Gospel of John, enunciated views which they regarded as unsound, and as at least tending towards Sabellianism, on the doctrine of the Trinity and the Eternal Sonship of our Redeemer. The passages objected to only appeared in the first edition,[18] and are to the following effect:—

"'In the beginning was the Word.' Let us observe: There was not a beginning before the Word, but the Word was in the beginning. The mind of God is the same as His will, and His will the same as His Word, for He does not change, and He willed, before either the world or an angel was in existence, to give Christ to be the Head of the Church. Therefore God is Father, Son, and Holy Ghost from eternity, in His own everlasting will; not 'as a necessary mode of existence, if no man were to be saved, or no sinner were to be sanctified,' as some unwisely say, but because He willed to save and to sanctify. For Christ in whom, above all, the wisdom of God is manifested, was the Father's delight daily in the beginning of His ways, and is the Alpha and Omega of all His works. Agreeably with which will, the Word, in the fulness of time, was made flesh, and dwelt among us, and some beheld His glory, and believed that Jesus is God; not 'God by appointment,' as some vainly talk, but that He is the only true and living God, for the Scripture testifies that the man Jesus is the eternal Father."

From the above extracts it appears that Mr. Williams regarded the Trinity of Persons in the Godhead, not as the necessary mode of the Divine existence, but as the result of the Divine will, as much so as the incarnation of the Second Person,—that He is the Father, Son, and Holy Ghost not in His own nature, but because He has willed to be so, that man might be saved. In the "Vindication" which he published some years after the beginning of the controversy, he expressed precisely the same sentiments, as will be seen from two short extracts:—

"I dare not say that a Trinity is necessary to the existence of God, as some presumptuously assert, but I do say, and believe, that a Trinity is essentially necessary to the revelation of God unto the heirs of eternal life."—"Let us remember that the names Father, Son, and Holy Ghost are given, not to signify a mode of existence, but a mode of operation, and especially in the work of Redemption."

This is at least so like Sabellianism that it would be difficult for plain people to see a difference. Dr. Evans, in his *Sketch of the Denominations of the Christian World*, the first edition of which was published when the controversy we are speaking of was at its height, says, "The Sabellian reduces the three Persons in the Trinity to three *Characters* or *Relations*. This has been called by some a *Modal* Trinity, and the persons who hold it *Modalists*. Sabellius, the founder of the sect, espoused the doctrine in the third century. Of his tenets the accounts are various. Some say he taught that the Father, Son, and Holy Spirit were one substance, and one Person, with three names; and that in the Old Testament the Deity delivered the law as Father, in the New Testament dwelt among men as the Son, and descended on the apostles as the Holy Spirit." The author adds, no doubt with special reference to this controversy, "This opinion gains ground in the Principality of Wales."[19]

The controversy extended over several years, but it was not until Mr. Williams had published a Welsh edition of "John Canne's Bible," in 1790, that matters came to a crisis. Here he had taken the liberty of introducing several changes into the text, and some of his brethren charged him with making these alterations for the express purpose of favouring his own views. The Welsh Bible is not a translation from the English, as some of our good friends on the other side of the Severn have said and written, but from the original languages. It differs materially from the English version, and, as we think, for the better. "John Canne's" was an English Bible, and Mr. Williams, in many instances, thought it right to adhere to the English rendering. There is one instance in which this was done, which seems to give some ground to the charge which his brethren brought against him. In Heb. v. 9, it is said in the Welsh version that our Redeemer "*was made* the author of eternal salvation to all those who obey him;" but the English version says that He "*became*" so, and Mr. Williams gave the English rendering. Great and bitter were the contentions that followed, and the result was, that this eminent man was, in his old age, expelled from the Connexion in which he had so long and faithfully and successfully laboured.

The Calvinistic Methodists of those days regarded the

views enunciated by Mr. Williams as serious errors, and yet they bore with him for many years; but since he persisted in refusing to retract anything that he had said or written, they felt it to be their duty to do as they did, and, painful as the duty was, they discharged it. It was a sad thing to do, but, under the circumstances, we are unable to see how it could have been avoided. We have not the least shadow of a doubt that the upright and conscientious old minister and his equally conscientious brethren now see eye to eye.

The rupture between Howel Harris and Daniel Rowland was followed by a long season of spiritual drought in that part of the Connexion which had adhered to the latter. During the fifteen years that had passed since the beginning of the movement, there had never been wanting conclusive evidences that the Lord was blessing His own Word. Great awakenings were taking place here and there all over the Principality, which made that period one of uninterrupted progress. But now everything seemed to have come to a stand. The Gospel was preached, and other means of grace continued to be employed, but there was no awakening anywhere; sinners were not converted, and many of those who had been once regarded as saints were falling away. Large numbers continued to assemble at Llangeitho on the Communion Sabbath, but even there the refreshing showers of former years had ceased to descend. In North Wales, as well as in the South, all was alike dead. No new ground was gained, no new churches formed, most of the existing ones were dwindling away, and some ceased to exist at all. Thus it continued for eleven[20] years, but in 1762 the Lord was pleased again to visit His people. At that time a great awakening occurred in many places throughout the Principality. Preachers and exhorters were again endowed with the power which they seemed, for a time, to have for ever lost; Christians began again to feast on the joys of salvation; thousands were converted to God, and the brethren who had been estranged from each other by the painful disputes of past years, were now rejoicing together in the glorious triumphs of the Redeemer's cause. Daniel Rowland had so far been allowed to retain his curacy at Llangeitho, and had the drought which we have spoken of continued it is not likely that he would have been disturbed; but the great revival of 1762 drew towards him the unfavourable notice of the authorities, and he was turned out of the Church in 1763. The people went out with him, and a spacious chapel was built for him a short distance from the parish church, and here he continued to labour with great earnestness and success until, full of years, he was called to his reward in 1790.

NOTES

1 [A. C. H. Seymour], *The Life and Times of Selina [Hastings], Countess of Huntingdon,* I (London: 1839), p.482.

2 *Ibid.,* vol. I, p.84.

3 Pet lambs

4 Strive for, scruple over

5 [Seymour], *Countess of Huntingdon,* II, p.92.

6 *Ibid.,* II, p.93.

7 Williams has the following footnote: "We do not know the name of this gentleman, but he seems to have been only appointed *pro tem,* when Mr. Easterbrook left."

8 [Seymour], *Countess of Huntingdon,* II, p.97.

9 *Ibid.,* vol. II, p.98.

10 *Ibid.,* vol. II, p.100.

11 The estrangement had in fact come to an end officially in 1763; during the second half of the 1750s the two sides had been moving gradually closer to each other. G.M. Roberts, *Y Deffroad Mawr,* pp.393-402.

12 The Minutes of 1770, drawn up by John Wesley, sought to curb Antinomianism. In effect, however, they could be construed as supporting a form of justification by works, and gave offence to even moderate Calvinists. Fuel was added to the flames of the resulting controversy by the

immoderate accusations made by two men otherwise remarkable for their godliness, namely John Fletcher on the Arminian side and Augustus Toplady on the Calvinistic side. E. J. Poole-Connor, *Evangelicalism in England* (1951; revised ed., Worthing: H.E. Walter, 1966), 170-1; [Seymour], *Countess of Huntingdon*, II, pp.232-50.

[13] A. M. Toplady, *The Posthumous Works of the Late Reverend A. M. Toplady* (London: 1780), p.386.

[14] *Ibid.*, pp.175-6.

[15] *Ibid.*

[16] *Ibid.*

[17] The first edition was issued in parts between 1768 and 1770; the second edition appeared by similar means between 1779 and 1781. G.M. Roberts, *Peter Williams*, pp.64, 70, 199.

[18] This was not in fact the case. *Ibid*, pp.75 , 78, 199.

[19] John Evans, *A Sketch of the Denominations of the Christian World* (1795; 14th ed., 1821), p.92 (article: "Sabellius").

[20] Twelve; see note 7, p.156.

CHAPTER XII

Concerning Welsh Revivals.

WE have seen and heard much of revivals within the last few years. A great awakening took place in America in 1858, and it visited this country, and spread more or less throughout the British islands in the years 1859 and 1860. Since that time it has been usual to hold what are called "Revival Services." Possibly there is not a neighbourhood in the kingdom where these are unknown. Series of prayer-meetings are held, in which earnest prayers are offered to God to revive His work, and stirring appeals are addressed to men, urging them at once to come to Christ and accept the proffered salvation. We have had professional "Revivalists" going about to hold these services, and some of those good people advertised as converted colliers, converted shoemakers, or converted something else. Some of them were men of sufficient spiritual discernment to ascertain the exact number who, at a particular service, had been brought under conviction. We have heard the converts classified after the following fashion:—"Wednesday evening—twenty-four cried for mercy, and eighteen found peace." Far be it from us to say anything uncharitable or unfriendly of attempts to get up a revival, for we reckon that every religious service ought to be an effort in that direction. We have seen some of those revival meetings followed by unmistakably beneficial results, and have seen some of them turning out very flat affairs indeed. A popular minister once related to us how he had produced a revival, and sought to impress us with the idea that it was a very simple process, and such as we ourselves could very easily carry out; but we wish our readers to understand that the revivals which we have to speak of as having taken place in Wales were very different from all this. The phrase which we have quoted above about a certain number crying for mercy, etc., is an importation from England, and we believe we are right in saying that it has not hitherto been translated into the Welsh language. Those revivals usually occurred, not as the result of any predetermined and special effort to produce them, but in the ordinary means of grace, and were frequently unexpected by the great mass of the congregation. As it was on the day of Pentecost, when the disciples "were all with one accord in one place, suddenly there came a sound from heaven as of a mighty rushing wind, and it filled all the house where they were sitting," it has often happened in Wales. When the congregation had assembled together to hold the usual service, and while that service was proceeding in the usually quiet manner, the preacher would suddenly find himself under some *unusual* influence—felt at liberty to relinquish the string of his discourse, and to utter words which were not on his paper, and thoughts which had not occurred to him in his study. Some of the oldest brethren and sisters would soon recognise the sound. John would remark to his brother Simon, "It is the Lord!" and possibly follow the glad announcement with the shout, "Gogoniant!" to which Simon would respond with "Diolch iddo byth!" Presently the whole congregation was ablaze. Christians shouted for joy that their good Lord had again visited them, while numbers who had been so far indifferent to their souls' salvation would send forth the distressing cry, "What shall we do to be saved?" It was no transient feeling. It would be present at the next service, and the next afterwards, and for months to come. It would spread to the adjoining districts, perhaps over the whole country, and possibly over the greater part of Wales. There is a wild and mountainous tract of country lying between the counties of

Brecon and Cardigan, where, for many miles in every direction, there are no human habitations, save here and there, in a deep dingle, just one house, the residence of the sheep-farmer, with three or four small cultivated fields in its immediate vicinity, and at some distance up the slopes of the mountains an occasional shepherd's hut. Crossing the range there is a bridle road leading from Llanwrtyd Wells, in the valley of the Irfon, to Tregaron, in the valley of the Teifi—a distance of about eighteen miles "as the crow flies," but of considerably more as the rider must travel. It is a magnificent ride, through scenery of the wildest grandeur. From the highest points in his progress the traveller will descry nothing but a sea of mountains, some rounded, and some rugged and precipitous, extending in every direction—bluff after bluff, and precipice beyond precipice, and, as it seems to him, interminable. Here are the "Wolves' Leaps," where the Irfon, before it has become a river, has worn its rocky channel to an enormous depth, and rushes and gurgles in the dark caverns and recesses beneath, while the rocks on the surface on both sides nearly touch each other. Here, too, are the "Cock's Paces," where the Tywi, many miles before reaching the plain, does the same thing on a greater and grander scale. Here, likewise, near the spot where the Doethïe and the Tywi rush, with a deafening roar, into one another's embrace, and more than half way up a rugged and rocky cone, is "Twm Siôn Cati's Cave," from whence, a couple of centuries ago, that celebrated outlaw was wont to issue forth, to spread terror and rapine through the surrounding districts. It is not a mountain at all that one traverses here, but a country of mountains. It is a path that a stranger would better not attempt alone, for the chances are that he would soon find his way into some place from which it would be exceedingly difficult to find his way out, and he might shout until he could do so no longer without making himself heard by any human being. In the heart of this wild district there is a comfortable chapel, into which worshippers gather from distances varying from two to eight miles. We attended a service in this chapel on a Sabbath morning some years ago. The building was filled with attentive worshippers, and the adjoining yard was occupied by some fifty or sixty ponies, that had borne as many people to the place. The first Methodists preached in the farmhouses among those mountains, and God bore witness to the Word of His grace, and a church was formed in the year 1747, which sometimes held its meetings at a homestead called Cwm-du, and sometimes at another called Bronyrhelem.

In the year 1779 a remarkable awakening began in this out-of-the-way place. A homely exhorter, of very ordinary preaching talents, but of great piety, Jack Edward Watkin by name, was preaching at the place on a Sabbath afternoon, when suddenly the fire kindled, and numbers who had been so far hearers only became deeply concerned for their everlasting safety. Daniel Rowland heard the glad tidings, and he resolved to ascend the mountain to see this thing which the Lord had wrought. He preached, and *the power* was still present, and even mightier than on the preceding Sabbath. On his return home he said to his friends, "It is a heath fire and will spread abroad." And it *did* spread from these dreary mountains to the valleys and plains around, until it had reached many and far-distant localities in South and North Wales, and thousands were brought earnestly to seek everlasting life.

One of those great revivals began at Llangeitho, not in the public service, but in several families in the neighbourhood simultaneously. When the brethren worshipped God with their own households, they felt a gracious and mighty influence descend upon their souls. They carried the fire with them to the chapel, where it became a blaze which spread far and wide through the surrounding country, and resulted in the salvation of many souls.

The Rev. Thomas Charles refers in a letter to a revival which took place in 1791, in the following terms: "Here at Bala we have been blessed with a great, mighty, and glorious outpouring of the Spirit upon the congregation, and especially upon the children and young people. Scores of the wildest and most thoughtless young men and women have been converted. The convictions are manifest and deep, and in the case of some persons so mighty that they are brought to the very brink of despair. Their comforts likewise are similar. If the Lord will please to continue to work as He has done for some weeks past, the kingdom of the devil will be in ruins. 'Go onward! Go onward, thou King of Glory!' is the earnest prayer of my soul day and night. I verily believe that the Lord intends to give a terrible shake to the kingdom of darkness, for He takes away its pillars. Some of those who were foremost in the service of Satan, and in rebellion against God, are now foremost in seeking liberty through the blood of the Lamb. It is easy work to preach the Gospel here at the present time. Divine truths lay hold on the minds of the people, in their own greatness and importance. Divine rays and irresistible power accompany all the truths that are delivered. It is delightful to see how the most stubborn hearts are bent, and the hardest melted. I would not have died without seeing what I have lately seen—no, not for the whole world. The free schools are greatly blessed. The children, who were like pearls hid in the dust and mire, now shine with great brilliancy and beauty. Little children from six to twelve years of age are melted and overcome. Their little minds are full of spiritual things night and day. All this is undeniable fact; I do not use exaggeration, but, on the contrary, have only selected a small part of that which is. The Lord has done great things for us, and to Him be the praise!"[1]

Besides those seasons of refreshing which spread thus from place to place, there were frequently mighty influences descending on particular services, and making one sermon the means of conversion to great numbers of souls. There are many instances of such sermons in the early history of Welsh Methodism; sermons long remembered in the localities in which they were delivered, and the fame of which has been handed down from generation to generation, to the present day.

There was a preacher living at Lledrod, in Cardiganshire, and afterwards at Tŵr-gwyn, in the same county, whose ministry was frequently owned in this remarkable manner. His name was David Morris. His son Ebenezer Morris, of whom we shall yet have occasion to speak, far surpassed him in preaching talent, but the father was a man of note, and especially made so by the mighty power of God which frequently attended his ministry. He made frequent visits to North Wales, preaching two or three times a day as he went along, and some of those evangelistic tours were remarkably successful; so much so that there was scarcely a sermon delivered by him that was not the means of conversion to some souls, and in several instances to a great number. On one of those journeys he preached at a place near Pontrhypont in Anglesey, from the words, "What shall it profit a man, if he gain the whole world, and lose his own soul?" A wonderful influence descended upon himself and upon the congregation. His heart within him melted with compassion towards the lost souls before him, and he burst into a loud and dolorous shout, while every line of his countenance expressed the deepest and most intense feeling—"O bobl y *golled fawr!*—*y golled fawr!*" The English for which is—"O ye people of the *great loss*—the *great loss;*" but that does not convey half the idea. The people bent before him like reeds before a mighty tempest; multitudes joined the neighbouring churches under impressions received from that sermon, and it is talked of to this day in the locality as "the sermon of the *great loss.*"

In the year 1818, there was in the village of Beddgelert, Caernarvonshire, besides the parish church, a small

Calvinistic Methodist chapel, to which belonged a church numbering about forty communicants. For more than twenty years this little flock had stood at about the same number, just maintaining its ground, and gaining enough from without, to fill the gaps made by deaths and removals; and at the beginning of 1818 there was nothing to indicate that any change was approaching in the state of things which had so far existed.[2] But gradually, as the year went on, a new feeling began to pervade the assemblies. It became easier to preach the Word, and more pleasant to hear it. The ministry seemed to tell more than usually on the congregations, and, what had not been known at the place for a long time before, two or three came forward asking to be admitted into the fellowship of the church, and showing hopeful evidences of conversion. An unusual influence, likewise, began to be felt in the Sunday School. One Sabbath, a young female teacher and her class of girls were reading the concluding chapters of St. John's Gospel, when one by one they began to weep, and so strong did the emotion become that they were unable to continue the reading. At the close, one of the brethren, Richard Roberts, of Cae-y-gors, stood up to address the school, and earnestly exhorted the young people to conduct themselves properly at a fair which was to be held in the neighbourhood during the ensuing week, and all at once, to the astonishment of his hearers, and of none more than himself, he became eloquent. He quoted a verse of a Welsh hymn, the concluding line of which, being translated, is, "The firmer hold's above."[3] The word "above" took possession of his whole mind, and for a long time he rang the changes upon it. "It is from *above* that everything precious comes to us. The light comes from *above*, and the heat and the rain. The blessings of salvation came to the world from *above*. It is from *on high* that God pours His Spirit. There is hope for the hardened sinners of Beddgelert *above*. If it is dark here, it is light *above*. If it is feeble here, it is mighty *above, above, above.*" While he spoke the power descended from above, and every soul in the place felt it. All became conscious of a great and mysterious presence; many of the children were filled with dread, and one lad ran to his father, exclaiming, "Oh, my dear father! here is the day of judgment! It has come!" There was universal weeping, and when the school separated it was in tears.

Religious services were statedly held at two out-stations lying in different directions, at distances of two and three miles from the chapel. One of these was at the small village of Nantmor, and the other at a farmhouse called Hafod-y-Llan, standing in the Gwynant glen, which winds up from Beddgelert, along the base of Snowdon. The ministry of those days was wholly itinerant, and continues to be so to a large extent among the Calvinistic Methodists.[4] On the Sabbath to which reference has been made, the supply at Beddgelert was a very humble "exhorter," one Richard Williams of Brynengan. Under ordinary circumstances he would have held services in the two out-stations in the morning and afternoon, and at the chapel in the evening; but on this occasion it was arranged that he should preach in the morning at Nantmor, in the afternoon at the Chapel, and in the evening up the glen at Hafod-y-Llan. The reason for this departure from the usual course was that the renowned John Elias, then in the zenith of his power and popularity, was to preach that evening at Tremadog, seven miles distant, and the chapel at Beddgelert was closed, that the congregation which usually assembled in it might be free to go to hear him. A large number of people usually assembled at the farmhouse, but it was very rarely that all, or even the majority of those who had come together took any part in, or paid any attention to the service. The district was sparsely populated, people came together from great distances, and they looked at the meeting at Hafod as a good opportunity to see one another, and to have a talk. A few of the more thoughtful would join in the service, while others sat in the parlour, or stood in groups about the court, busily engaged in conversation on things which were much more interesting to them than hymns, prayers, and sermons. It was so on this occasion. Richard Williams stood on a bench in the kitchen; in front of him was a square table, and on the top of that a small round one, doing duty as a reading-desk. He introduced the service in the usual way, but with more than usual fervour and unction, and the subject of his discourse was, "Coming to Christ." He had a sermon in his mind, and one with which he was perfectly familiar, for he had frequently preached it before, but when he had spoken for about a quarter of an hour he lost it quite, and began to say things that he had never thought of. It was not his own thoughts that he spoke now, and those which he uttered were not expressed in his usual style, nor with his usual voice. He felt that some one "was speaking through him," and for some time he was in doubt whether it was he himself that was preaching, or whether he was listening to another. The giddy ones that were talking in the parlour and outside became conscious that there was something unusual going on, and rushed into the kitchen with one accord. There they stood spell-bound and awe-struck, listening to the mighty words. Not one uttered a voice. No one wept. The feeling of awe upon every one present was too great for shouts, and even for tears; and when, at the close, the preacher gave out a hymn, no one was able to sing. The congregation separated in silence, and every one went his way to his own home, thinking, and afraid. What was it? It could not have been anything else than this which has been written, "The Holy Ghost fell on all them which heard the Word."

In the course of the ensuing week a church meeting, or as it is usually designated in Wales a "society," was held at the chapel. Those meetings were weekly, and were usually held at 10 o'clock or at noon on a working day, for many of the members lived at great distances, and had to reach their homes along paths that were anything but pleasant to travel on in the dark. The Calvinistic Methodists had not then, nor have they ever had, a hard-and-fast rule of procedure in the reception of members. In some cases those who express a wish to join the church are proposed, seen, and conversed with by some of the elders, reported on by them to the church meeting, and, if thought suitable, accepted; but very frequently such persons, without giving any formal notice of their intention, present themselves at the church meeting, and hence when any one has made a profession of religion, it is very usual in Wales to say that "he has gone to the society." On this occasion two of the elders who had arrived early were waiting at the chapel-house for the people to assemble. By-and-by, one of them looked into the chapel to see whether any had come, and immediately returned to his friend, saying, "Sure enough the people have made a mistake, there is a large congregation. It seems to me as if the whole parish had come together. They must be expecting a sermon." But it soon appeared that it was not a sermon that they had come to seek, but salvation; and at the singing of the opening hymn many of them saw a gleam of hope that, lost sinners as they were, they should find it by the mercy of God in Christ Jesus, and their pent-up feelings burst over all bounds. It was not possible to converse with any one, for nearly all were shouting with all their might. Tidings of this went out to the village and to the scattered dwellings beyond; people rushed to the chapel to see, and as soon as they arrived caught the infection, and began to shout like the rest. And thus they continued hour after hour throughout the day and late into the night; and when at length they retired to their homes, some of their own accord, and others led by friends who were more self-possessed than themselves, the rocks which bounded the gorges through which they had to pass echoed and re-echoed their shouts of praise.

It was thus that this great revival began, and it continued thus for many months. At every religious service the same wonderful influence was felt, and frequently at the singing of the first hymn a fire kindled, which made public prayer and preaching impossible. When the preacher was allowed to proceed as far as the beginning of his sermon in comparative quietness, if he wished to give it all he must be very cool and cautious, for the least spark would produce an explosion which would make it useless for him to speak any more on that occasion. And it was not in the public services only that these influences were felt. They came upon people in an unaccountable manner when alone or in company, or when they were following their daily avocations, and when, as far as men could see, there was nothing to induce them. A young woman, who was remarkable for her personal comeliness, was engaged in milking her father's cows when thoughts came into her mind which filled her with fear, and sent her home crying, "What shall I do to be saved?" She found the answer, *was* saved, and lived to "adorn the doctrine of God our Saviour." Two young people, the son and the servant of one of the elders of the Church, were bringing a cart into Beddgelert, when they began to sing a hymn quietly together. As they were singing the fire kindled, and they were drawn into the village shouting and praising in the cart, the horses having been left to guide themselves. It was hay-carrying day at one of the neighbouring farms, and the man who made the mow finding a longer interval than usual before the arrival of a fresh load, looked towards the field, and lo! the haymakers had thrown away their pitchforks and rakes, and were "leaping and praising God." It may be said that all this was very disorderly, and a sad breach of the decorum which ought to characterise the worship of God, and very probably that is true. But there is one thing to be said in favour of those poor people; they could not help it.

The influence soon began to spread to other districts. In many instances people came to Beddgelert to see the wonder, caught the fire, and took it home with them. A number of young people crossed the mountain from Dolwyddelan, rejoicing in anticipation of the "fun" they were going to have. They were disappointed in the fun, but they found salvation; and one of them, Cadwaladr Owen, became a minister of the gospel, and was for many years one of the most useful in the Principality. But while it spread into Merionethshire on the south, and the Isle of Anglesey on the north, it was on Caernarvonshire and especially on that division of it that is called Arfon, that it made the deepest impression, and produced the greatest change. Previous to 1818 there were in this district only fifteen Calvinistic Methodist chapels, all of which, with two or three exceptions, were small and poor, but in a very short time all these were rebuilt and enlarged, and twelve new places of worship were erected in localities where there were none before. The impetus then given to religion has never wholly subsided, and there are now in that district seventy-eight Calvinistic Methodist Churches, with 14,795 communicants. Besides this, there were men born again in that revival who became eminent ministers of the Gospel of Christ, and were the means of turning many to righteousness, and whose names will be household words in the principality for ages yet to come.[5]

There are some who are wise enough to account for all this on natural principles. They are by no means the discoverers of the theories which they enunciate on this subject. There were remarks made on the Revival, in the days of Daniel Rowland, equally wise, enlightened, and intellectual with those which are made in the present day. It is easy to say that "it was all excitement." There was excitement, we admit, and much of it; but we scarcely believe that there is any one prepared to say that there was none on the day of Pentecost. But to say that it was all excitement is quite another matter, if by that it is intended to imply that it was a momentary feeling, which passed away without leaving any lasting beneficial effect on those who experienced it. There is abundant and conclusive evidence in thousands of instances, that that idea is quite a mistaken one. There may be different opinions as to the propriety of those manifestations. The Rev. Rowland Hill, during one of his visits into Wales, witnessed some of these scenes, and said, "I like the fire; but don't like the smoke." It was prettily said, and quite in character with many of the other sayings of that eminent man; but perhaps it would have been too difficult, under the circumstances of the time, to get the one without the other. It is possible that the people allowed themselves to be too much excited,—that they ought not to have shouted, and that it was very blameworthy in them to jump. We are not at all disposed to argue that point; but it is certain that thousands of those who were thus excited, and who expressed their feelings in cries of distress, and in shouts of gratitude, underwent at the time the great change, and proved themselves for the remainder of their lives to be new creatures.

The idea has gone abroad that the preachers of those days encouraged such manifestations, and made every effort in their power to produce them. Some excellent men seem to have been under the impression that the preacher had only to say "Shout," and that the people shouted, and to say "Jump," and that they jumped accordingly. Dr. Evans, in his *Sketch of the Denominations of the Christian World,* designates one of his "Denominations" "Jumpers." He gives a description which, no doubt, was satisfactory to himself, of what he calls "this kind of worship." He administers a very just castigation to the miserable thing which his own imagination, or that of his informant, had created; and while admitting that "there were some sincere and pious persons to be found among this class of people—men who think they are doing God service, while they are the victims of fanaticism," he generously declares that "these are the objects of compassion;" and it is comforting to find him expressing his conviction that "they doubtless will find it in God."

But it is all an absurd caricature. It is a mistake to assert that these manifestations were only known in Wales; and another mistake to intimate that they were regarded by the founders of Welsh Methodism as necessary accompaniments of true religion. It is true they were defended, or rather apologised for, by W. Williams of Pantycelyn; but how? Not by attempting to show that they were necessarily connected with earnest religion, but by endeavouring to prove that they were not inconsistent with it. David leaped before the ark, and so we *may* do; but there was no attempt made to show that we ought to do so. We are not greatly in love with these things ourselves; and yet these cold times make us feel that, if we could only get the "fire," we would not very strongly object to a little of the "smoke."

NOTES

[1] The original version, first published in *The Christian's Magazine*, may be found in D.E. Jenkins, *The Life of the Rev. Thomas Charles B.A. of Bala*, (Denbigh, 1908), II, pp.88-91.

[2] The Beddgelert revival is usually reckoned to have begun in 1817. Eifion Evans, *Revival Comes to Wales* (Bridgend: Evangelical Press of Wales, 1979), p.14.

[3] This translation does not really bring out the steadfast hope expressed in the original Welsh. It might be expanded and paraphrased as 'My confidence lies in the fact that God has hold of me most surely from above'.

[4] This practice gradually ceased during the second half of the nineteenth century. D.D. Williams, *Llawlyfr Hanes Cyfundeb y Methodistiaid Calfinaidd* (Caernarfon: Cyfundeb y Methodistiaid Calfinaidd, [1927]), pp.206-14.

[5] Williams here refers his readers to *Y Drysorfa*, 1878, pp.377, 411, and to the *Catholic Presbyterian*, II, p.89.

CHAPTER XIII

The Rev. T. Charles of Bala—At Llanddowror School—At Carmarthen College—At Oxford—Ordination and first Curacy—Marriage and Settlement at Bala—Circulating Schools—Sabbath Schools—Letters from Mr. Charles—Owen Jones and Robert Davies at Aberystwyth—A Farewell Meeting and its Effects—Owen Jones at Llanidloes—At Shrewsbury—Ebenezer Richard—Establishment of the British and Foreign Bible Society.

WE have already referred to the Rev. Thomas Charles of Bala, and have given an extract from a letter which he wrote on the revival in the year 1791. It was six years before that letter was written that he had joined the Connexion.[1] He was the son of a farmer in the parish of Llanfihangel Abercywyn, Carmarthenshire, and was born October 14th, 1755. His parents intended him for the ministry, and when he was between ten and twelve years of age he was sent to a school that was held in the neighbouring village of Llanddowror, where the Rev. Griffith Jones had so long and devotedly and successfully laboured. Mr. Jones had gone to his rest some five years before the young lad joined the school; but the influence of his work and of his character was still present in the place, and the mind of Thomas Charles was deeply impressed by it. The conversation of an old disciple of Griffith Jones, named Rhys Hugh, was greatly blessed to him. He was led to make a public profession of religion; and while yet a boy he introduced family worship into his father's house. When he was fourteen years old he was sent to the Presbyterian[2] College at Carmarthen, where, to preserve himself from the bad influences of association with the careless and

189

indifferent young people around him, he gave as much as possible of his time to the reading of religious books. On the 20th of January, 1773, when he was in his eighteenth year, he heard Daniel Rowland; "and that day," he writes, "will be memorable to me as long as I live. From that day I found a new heaven and a new earth to enjoy. The change experienced by a blind man on receiving his sight is not greater than that which I felt on that day."

In his twentieth year he went to Oxford, and three years later he received Deacon's Orders, and was appointed to a curacy in Somersetshire. There was a friend of his, the Rev. Simon Lloyd, living at Bala, who, like himself, was of a Methodistical turn, and he paid him a visit in the interval between his ordination and his settlement in his curacy. The two friends took a tour together of several weeks, taking Llangeitho in their way that they might have the treat of hearing Daniel Rowland, and finished their journey at the house of Mr. Charles's father. During their stay there, the young clergyman had the privilege of preaching at the church of his native parish. We know not how long he retained his Somersetshire curacy, but a portion of that time was spent by him at Oxford, where he took his B.A. degree.[3] An event had, however, transpired during his visit to Bala which gave direction to the whole of his future life. While there, he became acquainted with a young lady in the place, a Miss Jones, and that acquaintance led in process of time to her becoming Mrs. Charles. After his marriage he made his home at Bala, and served several curacies for short periods; but in every case his Methodism was objected to, and he was consequently dismissed. He offered to serve gratuitously in a neighbouring church, but was refused. The doors of the Establishment having thus closed against him, he resolved to cast in his lot with the Welsh Methodists, and this was done in the year 1785.[4] The Connexion had now existed for nearly half a century, but the accession of Mr. Charles to the number of its ministers cannot but be regarded as an era in its history, for in the event it exerted a mighty influence on its destinies, and contributed in no small measure, by the grace of God, to make it a greater blessing to Wales than it had ever hitherto been. Daniel Rowland, after he had heard him preach for the first time at an Association at Llangeitho, only expressed a small part of the truth when he said, "Mr. Charles is the gift of God to North Wales."

He was an eminent preacher, and there are many instances in which his ministry was accompanied with great power, and it is certain that it was made the means of turning many to righteousness; but it is in another department of the work of the Lord that his labours were most abundant, and stood forth in the greatest prominence. In going about to preach from place to place, he was struck with, and greatly distressed by, the great ignorance of the people everywhere. He found that there was scarcely a neighbourhood in which one out of every twenty of the population could read the Word of God, while there were some localities in which it was difficult to find a single person who was able to do so. He applied himself to remedy this deplorable state of things with all his heart and soul. He resolved to attempt the establishment of circulating schools similar to those which had been established many years before by the Rev. Griffith Jones of Llanddowror. Mr. Jones's schools had proved a great benefit; but they had been confined chiefly to South Wales,[5] and had by this time, twenty-five years after the good man's death, nearly all disappeared. The plan was to send a teacher to some locality where he would stay long enough to teach as many as were willing to learn, young and old, to read Welsh, and then to remove him to some other neighbourhood. Mr. Charles applied in every direction for help to put this idea in practice. He began with only one teacher, but as assistance from friends far and near flowed to him in greater and still greater abundance, he was before long enabled to increase the number of his agents to twenty. In acknowledging a subscription from a lady in England towards this object, he wrote in 1796, "In travelling through different parts of the country more than nine years ago, I found that extensive districts in the mountainous parts of North Wales were sunk in the deepest ignorance. The number of those who were able to read was very few, and equally few were those who had the Word of God in their houses. I seriously began to consider how it would be possible to remove so great an evil, and I could think of no other plan which was likely to answer the purpose than to set schoolmasters to work according to the aid which I would receive, and send them to dark districts to teach freely all who would come to them, to read the Bible in their own language, and to instruct them in the first principles of the Christian religion. By the help of kind friends to whom I made known this plan it was set on foot, and has succeeded far beyond my expectations. The demand for schoolmasters has gone on increasingly, and there is a manifest change in the sentiments and morals of the people where those schools have been at work. I established Sabbath and night schools for the sake of those who were too much engaged or too poor to avail themselves of the day schools. The attempts which I have made in this direction have been marvellously successful. The country is filled with schools of one kind or another, and all are taught simultaneously. And there are blessed results following the instruction,—a great and deep interest in spiritual things has been awoke in many localities; many have been made sensible of their sinful state and of their need of Christ, and are now, I have every reason to believe, His faithful followers. The schools have now been in operation for nearly ten years, and the results are similar in a greater or less degree. The number of teachers have been increased or diminished according to the means at my disposal. All that I get for my ministry I devote to this purpose, while the wants of my own family are provided for by the industry of my dear wife.[6] At present I pay £12 per annum to each schoolmaster. They remain in the same place from six to nine months, and are then removed to another locality. We find that nine months is amply sufficient to teach the children to read their Bibles fluently in the Welsh language. I visit the schools myself, when I catechise them publicly, and have the unutterable pleasure of seeing the general aspect of the country marvellously changed. The desert blossoms as a rose, and the dry land has become streams of water. By means of the schools, and the preaching of the Gospel, religious knowledge spreads in every direction. Bless the Lord, O my soul!"[7]

The following extract from a letter written by Mr. Charles, to a member of the Society for the support of Gaelic schools, and which was published in the *Evangelical Magazine* for 1816, page 354, will give considerable light on the difficulties with which he had to contend, and the manner in which they were met and surmounted.

"At first, the strong prejudice which universally prevailed against teaching them to read Welsh *first*, and the idea assumed, that they could not learn English so well, if *previously* instructed in the Welsh language; this, I say, proved a great stumbling-block in the way of parents to send their children to Welsh schools, together with another conceit they had, that if they could read English, they would soon learn of themselves to read Welsh; but now these idle and groundless conceits are universally scouted. This change has been produced not so much by disputing, as by the evident salutary effects of the schools, the great delight with which the children attended them, and the great progress they made in the acquisition of knowledge. The school continues usually at one time in the same place six or nine months, which depends on local circumstances, the number of children, and the progress which the children make. In some districts they learn with much greater rapidity than in others: the causes of this are various, which I cannot enumerate here. This has been my mode of proceeding, subject to some local variations, for above twenty-three years; and I have had the only satisfaction I could wish, that of seeing the work by the Lord's blessing, prospering far beyond my most sanguine expectations. The beginning was small, but the little brook became an overflowing river, which has spread widely over the whole country in Sunday Schools, the wholesome effects of these precious institutions fertilising the barren soil wherever it flows.

"As to the *expediency* of teaching young people, in the first place, to read the language they generally speak and best understand, if imparting religious knowledge is our primary object, as it most certainly *ought* to be, in instructing *immortal* beings, it needs no proof, for it is self-evident. However, I beg your attention for a moment to the following particulars, making no apology for the great length of this letter, as you desired me to be particular.

"1. The time necessary to teach them to read the Bible in their *vernacular* language is so short, not exceeding six months in general, that it is a great pity not to give them the key immediately, which unlocks all the doors, and lays open all the Divine treasures before them. Teaching them English requires two or three years' time, during which long period they are concerned only about dry terms, without receiving one idea for their improvement.

"2. Welsh words convey ideas to their infant minds as soon as they can read them, which is not the case when they are taught to read a language they do not understand.

"3. When they can read Welsh, Scriptural terms become intelligible and familiar to them, so as to enable them to understand the discourses delivered in that language (the language in general preached through the Principality), which, of course, must prove more profitable than if they could not read at all, or read only the English language.

"4. Previous instruction in their native tongue helps them to learn English *much sooner*, instead of proving in any degree an inconveniency. This I have had repeated proofs of, and can confidently vouch for the truth of it. I took this method of instructing my own children, with the view of convincing the country of the fallacy of the general notion which prevailed to the contrary; and I have persuaded others to follow my plan, which, without one exception, has proved the truth of what I conceived to be really the case.

"5. Having acquired new ideas by reading a language they understand, excitement is naturally produced to seek for knowledge, and as our ancient language is very deficient in the means of instruction, there being few useful books printed in it, a desire to learn English—yea, and other languages also—is excited, for the sake of increasing their stock of ideas, and adding to their fund of knowledge. I can vouch for the truth of it, that there are *twenty* to one who can now read English, to what could when the Welsh was entirely neglected. The knowledge of the English is become necessary, from the treasures contained in it. English books are now generally called for; there are now a hundred books, I am sure, for every one that was in the country when I removed from England, and first became a resident in these parts. English schools are everywhere called for, and I have been obliged to send young men to English schools to be trained up for English teachers, that I might be able, in some degree, to answer the general demand for them. In short, the whole country is, in a manner, emerging from a state of great ignorance and ferocious barbarity to civilisation and piety, and that principally by means of the Welsh schools. Bibles without end are called for, are read diligently, learned out by heart, and searched into with unwearied assiduity and care. Instead of vain amusements, dancing, card playing, interludes, quarrelling, and barbarous and most cruel fightings, we have now prayer-meetings; our congregations are crowded, and public catechising is become pleasant, familiar, and profitable. One great means of this blessed change has been the Welsh schools.

"6. By teaching the Welsh first, we prove to them that

we are principally concerned about their souls, and thereby naturally impress their minds with the vast importance of acquiring the knowledge of divine truths, in which the way of salvation, and our duty to God and man, are revealed, whereas, that most important point is left totally out of sight, by teaching them English; for the acquisition of English is connected *only* with their temporal concerns, and which they may never want, as they may, as the majority do, die in infancy. In my opinion, in the education of children it is of the utmost importance, in the first place, to impress their minds with a sense that they are candidates for another world, and that the things pertaining to their eternal felicity there, are of infinitely greater importance to them than the little concerns which belong to our short existence. The neglect of this is, I apprehend, a very great defect in the education of children."

It was no light labour that devolved on Mr. Charles in connection with this great movement. He had to find localities to receive the schools as well as suitable teachers for those localities, and there were not a few whom he was obliged to instruct himself, before they were qualified to teach others. He had to be president and sole teacher of what was in effect a Normal College, as well as general superintendent of a large number of schools spread far and wide throughout the country; and he had to be secretary, treasurer, committee, and collector of the fund which was necessary to keep this vast machinery from coming to a stand. But this was not all. Teachers and children cannot make a school without books; and where were they to come from? Mr. Charles found it necessary to write and bring through the press three elementary spelling and reading books and two catechisms. One of the latter, *The Instructor in the Principles of the Christian Religion,* has passed through a great many editions, and continues to this day to be extensively used in the Principality.

He exercised great care in the selection of his masters. He

sought men of moderately good parts; but they must be humble men, well conducted, of winning ways,—and not proud, lazy, or talkative; but above all they must, as far as could be judged by their life and conversation, be godly men.

Mr. Charles would, first of all, fix upon a locality in which to establish a school, and would then visit the place, call a meeting of the inhabitants, and impress upon their minds the importance of having their children taught to read the Word of God, and then signify his intention to send a teacher among them, who, without fee or reward, would instruct all who were willing to come to him on week-days, or in the evenings, or on the Sabbath-day. In conclusion he would urge the parents to send their children to school, promising to give books gratuitously to all those who were too poor to purchase them. The master was instructed not to receive any money on account of the children whom he taught—not to be burdensome to any of the parents—not to go to any house to eat and drink unless he were specially invited, and was expected, when he remained at any house for a night, to read and pray with the family before going to rest, and also before he left on the following morning. He was likewise instructed to lead the conversation to his own special employment, and to be careful not to let it drift into vain and useless talk. These schools continued in operation for upwards of twenty years, and it is not strange therefore, that, with such means and such men, "the whole aspect of the country was marvellously changed."

It was in the year 1782 that the Sabbath-school was begun at Gloucester by Mr. Robert Raikes, and it was only a few years later when a similar institution was inaugurated in Wales in connection with Mr. Charles's circulating schools.[8] His teachers gave instruction on the Sabbath to those who were unable to attend in the week; and those schools were the means of qualifying great numbers throughout the country to become in their turn teachers themselves. Mr. Charles saw this advantage, and was not slow in availing himself of it. He advocated the establishment of a Sunday-school in connection with every congregation, and though he was opposed at the outset by many conscientious brethren, who regarded teaching people to read as "work," and therefore a thing forbidden by the commandment of God, his mild spirit and kind persuasions ultimately prevailed. Schools sprang up thickly in every direction, and from that day to this the Sabbath-school has been one of the most important and efficient means of grace in the Principality.[9]

We want at this point to give to those of our readers who are unacquainted with Wales some idea of the Welsh Sabbath-school, for it is a very different affair from anything called by that name which they can find in England. It is not an institution of teachers and children merely, but a meeting where the great bulk of the congregation connected with the particular place of worship to which it belongs assemble together to instruct one another in Divine things. It is very frequently the case that the first evidence of a change in a so far thoughtless man, is his beginning to attend the Sunday-school. The majority of attendants are above fifteen years of age, and they range between that and eighty or ninety. Of course the children of the congregation attend, but they are outnumbered in most cases by the seniors. We could take our reader to many a school in Wales where he would find more pairs of spectacles than in any ten in the metropolis together. There is a female class in the corner of the room, the teacher of which is a matron of seventy-two. Perhaps she has been there every Sabbath, with very few exceptions, for the last forty years. Her dear old teacher went to heaven twenty years ago, and she has occupied her place ever since. The class is numerous, and her oldest pupil is perhaps eighty-five years of age, and her youngest approaching sixty. Of course she is under no necessity to teach them to read; that they have been able to do for many years,—indeed, long before we were born; but they read a portion of the Word of God together, and then talk. A thought has occurred to one of them in reading, another to another, and each in her turn expresses her thought. Possibly the conversation drifts more in the direction of experience than in that of exegesis, but it is by no means uncommon for the whole host of spectacles to be considerably dimmed, and for the dear old sisters to go home more refreshed than they have been under many a sermon. There is a class of men of similar ages in the other corner, who possibly will go deeper into doctrine than their sisters opposite. Then there are classes of middle-aged, and of young people of both sexes, discussing, it may be, "The fall of man," "The universality of the Flood," "The journeys of Israel," "The travels of St. Paul," "Justification by faith," "The difference between regeneration and adoption," or any other imaginable biblical or theological subject. It is this that accounts for the fact that such a large number of the common people in Wales are so much at home in the Holy Scriptures, and so well versed in theological knowledge. We do not mean to assert that all the Welsh people are thus, nor even the greatest part of them, but we believe we are right in saying that it is so in the case of a larger proportion of the working classes than in any other part of the kingdom. Some time ago we passed three working men, we believe they were colliers, sitting together on a heap of stones by the roadside, and earnestly discussing the question "How to reconcile the sovereignty of God with the responsibility of man." It struck us at the time that people of that class do not usually discuss such subjects anywhere out of Wales. Perhaps we were mistaken; but we are certain that they would not have done it, and would not have been able to do it, in Wales, if it had not been for its peculiar system of conducting the Sabbath-school.

To Mr. Charles belongs the honour of having been the father and founder of the Sabbath-school in Wales. It was the circulating day and evening schools which he had established and kept in operation by an enormous amount of labour and self-sacrifice, that produced a class of men and women capable of instructing others. It was he that urged that class to utilise the powers and capabilities which they had thus acquired for the benefit of their neighbours, young and old, by collecting them together to teach them on the Sabbath; and it was he who, by his unflagging perseverance, and kind and winning ways, completely overcame the strong prejudice against that kind of "work," that was felt by a great many earnest-minded people. But he was followed by many other zealous and successful labourers in the same field, one or two of whom we will take the liberty of introducing to our readers.

Owen Jones was born at Tywyn, in Merionethshire, in the year 1787. When between seven and eight years of age, he was sent to school to a Mr. J. Jones, Pen-y-parc, who seems to have been a very efficient schoolmaster, and who was withal an earnestly religious man. He took a great liking to young Owen for his quickness in learning, and especially for the readiness with which he would at any time drop his play in order to accompany him to a religious service. After having been for some years under Mr. Jones's instruction, the lad was sent for a short term to a school in England. Soon after his return home, the master of a free school at Tywyn had occasion to leave for a time, and young Owen Jones was requested to take charge of his pupils during his absence. Though only a boy himself, he accepted the work, and did it well. During the brief period of his oversight of this school he adopted the custom of examining the children every evening on the subjects which they had studied during the day, and there he discovered in himself, and began to make known to others, that power for which he became afterwards so renowned,—the power to convey instruction by means of questioning his pupils. We hesitate not to say that Owen Jones was the greatest catechist that Wales ever produced.

Soon after this he was apprenticed to a saddler at Aberystwyth, and it was in that town that he began his marvellous career in connection with Sabbath-schools. In the year 1799, the Rev. Mr. Williams, a clergyman of the Church of England, and a zealous advocate of Sabbath-schools, paid a visit to Aberystwyth. During his sojourn in the place, he was distressed to see a great number of people of all ages loitering about on the Lord's Day, and he resolved to gather as many of them as he could together, to give them religious instruction. He prevailed upon a number of them to assemble in a room which he hired for that purpose, and taught them for two Sundays. But he was only a visitor in the place, and when the time of his brief sojourn was coming to its close, he looked about him for some one to carry on the work which he had begun. He was directed to a young lad named Robert Davies, who was already connected with a small school, which had been for some time carried on in the town by the Methodists. Young Davies readily consented to do what he could, but before entering upon the work, he sought and obtained the assistance of his friend and cousin, the saddler's apprentice. It was generally anticipated that the work which had been successfully begun by the good clergyman would soon collapse in the hands of two boys. But those were not ordinary boys. It flourished greatly under their care, and soon began to attract large numbers of all ages. Finding the Sabbath hours too short to do all that was in their heart to do, they conducted classes in several houses in rotation on every evening in the week but Saturday. Owen Jones's lively method of teaching, and his tact in catechising the children, attracted the notice and won the admiration of all classes throughout the town. Neither of the cousins had at the time made a profession of religion, but they always opened and closed the meetings of their school with prayer. By-and-by, however, they both became deeply impressed with the importance of personal religion, and offered themselves, and were gladly accepted, as members of the Methodist Church. The deep earnestness which had thus possessed their own souls soon spread to many of those who were under their charge. But while Owen Jones was thus in the full tide of usefulness, he received an intimation from his father that he must leave Aberystwyth and return to Tywyn. The prospect of leaving his beloved work was to him a most painful one, and that of losing him was equally so to hundreds at Aberystwyth; but there was no help for it. An evening was fixed for him and the scholars to take leave of each other, and that proved an evening long to be remembered. He offered up a prayer at the opening of the meeting, and a mighty prayer it was. Earnestly, even agonisingly, did he plead with God for his own life and that of his dear, *dear* scholars, and there descended an overpowering influence which spread through the place, and extended to the crowd which had assembled outside. About eighty members were added to the Church at Aberystwyth, who had been brought under impressions on that memorable evening. The awakening which thus began mightily spread to the neighbouring districts. We give an extract from a letter which appeared in the *Evangelical Magazine* for May 1805, from the Rev. T. Charles:—

"I am glad to say that there is a happy revival of religion in some parts of Wales. At Aberystwyth and the neighbouring districts there is a general and mighty awakening among the young people and children, and some hundreds have joined the religious societies in those parts. I was lately at an Association of the Calvinistic Methodists at Aberystwyth, and it was estimated that the multitude assembled together amounted to, at least, twenty thousand. It was a happy sight to a Christian. The sermons were with the demonstration of the Spirit and with power. There were hundreds of children from eight years old and upwards to be seen in the congregation, listening with as much attention as the most earnest Christians, and bathed in tears. This work began in a Sunday-school which was conducted by two young men. Soon after the commencement of this school, both teachers and scholars were brought under deep impressions, and the work has now spread over a district extending fifty miles in length and twenty in breadth. In going along the road, it is pleasant to hear the ploughmen and the lads who drive the horses singing hymns at their work. There is nothing else to be heard all over the country. This I can testify with gratitude and joy."[10]

When the day came for Owen Jones to leave Aberystwyth, he was escorted by all the scholars, together with a large number of men and women, some miles from the town; and when this great escort could proceed no farther, and the poor sorrowing lad was obliged to trudge on alone, they followed him with their eyes to a considerable distance, and saw him fall on his knees to pray three times before his path had taken him out of their sight. When he was eighteen years of age we find him at Llanidloes, and hard at work instructing and catechising the young. While residing at that town, he visited several places in the surrounding districts in pursuit of his great object, and extended his labours as far as Rhaeadr, where he succeeded in planting a large and flourishing Sunday-school. When he found parents indisposed to send their children to be instructed, he would ask permission to bring a number of his young folks to their house, that he might catechise them in their hearing, and that they might see what progress they were making in religious knowledge. This device scarcely ever failed to succeed.

When in his twentieth year he came to Shrewsbury, and his first care in that town was to gather the Welsh people together to receive instruction; and not finding sufficient materials among his own countrymen, he resolved to try what he could do for the English, and by going about from house to house he succeeded in establishing an English Sunday-school, numbering between a hundred and a hundred and twenty children, which he conducted with great success as long as he remained at Shrewsbury. When he left the place, his school was taken charge of by the Rev. Mr. Nunn, incumbent of St. Chad's, and became the beginning of the Sunday-school connected with that church.

When Mr. Jones married he settled at Gelli, in Montgomeryshire, and became a popular preacher of the Gospel; but it was as an organiser of schools and a catechist of the children that he excelled to the end of his life; and whenever he came on his evangelising mission to any locality, his visit never failed to give new life to the Sunday-school.

Another zealous and successful labourer in the same field was the Rev. Ebenezer Richard of Tregaron. The enthusiasm of this great and good man in the cause knew no bounds, and the excellent "Rules" for the conducting of Sabbath-schools and Sabbath-school unions, which he wrote and published, as well as his unceasing and affectionate advocacy everywhere of the claims of this beneficent institution, resulted in valuable blessings not only to Cardiganshire, but likewise to the whole of South Wales. Will those of our readers who do not call the Principality their own dear country, pardon us if we say that England is indebted to the Welsh Sunday-school for one of its most glorious institutions, and that the world is indebted to it for one of its greatest blessings? We believe that we are fully warranted in saying that such is the truth. Before the beginning of the Sabbath-school movement the number of Bibles in the country was too few for each of those who were even then able to read to have a copy. What then must have been the state of the case after readers had been multiplied more than a hundredfold? There was quite a famine in the country—a famine for the possession of the Word of the Lord.[11] Mr. Charles applied to the "Society for Promoting Christian Knowledge," and succeeded in obtaining from that excellent institution a grant of ten thousand Welsh Bibles. But what were they among so many? Another application was made to the same Society, and then another; but in vain. Every effort to procure any more supplies from that source proved unavailing. The promptitude with which the Society responded to the first application conclusively proves that it was not from any unwillingness on its part to help the Welsh people, that future applications were unsuccessful.

Mr. Charles was thus constrained to cast about for some other means to supply the great and increasing want of his country. He went to London to consult a few friends with a view of establishing a Society to supply Wales with the Holy Scriptures. Most of our readers, we presume, are aware of the fact that it was at a meeting which had been called together to consider that subject, it was resolved immediately to establish "The British and Foreign Bible Society." Before that Society had been in existence ten years it had supplied Wales with a hundred thousand copies of the Word of God.

NOTES

1 Seven years; see note 4 below.
2 The College was during this period a stronghold of Arianism and a breeding-ground for Unitarianism. Dewi Eirug Davies, *Hoff Ddysgedig Nyth* (Abertawe: Tŷ John Penry, 1976), p.66. The former College building is now the home of two evangelical churches (one Welsh, one English).
3 Thomas Charles originally served the parish of Sparkford; South Barrow and Lovington were later added to his charge, and he also assisted his friend John Lucas in an unofficial capacity at Milborne Port. D.E. Jenkins, *Thomas Charles*, I, pp.96, 104, 154, 288-90. He returned to Oxford very briefly on only two occasions, firstly to graduate and subsequently to be ordained a priest. *Ibid.*, pp.114-5, 185-7. After nearly five years in Somerset, he left for north Wales on 23 June 1783. *Ibid.*, p.415.
4 The date was rather 2 July 1784. *Ibid.*, p.496.
5 This statement is misleading. See p.56 above, and cf. M.G. Jones, *The Charity School Movement* (1938; republished London: Cass, 1964), pp.390-407; R. T. Jenkins, 'A Conspectus of Griffith Jones's Schools in North Wales, 1738-

1761', *Bulletin of the Board of Celtic Studies,* V (1929-31), pp.354-79; Hugh Jones, 'Gruffydd Jones's Circulating Schools in Anglesey', *Transactions of the Anglesey Antiquarian Society* (1936), pp.94-109.

6   Charles's wife, Sally, inherited a shop at Bala which sold grocery, drapery, and general household goods. D.E. Jenkins, *Thomas Charles,* I, pp.418-9. For Charles's wife, see Gwen Emyr, *Sally Jones: Rhodd Duw i Charles* (Pen-y-bont ar Ogwr: Gwasg Efengylaidd Cymru, 1996), 53pp.

7   The letter was written not in 1796 but on 5 August 1797. It is reproduced in full in D. E. Jenkins, *Thomas Charles,* II, pp.162-3; the quotation given in the present volume seems to be a translation from a Welsh version of the letter.

8   Raikes's first school was established in 1780, not 1782. Thomas Charles was almost certainly aware of the existence of Sunday schools in England when he became actively involved in promoting them in Wales from 1787 onwards. *Ibid.,* II, pp.1-28.

9   Williams has the following footnote: "Jenkin Morgan, a schoolmaster and exhorter, had taught a number of people on the Sabbaths at Tyn-y-fron, Crawlom, Montgomeryshire, as early as the year 1770 or 1771; but since that was an isolated effort it cannot be regarded as the beginning of the Sabbath-schools." Williams's statement is based on an essay quoted in John Hughes, *Methodistiaeth Cymru,* II, p.361. No corroborative evidence is provided. A Methodist exhorter named Jenkin Morgan had been one of Griffith Jones's schoolmasters and had held schools in Montgomeryshire, but he died in 1762. *Dictionary of Welsh Biography,* p.646.

10 This quotation again appears to be a translation from a Welsh version. The original English version may be found in the *Evangelical Magazine* (1805), p.235, and in D. E. Jenkins, *Thomas Charles,* III, p.114.

11 This is the background to Mary Jones's well-known quest for a Welsh Bible. The story has been overlaid with much whimsical fiction, and it should be remembered that her quest was far from unique, but the basic truth underlying the story of her journey to Bala to obtain a Bible is undeniable. *Ibid.,* II, pp.492-5, 518-9.

CHAPTER XIV

THE first ten or twelve years of the present century was the most critical period that the Welsh Methodist Connexion ever passed through. Its position with regard to the Establishment from the beginning of its existence was an exceedingly anomalous one, and it was becoming increasingly so as it increased in numbers, and as its first founders were one after another passing away. It was not a Dissenting Body, and it took great pains to convince the world that it was not. But what was it? Was it a part of the Establishment? It regarded itself in that light, but the Establishment did not recognise it. Several of the clergymen who were at its head had been turned out of the Church for their Methodism, and their brethren who were allowed to retain their place in the Establishment found their position anything but comfortable. In going beyond the limits of their own parishes, and ministering in unconsecrated places, they transgressed the laws to which they were amenable, and might any day be called upon to suffer the penalty. And these brethren, while subject to the courts and the laws of the Establishment, assisted, indeed took the leading part, in constituting courts and framing laws and regulations which the Establishment did not recognise. All the members of the Methodist body regarded themselves as members of the Established Church; but there were multitudes belonging to that Church who would not on any account have been received, as they were, into the Methodist body. We have seen how careful they were to avoid, as far as possible, everything that looked like seceding from the Church. When they built a place of worship, it was called "a Society house," or "a house for religious purposes," or anything else which they could think of that was most likely to make the impression that they had no desire to secede from the Church. They communicated in the Established Church; but in very many instances the clergyman of their own parish was not such as they felt at liberty to receive the Communion from, and many of the communicants were not such as they felt at liberty to communicate with. Was it right, they could not help asking, that, after withdrawing from the ungodly and immoral people of their neighbourhood, they should meet them again at the Lord's Table? In some instances, after the brethren of the Methodist Society had expelled a member for immorality, they would have the mortification of meeting him again at the Communion in the parish church. To avoid such offences they had either to remain for many months, and in some cases for years, without the privilege of partaking of the Lord's Supper, or to travel many miles in order to obtain it. The Methodist clergymen, as those of their ministers who had been episcopally ordained were designated, were few in number,—about sixteen in South Wales at the close of the last century; but most of those confined themselves to their own parishes, and for many years there were only six other places in the whole of South Wales where the Methodists were in the habit of solemnising the Lord's Supper. Some of those were places belonging to the Establishment, such as Gyfylchi Chapel in Glamorganshire, and Llanlluan Chapel in the county of Carmarthen, and some were "Society houses" to which the privilege had been extended by the favour of the Association. In North Wales there was a still greater dearth of clergymen,—three being the largest number of this class that had ever existed together in that portion of the Principality. A great number of able preachers had by this time risen in the body; but they were not ordained. Sometimes an ordained clergyman and an unordained exhorter would preach in succession to the same audience; the former inside, and the latter outside the church. There was a room built against Gyfylchi Chapel, near Neath, and a door was opened leading from it into the chapel. Clergymen officiated in the chapel, but exhorters in the room; and when two of these different classes of teachers met, as it frequently happened, the former would address the audience from the pulpit, and the latter from the doorway, taking great care that his feet should stand within the room.

All these privations and inconveniences suggested to some of the brethren the idea of ordaining ministers of their own; but it was not without fear and trembling that this thought was first expressed. It would he a momentous step; in fact, nothing less than a secession. Nearly all the Episcopal clergymen met the first proposals in that direction with the most determined opposition. Nathaniel Rowland, a son of the great reformer of Llangeitho, had married the daughter of Howel Davies, the great reformer of Pembrokeshire, and he seems to have supposed that being son of one of those eminent men, and son-in-law of the other, gave him the right to rule in the Connexion which they had done so much to bring into existence and to foster. We have not been able to find out that he possessed qualifications to exercise dominion; but it is certain that he did rule with a high hand for some time in the Associations of South Wales. Although a large number of chapels had by this time been erected in the south, there were only some three or four in which permission had been obtained to solemnise the ordinance of the Lord's Supper, and Mr. Rowland opposed with all his might every attempt to increase the number of those

privileged places of worship. At an Association held at
Carmarthen, there was something like a scene in connection
with a request for leave to communicate in the chapel of
that place. Mr. D. Charles, brother of Mr. Charles of Bala,
who was a deacon of the Church, and who afterwards
became an eminent minister, rose up and said, "The church
in this place has requested me to ask permission to
commemorate here the death of our Redeemer." Upon this
Mr. Nathaniel Rowland sprang to his feet, and said in a
determined voice, "You *shall not;* Llanlluan Chapel is
sufficiently near for you." This chapel was ten miles off. "I
ask again," said Mr. Charles, "shall we have this privilege?
We are permitted to preach Christ, to believe on Him, to
profess Him; shall we commemorate His death for us?"
"You shall *not* in this place," said N. Rowland. "It so
happens," said Mr. Charles coolly, "that it was not *your*
permission that I was requested to ask." Things were
beginning to look serious, when the Rev. David Jones of
Llan-gan got up and exclaimed, "You shall, dear David, you
shall. When do you wish it to be? I will come over myself to
assist you." And so in process of time it came to pass; but
this concession on the part of the eminent clergyman of Llan-
gan brought upon him, on the spot, a furious onslaught from
Nathaniel Rowland. It could not but be expected that this
man would have determinedly opposed any step of the kind
which we have above indicated; but in the year 1807 a
charge of misconduct was brought against him, and this led
to his expulsion from the Connexion over which he wanted
to be king. Mr. Jones was Vicar of Llan-gan, in Glamorganshire, and had settled in that place in the year 1768. His
ministry soon began to attract great congregations, and it
was not long before Llan-gan became that which Llangeitho
had been for many years before,—the centre of great
gatherings from the surrounding districts, especially on the
Communion Sabbath. He did not confine himself to his
church, but went about doing good, preaching in the

surrounding villages, and taking occasional tours to distant parts of the Principality. He was intimately acquainted with the Countess of Huntingdon, and it was by her influence that he had been presented to his living. He paid periodical visits to London to preach in her ladyship's chapels, and in other places, and was one of the most zealous and active among the founders of the London Missionary Society. On the second anniversary of that great Institution he was appointed to preach the anniversary sermon at Zion Chapel. This was on the 13th of May, 1796, and two months before the first batch of missionaries sailed for the South Sea Islands. Wherever he preached he drew together a great concourse of people, and his ministry was generally overpowering in its effects. His first visits to North Wales were made before the scum of the people had quite given up mobbing Methodist preachers, and disturbing their services; but the mild accents of his voice never failed to melt the hearts of even those who had come within its reach for the purpose of making a disturbance. He once preached at an Association at Rhuthun, where a disturbance had been planned, which was to be led by a burly butcher. Mr. Jones's text was, "No man ever spake like this man." The butcher stood to listen, and, as he listened, his courage to attack the preacher was getting smaller and smaller, and at length he exclaimed, "By—! no man ever spake like *you* either. Never in my life before have *I* been so completely mastered." Complaints were made against him more than once to his bishop, and, on one occasion, at a visitation at Cowbridge, he was called to account for his irregularities. The bishop earnestly remonstrated with him, and begged him to desist in future from those Methodistical practices. Mr. Jones was very sorry that he could not yield to the persuasions of his superior, but he really could not. He must go about to preach the Gospel to perishing sinners: and, as to preaching in unconsecrated places, he did not believe that any place was unconsecrated. His belief was, that when the blessed Saviour had put His foot on this earth of ours, He had consecrated every inch of it. That bishop was too good and kind a man to wish to do any injury to the earnest evangelist, and finding that he was prepared to suffer any pains or penalties rather than give up his Methodistical ways, he only begged him to be careful not to intrude into two particular parishes in the Vale of Glamorgan, adding, that the clergymen of those parishes were very much annoyed by his interference with their charges. This Mr. Jones readily promised to do, regarding of course the prohibition to go to those parishes as good as a license to go to all the world besides. When this interview was over, there were many who were astonished, and some not a little chagrined, to see the bishop walking along the street with Mr. Jones leaning on his arm.

The loving and liberal spirit of this great and good man made him immensely popular among all the Methodists, especially in South Wales; and this was a very serious difficulty, perhaps indeed the most serious of all, in that portion of the Principality, that was lying in the way of the ordination of ministers. It was well known that he was opposed to it, and the friends felt a great disinclination to take any step that would be painful to the feelings of the good, kind Mr. Jones. There were other clergymen who stormed and threatened—that the brethren did not much mind; but Mr. Jones wept and entreated, and that was something serious to withstand. "I have risked my bread," said he at one Association where this subject was discussed; "I have risked my bread in order to be with you, and with you, so far, I have been permitted to be; but if you are resolved thus to break up the cause, you shall, as far as I am concerned, go along by yourselves; I will remain with you no longer." Again and again he entreated the brethren not to take such a step while he lived, and if a sense of duty to God and to the thousands who were deprived of religious privileges had constrained them to deny the request of one whom they so greatly loved, it would have been with the deepest sorrow; but the

Providence of God spared them and him the trial which seemed inevitable, by taking Mr. Jones to his rest some time before the step had been fully decided on. He died in perfect peace at his own residence, Manorowen, on the 12th of August, 1810, in the seventy-fifth year of his age.

There was another clergyman in Pembrokeshire, the Rev. D. Griffiths of Nevern, whose high position in society, extensive family connections, great preaching talents, and blameless character, gave him great influence in the Methodist Connexion. He determinedly opposed the ordination of ministers, and not always, perhaps, in the best temper. The subject was brought before an Association, held at Cardigan, by Mr. Evan Davies, one of the deacons of that county. Mr. Davies had attempted to broach the matter at a previous Association, but had been summarily put down. As soon as he began to speak on this occasion, Mr. Griffiths stood up and said with great warmth, "Turn out that man who follows the Associations to create a disturbance and injure the cause—out with him!" "Mr. Griffiths", was Mr. Davies's cool reply, "the chariot of God is going onward. Beware of standing in its way, lest you be crushed, as it happened to that prince in the gate of Samaria." There were not a few painful scenes, which we do not care to describe, at the Associations and Monthly Meetings of those days, in which the chief actors were the deacons, or, as they were then called, leaders, who desired the change, and the ordained clergymen who opposed it. Most of the preachers were in favour of it, but they were under a necessity to keep comparatively silent, for any warm advocacy on their part would be naturally regarded as the result of a desire for the honour it would confer on themselves.

We are not at all disposed to find fault with the Episcopal clergymen for opposing the measure that was now in contemplation. Most of them retained their places in the Church, but had suffered not a little in consequence of their Methodism. They were for the most part able men, and therefore more likely than many to obtain preferment in their own Church; but they had sacrificed every such prospect to their attachment to the Methodist body. They considered that body as a part of the Church, and regarded their labours in its behalf in the light of labours for Church extension. This was their excuse to their bishops, to their Episcopal brethren, and to their own consciences, for persisting in practices which they admitted to be irregular. But the ordination of ministers by the body itself would place them in an entirely new position, and oblige them either to give up their connection with people whom they greatly loved, and relinquish labours to which they were strongly attached, or to leave the Establishment. They could not remain ministers of the Church *and* ministers of that which would now be an avowedly Dissenting denomination. It was the necessity of the case that had brought matters to this painful crisis. The body had become by far too numerous to be supplied with ordinances by the few Episcopal clergymen who had identified themselves with it. The people had become many thousands, scattered over the whole of Wales, and the great majority of them would prefer communicating in the Dissenting Chapel to receiving the ordinance from such men as the greater number of the then parish clergy were. They must either have ministers of their own, or suffer a most important ordinance, which the Redeemer had instituted in His Church, to fall into comparative desuetude, or offend their consciences by receiving the ordinance from ministers whom they regarded as anything but earnest servants of Christ, and in company with people whom they knew to be ungodly, or go over to the Nonconformists. Some Churches had already taken the last course—had ordained ministers for themselves, and from that day become Independent Churches. But the body decided upon taking the first of the courses which we have indicated, and it is to its having done so it is indebted for its separate existence.

But let not our brethren of the Establishment imagine that, if that step had not been taken, the Church would have been one whit stronger in Wales at the present day than it is. There is one Dissenting denomination the more, and, as we believe, a greater number of religious people in consequence; but if that had not been, it is the other Dissenting denominations, and not the Church, that would have been more numerous. The position of the Church has been made, not by any steps which have been taken outside of it, but by the character of its own ministers.

There were a few clergymen who had already either been compelled to relinquish their connection with the Establishment, or had left it of their own accord, and had fully identified themselves with the Methodists; and there were others who did so when the decisive moment came. Among the latter was the Rev. John Williams, the parish minister of Lledrod, in Cardiganshire. He was a good and earnest man, and does not seem to have ever been strongly opposed to the ordination, and whatever objections he had felt to it were completely overcome at an Association which he attended at Bala. On his way home from this assembly he resolved, after a severe mental struggle, to cast in his lot with the Methodists, and to throw himself on the Providence of God for the means of subsistence; after this, he reasoned and preached in favour of the contemplated movement. To some of the members who opposed it he said, "You are strange people; you are not satisfied with a regular clergyman, and a Dissenting minister won't do for you: nothing will satisfy you but an expelled parson."

Mr. Charles was at first opposed to this step, but he was gained over at the same Association as Mr. Williams. He was chairman at the time, and the subject was discussed with some warmth on both sides. Mr. Ebenezer Morris was present, and while the discussion was going on he rose from his seat and stood leaning against one of the pillars that supported the pulpit. At the first pause every eye was turned towards him. For a while he remained silent, but at length, said, with his deep, solemn, and commanding voice, "I have a question to ask the chairman." After another pause he went on. "I am here representing hundreds of people in this congregation and elsewhere, and I call on Mr. Charles to answer me, adjuring him to give an honest and straightforward answer to my question—Which is the greatest and most important work? Is it the preaching of the gospel or the administering of the ordinances of Baptism and the Lord's Supper?" Mr. Charles rose at once from his seat, and answered, "The greatest work is preaching the Gospel." "Then," exclaimed Ebenezer Morris, "we are one. Satan had thought to divide us, but thanks be unto God, we are one." With these few words, slowly and solemnly uttered, a thrill of feeling passed through the whole congregation, and all felt that the struggle was over. And so it was. It was unanimously resolved to proceed, and to send a letter to the brethren in South Wales announcing the decision which had been arrived at, and inviting them to take the same course. The subject was accordingly brought before an Association held at Swansea in the year 1810, where there was a long, and, on the part of one or two, a rather angry discussion. The Rev. Rowland Hill was present, and warmly and eloquently advocated the ordination, and it was eventually resolved to endorse the decision arrived at by the brethren in North Wales. Pursuant to this resolution, eight brethren chosen from among the preachers of North Wales were ordained at an Association held at Bala, on the 20th of June, 1811, and thirteen chosen from among those of the South were ordained at an Association at Llandeilo Fawr in the month of August in the same year. The brethren from the North were Thomas Jones and John Davies, Denbighshire; John Elias and Richard Lloyd, Anglesey; Evan Richardson, Caernarvonshire; John Roberts, Merionethshire; and Evan Griffiths and William Jones, Montgomeryshire.[1] Those ordained in South Wales were, from Carmarthenshire, John Evans, David Rees, Arthur Evans, and David Charles. The first of these had previously received Deacon's Orders in the Church of England, and the last was brother of Mr. Charles of Bala. From Breconshire there were James James, David Parry, and Evan Evans; from Cardiganshire, Ebenezer Morris, John Thomas, and Ebenezer Richard; from Pembrokeshire, Evan Harries; from Glamorganshire, Hopkin Bevan; and from Monmouthshire, John Rees.

We have before us a report of the proceedings at the former of these solemn occasions, which we subjoin:—

"Mr. John Evans of Bala, the oldest and one of the most respected preachers in the Connexion, commenced the service by reading the third chapter of the First Epistle to Timothy, making appropriate remarks on the qualifications which, in that chapter, are pointed out as requisite in ministers of the Gospel, and then offered prayer in a very devout and solemn manner. The Rev. Thomas Charles then read the names of the persons who had been chosen by the monthly meetings of the several counties. Having done so, he asked the representatives of the different churches, of whom about three hundred were present, whether they wished him to put a few questions to the brethren who were to be ordained, on the fundamental articles of the Christian religion, and if that was their desire he requested them to signify the same by raising their hands, which all immediately did. Then he submitted the following queries to those who were about to be set apart, and obtained highly appropriate and satisfactory answers:—

"What are your views of—

"1. The Being of God and His attributes?

"2. The Trinity?

"3. The Word of God?

"4. The decrees of God, and Election?

"5. The Providence of God over the world?

"6. The Fall and Corruption of Man?

"7. The Moral Law?

"8. The Person of Christ?

"9. The Offices of Christ?

"10. The Sacrifice of Christ and Redemption?

"11. Justification?

"12. The Person of the Holy Ghost?

"13. The Work of the Holy Ghost in the plan of salvation?

"14. The call of the Gospel?

"15. Perseverance in Grace?

"16. The Resurrection?

"17. The general Judgment?

"18. Which are the ordinances of Divine appointment?

"19. What are your views regarding Baptism and the Lord's Supper: their end, their use, and their signification?

"20. Do you sincerely approve of the present order of the Welsh Calvinistic Methodist Connexion?

"21. Do you intend, as far as lies in you, to preserve the unity of the Connexion in the manner in which the Lord has so greatly prospered it? and do you purpose to withstand all useless and contentious debatings which have a tendency to create strife?"

Having obtained their solemn and enlightened replies to these questions, he asked the representatives whether they chose these brethren to administer the ordinances of Baptism and the Lord's Supper among them; and if they did, to signify the same by holding up their hands. This was done by all present, without exception.

"He then asked the brethren, whether they assented to the call of the Connexion, and whether they willingly yielded themselves to be faithful, laborious, and diligent, to feed the flock of God, by devoutly administering the ordinances according to the assistance which they should receive of God.

"They answered in a humble and serious manner, that they did, and earnestly desired the prayers of the whole Connexion in their behalf.

"The venerable brother, Mr. Robert Jones of Caernarvonshire, gave them in conclusion a word of exhortation and offered up an earnest prayer appropriate to the occasion."[2]

The same method was observed, and the same questions asked, by Mr. Charles, at the ordination of the thirteen South-Walian brethren a few weeks later, but the devotional portions of the service, on this latter occasion, were conducted by two Episcopally ordained clergymen, the Revs. John Williams, Pantycelyn, and John Williams, Lledrod, who had now, like Mr. Charles, finally seceded from the Establishment.

Ordinations in the Welsh Calvinistic Methodist Connexion are to this day conducted in the same manner, and have come of late years to be attended by vast congregations. Often have we found them "seasons of refreshing," and furnishing evidences which to us were most conclusive and satisfactory, that they obtained the sanction of the Great Head of the Church.

NOTES

[1] Robert Ellis of Flintshire also received authority to administer the sacraments, but was not ordained as such at the Association because he had already been ordained in the Countess of Huntingdon's Connexion. D. E. Jenkins, *Thomas Charles*, III, 283.

[2] This is the author's English translation of part of the historical section appended to the Welsh Confession of Faith. The official English translation is to be found in the English version of the Confession, *The History, Constitution, Rules of Discipline, and Confession of Faith of the Calvinistic Methodists, or the Presbyterians of Wales* (Caernarfon: D. O'Brien Owen for the General Assembly, 1900), pp.20-21.

CHAPTER XV

THOSE who opposed the ordination of ministers were
under the impression that that step would lead to very
disastrous consequences. They were themselves attached to
the Establishment, and supposed that the great mass of the
people were more like them in this respect than they really
were. The Episcopally ordained ministers had great
influence over the Connexion. They were much respected
and loved by the brethren universally, but it was more on
account of their personal worth than on account of the
precarious tie which held them to the Establishment. There
was scarcely one of them who had not suffered, in one way
or another, in consequence of his Methodism. It was well
known that they would be more respected by men of
position and authority in their own Church, and would be
much more likely to obtain preferment in it, if they were to
withdraw altogether from the despised sect, and this
consideration endeared them still more to the people. It was
to the *men* that the people were attached, and not to the
Church, and some of the very reasons for their attachment
to the former could not otherwise than lead to unfavourable
impressions with regard to the latter. Their love to these
sufferers was such, that they could not feel any strong
attachment to the system which was at the source of their
sufferings.

When the ordination was fully decided on, seven out of
the ten Episcopally ordained clergymen who had so far

laboured with the Methodists in South Wales, withdrew from them altogether, and among these there were a few of great ability and extensive influence; but notwithstanding the withdrawal of these eminent men, the great mass of the people everywhere adhered to the Connexion. Mr. Jones of Llan-gan, as we have seen, attracted to his church an enormous congregation. On the monthly Sabbaths several hundreds were in the habit of assembling from the surrounding country to partake of the Lord's Supper. Mr. Jones was called to his rest only a few months before the final step was taken. But what of his flock? Did they continue in their attachment to the Church after he had gone? Quite otherwise. We are well acquainted with Llan-gan, having been born and brought up within two miles of the place. At the time of our earliest recollection there was a small congregation assembling there, for the clergyman was somewhat of a Methodist, and held "societies" and prayer-meetings, but the churches of the surrounding parishes were nearly empty. Our own parish church was scarcely ever attended by more than the vicar, the clerk, and a couple of old women, while that of an adjoining parish was often for several weeks together without any service at all. But what had become of Mr. Jones's large congregation? We knew scores of them personally, and well remember the tears which some of them were wont to shed when they spoke of him or repeated some of his sayings; but as far as we can recollect there was only one of the whole number, a good old sister, who kept up her connection with Llan-gan church, while all the rest were connected with the Methodist chapels in the neighbourhood, such as Bridgend, Pen-coed, Aber-thin, Llyswyrnwy, and other places, and this was generally the case all over the country.

There were exceptions, however, and those were chiefly in Pembrokeshire, and in the southern portion of Cardiganshire. In those districts the great bulk of three or four congregations withdrew to the Church, and the chapels in which they were in the habit of assembling, to hold societies and prayer-meetings, and to hear the Word from the mouths of "exhorters," were lost to the Connexion.

Three of the Episcopal clergymen in South Wales remained with the Methodists—namely, the Revs. Howell Howells of Tre-hyl, John Williams of Lledrod, and John Williams, the son of the eminent reformer and hymnologist, Wm. Williams of Pantycelyn.[1] In North Wales there had never been more than three of this class connected with the body—namely, the Revs. T. Charles of Bala, Simon Lloyd of the same place, and William Lloyd of Caernarfon; and all these continued to adhere to it.

Welsh Methodism emerged from this important crisis. in its existence different, in several respects, from what it was before. It was a little, but very little smaller, and a trifle less aristocratic, for it had lost several wealthy and influential families in different parts of the country; but it was very much more compact, and more free. The men who now came to the front had already proved themselves to be able ministers of the New Testament; and they subsequently proved themselves competent to lead the Connexion, by the blessing of God, to usefulness and success. They watched over the churches, they travelled from place to place to preach the Gospel, they threw their hearts and souls into their great work, and their ministry was accompanied by rich outpourings of the Holy Ghost. God was bearing witness to the word of His grace; and in a few years the losses which had been sustained at the time of their ordination had been far, and very far, more than compensated. The leading men of the great Association were no longer with them—the fathers had gone to their eternal rest, and some of their most prominent leaders had now withdrawn from them; but there were among themselves men whom God had raised to be masters of the Assembly, and very frequently and conclusively was He pleased to give unto them evidences of His own presence.

When those great men were removed, there were others equally able and devoted to take their places, and thus it was that the Connexion went on increasing in numbers and in influence; and thus it is that it has continued to progress up to the present day.

When Harris, Rowland, and their coadjutors commenced their evangelistic labours, they had not the remotest idea of forming a separate Christian denomination, and therefore it is that the body, which was brought into existence by the blessing of God on their ministry, found itself without a constitution, and without any rules or regulations for its government. It has all these now, but they were not made at once. They have rather grown from time to time, as the various circumstances through which the body has passed have shown the necessity for them. The form it has assumed may be designated a *modified Presbyterianism.* Each church manages its own affairs, admits or expels its members by the vote of the majority of those who belong to it; so far it is Congregational. But there is an appeal from the decision of the individual church to the Monthly Meeting of the county to which it belongs, and then there is an appeal from the decision of the Monthly Meeting to the Quarterly Association of the province. Matters relating to South Wales are finally disposed of by the South Wales Association, and so of the North; but a few years ago a General Assembly of the whole Connexion was established, and the two Associations may agree to refer matters to that body, which meets once a year, for final decision. Churches *nominate* their own deacons or elders by the vote of the majority; but they can only be *appointed* with the sanction of the Monthly Meeting of their county, and by delegates sent by that body to the place for that purpose. Monthly meetings never interfere with the internal affairs of individual churches, unless their members fail to agree among themselves, or permit some manifest irregularity. Ministers can only be ordained with the approval of one of the Associations, North or South. They are nominated by delegates of the counties to which they belong at one Association, and if approved of are ordained at a subsequent one. These representative meetings are made up of ministers and deacons, and generally the latter preponderate in numbers. There is no rule made to preserve "the balance of power" in this respect, and happily there has not hitherto appeared any necessity for it. All the chapels are the property, not of the congregations worshipping in them, but of the Connexion. A constitutional deed has been enrolled in Chancery, securing to it the possession of all its places of worship, and all the leases and other transfers of property are drawn up in accordance with the provisions of that deed. Many of the chapels are in debt, but there is not one of them mortgaged; the security to the creditor in each case being a note of hand, signed by persons appointed to do so by the Monthly Meeting of the county to which the chapel belongs. These are the parties who are under the *legal* responsibility, but the whole community is understood to be *morally* responsible for the debt of each chapel.

All this, as we have intimated, did not come at once. "Rules regarding the proper mode of conducting the Quarterly Association" were drawn up by Mr. Charles, and agreed upon in 1790. The "Order and Form of Church Government, and Rules of Discipline," were first published in 1801;[2] but it was not until the year 1823 that the Connexion drew up in form and published its "Confession of Faith." The subject had been mooted in 1821, and after it had been discussed in several Associations, it was resolved to convene a meeting of delegates from North and South Wales in connection with an Association at Aberystwyth on the 11th of March, 1823, to revise and amend, should it be deemed necessary, such "Rules" as had been already promulgated, and to draw up a "Confession of Faith." We have before us the minutes of that important meeting, from the pen of the late Rev. Ebenezer Richard, the secretary at the time of the South Wales Association, and of which the following is a translation:—

"The delegates from North and South Wales began to assemble on Monday evening the 10th, but they did not enter upon their important work until Tuesday the 11th, when they assembled at the house of Mr. Robert Davies, Dark Gate Street, in a very convenient and commodious upper room. The proceedings commenced with reading and prayer by John Roberts, Llangwm. The committee was composed of the following brethren—viz., The Reverends John Williams (moderator), Ebenezer Morris, David Charles, Thomas Jones, John Roberts, John Elias, John Humphreys, and Michael Roberts, with Humphrey Gwalchmai and Ebenezer Richard as secretaries.

"First, the rules and objects of the private societies were taken into consideration, and after having been carefully and deliberately considered, and after a few changes and abridgements were made in them, they were unanimously adopted. Next, our brother, J. Humphreys, read a sketch which had been written by him of the rise and progress of the Connexion; and this, with some slight alterations, was agreed upon."

We have this sketch lying before us, and it comprises about eighteen pages duodecimo.

"Then the constitution of the body, written by Mr. David Charles, was read, and, with some modifications, adopted.

"The meeting then entered upon the consideration of the Confession of Faith. The portion from North Wales was read by the brother, John Elias, and that from the South by Ebenezer Richard. Every point and article was considered with the greatest solemnity, deliberation, and minuteness. In proceeding, selections, additions, abbreviations, and alterations were made according as it was deemed most suitable and necessary, until the whole of the articles had been gone through; and all unanimously adopted without wrath or doubting.

"Then it was resolved that the whole should be read at the general meetings of the Association, at two o'clock on the 13th, and at eight on the 14th; the rules and constitution of the body to be read by Ebenezer Richard; John Elias to read that portion of the Confession of Faith which had been prepared in North Wales, and Ebenezer Richard the portion prepared in the South. This was done as resolved, and the body unanimously, and with the completest and most pleasant harmony, adopted the whole without as much as one dissentient voice or one objection. BLESSED BE THE LORD GOD OF ISRAEL."[3]

This "Confession" comprises forty-four articles, and is in every important feature in unison with the Westminster Confession of Faith and the Articles of the Church of England.[4]

The whole of the Welsh-speaking portions of the Principality had by this time been pretty well filled with the Gospel, but those districts in which the English language prevailed continued in very much the same state as all Wales had been before the days of Howel Harris.

It is a curious fact that there are tracts of country lying far away from the border, where nothing but English has been spoken for several generations. The hundred of Castlemartin, the borough of Pembroke, the towns of Haverfordwest and Tenby, with considerable portions of the hundreds of Narberth and Rhos, all in the south of Pembrokeshire, and comprising almost a third of the area of that county, have a population as English as Derby or Dorset. It is the same with Gower, in the west of Glamorganshire; that peninsula lies between the Bristol Channel and the Byrri estuary,[5] from Swansea to the Worm's Head, and is about eighteen miles in length, and varying from four to six in breadth, and comprises sixteen parishes. These two spots, separated alike from each other and from England by many miles of country occupied by Welsh-speaking populations, have each been designated

"Little England beyond Wales." The people are supposed to be of Flemish extraction, and their presence in these parts is thus accounted for:—"About the year 1110 Henry I admitted into England great numbers of Flemings, who by the inundation of the sea in their own country were compelled to seek elsewhere for new habitations. He planted them at first in the waste parts of Yorkshire, but upon the complaints made to him after his return from Normandy, he removed them to the country conquered from the Welsh, about Rhos and Pembroke. Their posterity continue there to this day, retaining so much of their old customs as to distinguish them plainly from the Welsh, and to show that they are of foreign extraction."[6]

According to Caradog of Llancarfan, Gower was peopled with English from Somersetshire. "Swansea Castle was built in the year 1099, by Henry Beaumont, Earl of Warwick, who, acting on the system of the other Norman freebooters of the age, made war upon the sons of Caradog ap Iestyn, who then held the district of Gower, in order to enrich himself with the spoils he might be able to wrest from them. After the subjugation of Gower, he brought over a colony of English settlers from Somersetshire, to whom he gave a large proportion of the lands. Their descendants yet remain here, separated by their language and manners from the native population."[7]

Monmouthshire is regarded as an English county, but whatever faults it has are generally put down against Wales. The Chartist Riots of 1839 occurred in Monmouthshire, and resulted in a serious conflict at Newport, where several lives were lost. We believe that none took part in the affair but the people of that county, and yet that mad movement was designated at the time, and continues to be designated, "the Chartist riot *in Wales*." On the western side of this county the people talk Welsh, and on the eastern, English; but the former language continues gradually, but steadily, to recede before the latter. The whole of Radnorshire and a part of Breconshire in South Wales have become English-speaking, and so have portions of Montgomeryshire, Denbighshire, and Flintshire in the North. The English wave having rolled over the border, is steadily progressing westward, and it is generally anticipated that it will by-and-by have inundated the whole of Wales, and completely extinguished the dear old language of the country; we are afraid that this will come to pass, but it will not be just now, nor for many years to come.[8]

Home Missionary Societies were established in the early part of the present century for the benefit of these Anglicised districts. Isolated efforts were made in North Wales as early as 1808, by Mr. Thomas Edwards of Liverpool, and others, and in 1813 a Society was formed for the "propagation of religious knowledge on the borders of Offa's dyke." That Society still exists under the name of "The North Wales Home Mission," and employs from fifteen to twenty missionaries to labour among the people of the English-speaking districts.

The first impulse in this direction in South Wales was given by the Rev. D. Charles of Carmarthen, who, on his annual visits to the mineral springs of Llandrindod, Radnorshire, was distressed in witnessing the ignorance and ungodliness of the surrounding population. By his efforts Mr. George Griffiths of Llandeilo was settled as a missionary at Pen-y-bont; he only remained for a few months, and was succeeded by the Rev. D. Morgan, afterwards of Welshpool, whose stay was almost equally short. In 1821 the Rev. D. Howells of Swansea was appointed to the station, and continued to labour on it with great devotedness and marked success for seven years. These efforts began in 1819, but it was not until some years later that the South Wales Home Missionary Society was formally established. One of its first missionaries was Thomas Phillips of Llandovery, who was settled at Hay, at a salary of £30 a year, and who afterwards became widely known as the Rev. Dr. Phillips of Hereford, the indefatigable and marvellously successful

District Secretary of the British and Foreign Bible Society. The South Wales Home Mission has now under its charge twenty-nine English stations, containing about forty places of worship, but Pen-y-bont, and several other places which it once assisted, have become self-supporting.[9]

The field of these Societies' operations continues to enlarge with the spread of the English language. There is likewise a continuous stream of English people coming over to the manufacturing districts and large seaport towns, which makes it necessary to provide religious means in the English language in those places. This is done largely by other denominations, and the Calvinistic Methodists are making strenuous efforts in that direction. The latter labour, in this respect, under the disadvantage of not having "brethren in England " on whom to fall back for aid. They have expended an enormous sum, we believe more than a quarter of a million sterling, upon places of worship within the last twenty-five years, and there remains a heavy debt on many of those sanctuaries. This incubus is being gradually removed, and when it is gone, the Connexion will find no difficulty in making all the necessary provision to meet the spread of the English language. In the meantime, the need of such efforts is becoming increasingly felt, and there is more being done in the two provinces of the Principality than, under the circumstances, could have been expected.[10]

The Welsh Methodist Connexion existed for upwards of a century without a College of its own, though it never was without some men who had received a collegiate education. For many years it had among its ministers a few who had been trained for the Establishment. Some were educated at the Countess's College at Trefeca, and afterwards at Cheshunt, while others went for a time, either at their own expense or by the assistance of kind friends, to superior schools at Chester, Liverpool, and other places. There were a great many in the Connexion who, to say the least, were not favourably disposed towards a college-training for ministers, and they found some apology for their feelings in the fact that some of their most popular and efficient preachers were not collegians. They were men who had studied hard, and had acquired by their own unaided exertions more of those qualifications which are essential to the efficient discharge of the duties of the ministry than some who had received a collegiate training. While they themselves deplored their want of early advantages, there were not a few of their brethren who thought that they did quite as well, if not better, without them. But early in the present century, the want of an institution for the training of ministers became increasingly felt; and the first movement towards securing that object was made in North Wales, in the year 1817. It was resolved to open an academy at Llangollen; a house was taken for the purpose, and Mr. Owen Williams, a very pious and talented young man from Anglesey, who had distinguished himself as a scholar, was chosen to be the tutor. He was sent to Hoxton Academy to more fully prepare himself for the important charge; but while assiduously pursuing his studies at that place, he was taken ill and died. Some years later, Mr. Evan Rowlands, a young man of earnest piety, good education, and superior talents, was chosen for this purpose. He went to Belfast to complete his studies; but the brethren were again doomed to disappointment, for Mr. Rowlands's health broke down, and he was taken away.

After many unsuccessful attempts on the part of the Connexion to procure this first requisite of a College, the Great Master was at length pleased to provide tutors in every way qualified for the work. The Rev. Lewis Edwards, M.A., who had studied and taken high honours at Edinburgh, was led to settle at Bala, through marrying the grand-daughter of the renowned Thomas Charles. Her brother, the Rev. David Charles, B.A., returned from Oxford about the same time, and the two brothers-in-law joined to open "The Welsh Calvinistic Methodist Theological Institute," at Bala, in 1837,[11] and the North Wales Association, held at Caernarfon in September 1839, adopted this Institute as a College for the Connexion, and decided upon rules for its management and measures for its support.

The few survivors of the Trefeca "family," who were now the owners of the "house" which had been built by Howel Harris, presented this commodious edifice to the South Wales Association for the purpose of a College, and efforts were therefore made on the part of the brethren in the south to have the Institution that was at Bala removed to this place; but the northern friends could not be brought to assent to this proposal, and it was ultimately agreed that Mr. Edwards should remain at Bala, and that an additional College should be opened at Trefeca, to be presided over by Mr. Charles. Soon after his departure for the south, the Rev. John Parry was appointed to succeed him at Bala. That Institution has been growing in importance from year to year, and is still carried on successfully under the charge of Dr. Edwards as President and Theological Tutor, and the Revs. Ellis Edwards, M.A., and Hugh Williams, M.A., who were appointed after Dr. Parry's lamented death, in 1874, as professors. For many years it was supported by annual subscriptions from individual friends and collections in the churches; but these sources of revenue proving uncertain and precarious, it was suggested that a fund, which would be adequate for the permanent endowment of the College, should be at once collected. It was acknowledged by all that this was a grand idea; but then came the question, Where was the man to be found that would put it in practice? The Rev. Edward Morgan of Dyffryn undertook the gigantic task, and in about five years collected £25,000 from the Calvinistic Methodists of North Wales and of three or four large towns in England. When this had been done, it was resolved to collect another fund to erect a College building worthy of the Institution and of the Connexion to which it belonged. This edifice cost about £8,000, and Mr. Morgan had succeeded in collecting the greater part of this additional sum, when he was called to his rest, on the 9th of May, 1871, and when he was only fifty-three years of age. Few men devoted as much time and energy as he to the outward interests of the Connexion; and yet he preached as if all his mind and soul had always been entirely concentrated on the studying of sermons. For many years he struggled against very bad health, but his indomitable spirit raised him above all difficulties and disadvantages. Battling for breath, he worked on and worked hard, and continued to do so to the very last.

The College at Trefeca was opened in 1842, and Dr. Charles conducted it alone for twenty years. His self-sacrificing zeal and unwearied application to the onerous duties of his position made that College a great blessing to the Connexion in South Wales. In the year 1862 Dr. Charles found it necessary, to the regret of his friends, to resign the presidency of the College, and as it was resolved not to open it again without two tutors, the difficulty of coming to a satisfactory arrangement in this matter led to its being closed for more than three years. There was one highly qualified tutor whose services could be secured, but the difficulty was to find a second. At length all difficulties were surmounted, and the College was reopened in September 1865, with the Rev. William Howells, then of Liverpool, as president, and the Rev. J. Harris Jones, Ph.D., as classical tutor. The College remains under their able superintendence, and is eminently successful. Before the institution at Trefeca was first opened, a fund of six thousand pounds was collected in South Wales towards its support; but the success of Mr. Morgan led the South-Walian friends to resolve to raise their fund to an equal amount to that of Bala, and though they did not fully succeed in reaching that mark, the Trefeca fund has been raised to upwards of £20,000 by the efforts of the Rev. Edward Matthews, now of Bridgend.

The Welsh Calvinistic Methodists were among the most zealous of the friends and supporters of the London Missionary Society from its very beginning; but in 1840 they resolved to establish a Foreign Missionary Society of their own.[12] They fixed upon two fields of operation, one on the Kassian Hills in Assam, and the other in Brittany. The Rev. Thomas Jones was the first sent to Kassia. He found tribes of people without any form of religion and without a written language, but he soon mastered their tongue and reduced it to writing. Though some unhappy circumstances led to the withdrawal of Mr. Jones from the Society a few years before his death, he proved himself a most able and zealous worker. He was followed by the Rev. William Lewis, who laboured with much success among these tribes for twenty years. He has now retired to his native country in broken health, but has since his return completed the translation of the whole of the New Testament into the Khassee language. Several other missionaries have gone out to the same field, and, though the mission has met with some serious difficulties, God has blessed it with remarkable success. There are now on those hills 7 Missionaries, 11 Native Preachers, 62 Preaching Stations and 38 Churches, connected with which there are 2,417 members, 3,448 hearers, 3,189 in the Sabbath-schools, and 2,571 in the day-schools.

The Rev. James Williams was sent out to Brittany, and settled at Quimper, where he laboured hard for many years as minister, colporteur, or anything else that could further the interests of the Gospel. A chapel was built at Quimper and another at L'Orient. Mr. Williams's state of health compelled him some time ago to retire, but the mission is still carried on with hopeful prospects by the Rev. W. Jenkyn Jones, assisted by M. Le Groignec as evangelist and colporteur.

We have spoken throughout of two Associations, one in North Wales and the other in the South. Those have been to all intents and purposes two separate organisations, quite independent of each other. Ministers from the South would attend the North Wales Associations, and *vice versa;* but the brethren from one province did not feel that they had a right to take part in the business deliberations of the other. The two sections felt that they were one, and neither would take an important step without consulting the other; but there was no meeting held at which the whole body was represented. For a long time this deficiency was felt, and a few years ago measures were taken to supply it. After a conference of ministers and others from the two provinces, and a lengthened correspondence between the different Associations, it was resolved to establish a General Assembly of the whole Connexion, to hold its meetings alternately in the North and the South. The first meeting was held at Swansea in May 1864, and the twentieth at the same town in June 1883. This annual gathering is becoming increasingly important, and will, no doubt, ultimately become that which their General Assemblies are to the other Presbyterian bodies—the legislating body for the whole Connexion.

Nearly one hundred and fifty years have now passed away since the rise of Welsh Methodism, and we are glad that we can state that the Connexion as it increases in years does not show any symptoms of decay. Its progress during the last thirty-two years of its existence has been more marked than in any similar period from the beginning. The following figures will show the advance which it has made during that period:—

	1850	1882	Increase.
Ministers	172	616	444
Preachers	194	354	160
Chapels and preaching places	848	1,372	524
Communicants	58,678	122,167	63,489

Of the Communicants there are 8,186 connected with the

English Churches. There are also, in the United States of America, 173 *Welsh* Calvinistic Methodist Churches, with 86 Ministers and a number of Preachers.[13]

Truly can we say, "The Lord has done great things for us." There remains yet much to be done, but He is among us still, and with Him all things are possible.

NOTES

1 To this list should be added Richard Bassett of St. Athan and Llan-dow and, possibly, John Davies of Aber-nant and Cynwyl Elfed. Gomer M. Roberts, ed., *Hanes Methodistiaeth Galfinaidd Cymru: II, Cynnydd y Corff* (Caernarfon: Llyfrfa'r Methodistiaid Calfinaidd, 1978), pp.330, 332-3.

2 The title is incorrect; it was the 'Rules and Objects of the Private Society among the People called Methodists in Wales' that was published in 1801 (English version, 1802). *Ibid.*, pp.228-34. The 'Order and Form of Church Government, and Rules of Discipline' was not approved until 1823. D. D. Williams, *Hanes Cyfundeb y Methodistiaid Calfinaidd*, p.140.

3 Williams here refers his readers to *Y Drysorfa*, 1869, p.166.

4 In 1924 a 'Short Declaration on Faith and Life' was adopted as comprising the essential elements of the Christian faith as held by the Presbyterian Church of Wales. Nine years later, despite opposition from evangelical elements in the Church, an Act of Parliament was passed which released the Church from the clause in its Constitutional Deed binding it to the 1823 Confession of Faith. While not unorthodox as such, the 'Short Declaration' marked a significant departure from the former confessional standard by its reluctance to make specific statements on key theological issues. R. H. Evans, *Datganiad Byr ar Ffydd a Buchedd Eglwys Bresbyteraidd Cymru* (Caernarfon: Ymddiriedolwyr Darlith Davies, 1971).

5 It would be more accurate to speak of Gower as lying between the Bristol Channel and the estuary of the Llwchwr (or Loughor).

[6] C. A. Ashburton, *A New and Complete History of England* (London: 1791-94), p.119.

[7] T. Rees, *A Topographical and Historical Description of South Wales* (London: 1819), p.726. The first mention of a castle at Swansea is in 1116; it was probably built in the preceding decade. Caradog ap Iestyn and his sons held Blaenau Morgannwg between the Taff and the Neath, and were never lords of Gower. The creation of the "Englishry" of Gower was a gradual process in which the thirteenth and fourteenth centuries were particularly significant, and was far from being as sudden as the text suggests. T. B. Pugh, ed., *Glamorgan County History III: The Middle Ages* (Cardiff: Glamorgan County History Committee, 1971), pp.25-26, 36, 207, 215-6.

[8] For the sake of non-Welsh readers, it is worth pointing out that over 100 years after the original publication of the present volume the Welsh language is still very much alive. In the 1991 census over half a million people resident in Wales were recorded as being Welsh-speaking; this figure represents almost twenty *per cent* of the total population.

[9] The author himself served as both Secretary and President of this Society. *Y Geninen* (1901), p.46.

[10] It should be noted that this large-scale movement to establish English causes, not only among the Calvinistic Methodists but also among the other denominations, was fiercely opposed by those who foresaw—correctly as it turned out—that many Welsh-speakers would be drawn to the English churches and that the Welsh churches (and the Welsh language) would be seriously impoverished thereby. Trebor Ll. Evans, *Lewis Edwards: ei fywyd a'i waith* (Abertawe: Gwasg John Penry, 1967), pp.156-64.

[11] The venture began in fact as a private adventure school, not as "The Welsh Calvinistic Methodist Theological Institute". As the remainder of the sentence in the text indicates, only subsequently was the school officially adopted by the Connexion. Thomas Charles Edwards, *Bywyd a Llythyrau y Diweddar Lewis Edwards* (Liverpool, 1901), p.163.

12 The formation of the new society was attended by a certain amount of controversy. There was a general feeling that the domination of the London Missionary Society by the Congregationalists was detrimental to Methodist interests, not only because a number of Methodist missionary candidates had been rejected but also because Methodist churches were reluctant to take an interest in and shoulder responsibility for missionary work under the Society's auspices. Matters were brought to a head when a young Methodist, Thomas Jones of Berriew, came into conflict with officials of the L.M.S. over the country to which he was to be sent and the state of his health. John Hughes Morris, *Ein Cenhadaeth Dramor* (ail argraffiad; Liverpool, 1931), pp.11-12.

13 It has to be recorded with sadness that the Welsh Calvinistic Methodist Church, or the Presbyterian Church of Wales, has shared in the general decline in organized religion during the second half of the twentieth century, as the following statistics indicate:

	1993	Estimate for 2010
Ministers	148	90
Churches	977	740
Members	55,690	26,600

UK Christian Handbook 1996-1997 (Carlisle, O.M. Publishing, 1997), p.277.

CHAPTER XVI

Sketches of Ministers—Robert Roberts—John Elias—Ebenezer
Morris—Ebenezer Richard—John Jones—Henry Rees—
David Howell—Conclusion.

BEFORE laying aside our pen, we should like to enable
our readers to form an idea of some of those men whom
God raised at the most critical period of the history of Welsh
Methodism, and whose ministry was blessed by His Spirit
to make such a wide and lasting impression upon the
Principality. And here there is a serious difficulty meeting
us at the very outset. They are so many, that it would require
a large volume to give even a brief sketch of their history.
A list of the names of those who have occupied an important
place in the Connexion, and have done a great work in its
behalf, would itself fill several pages. We will select a few
of the most prominent, and our readers will understand that
they represent a great many more whose names we are
compelled to leave unmentioned. Our purpose will be
answered better by giving a comparatively lengthened
account of six or seven, than by devoting half-a-dozen lines
each to forty or fifty.

There was one in North Wales who had died nine years
before the Connexion ordained its own ministers, and who,
if he had lived, would have been among the first to be
selected for that purpose. This was Robert Roberts of
Clynnog (Fawr), in Caernarvonshire. He was originally a
slate-quarryman, and afterwards a farm-servant, before he
became a preacher of the Gospel. When sixteen years of age
he was brought to know the truth under the ministry of Mr.

Jones of Llan-gan, and began to preach when he was five-and-twenty. In his youth be contracted a severe cold, and this brought on a disease which so affected his spine as to make him quite deformed; but his face continued a thing of beauty and power. His course was very brief, for he died in his fortieth year; but it was one of great brilliancy and tremendous might. Nature had made him an orator of the first order, and grace made him an able minister of the Gospel of Christ. His commanding voice, intense earnestness, and many tears, gave him an irresistible influence over his audiences. His sermons moved him to the very depths of his nature, and therefore it was that he so mightily moved others. "Tell me," said one young man to another, who was standing by and listening to Robert Roberts, "tell me, is he a man, or is he an angel?" "An angel," was the other's reply. "Oh, well!" said the first, "how much better than a man an angel *can* preach!" When preaching on another occasion, and carrying the congregation along with him, he suddenly paused, and beckoning with his hand as if to command silence, he said, in a lowered tone, "Hush! hush! hush! What is this sound that I hear?" Another moment's pause, and then came the great shout like a clap of thunder, "Upon the wicked will he rain snares, fire, and brimstone, and a horrible tempest; this is the portion of their cup." The effect was overpowering. He had the power to describe things in such a vivid and graphic manner as to make his hearers feel as if they were then passing before their eyes. There is a great storm. A small ship is tossed upon the waves. The mariners pull this way and that way to no purpose. A man is thrown overboard. He is swallowed by a whale, and then the sea-monster rushes through the deep, marking its course with a great line of foam, and in its manner shouting, "Clear the way for the King's messenger!" while Jonah is inside, crying, "Temple! temple! temple!" When he failed to enjoy liberty in preaching, and the people seemed heavy and inattentive, he would stop in the middle of his sermon, and lift up a prayer to God for help and light. On one occasion, when the service was dragging heavily along, he paused, and stood like a man astonished; then lifting up his hands towards heaven, while tears ran down his cheeks, he cried, "O God, draw aside the veil! Draw aside the veil!" And it was drawn aside. An overwhelming influence descended upon himself and the congregation, until at length, almost overcome by his emotions, he cried, "O God, restrain! restrain! Close the curtain a little! It is too much for us to bear!"

We have before us a characteristic letter written by him to a friend just after his return from London, where he had been supplying the Welsh congregation in 1791. The following is an extract:—

"At Shrewsbury we mounted the wild coach, which seemed to be made to fly by the galloping of the swift-footed horses. I thought that those animals were shouting in their way, 'London! London! Let's hasten to be there!' I was poorly on my journey, in consequence of the rapid motion of the coach; but I was enabled to reach the end.

"I was in the great city for eight Sabbaths, and I think I can humbly say that the Lord helped me in the work. I feel it to be a great, great thing to be sometimes a few moments in God while speaking to the people, and can easily understand that I am of no use whatever anywhere else.

"As to the hearers, they were very numerous. If you had seen them, I know you would have wondered to behold such multitudes of Welsh people assembled in London.

"While there I heard many of the English preachers. In listening to them it is such thoughts as these that passed through my bosom: 'Behold wood and fire, but where is the Lamb of the burnt-offering?' 'Behold an altar, behold a sacrifice, but where is the fire?' 'Behold Whitefield's pulpit, but where is his God?' Sometimes such lamentations as these would resound between the lobes of my heart: 'Oh, unhappy assemblages! Is it the vibrations of organ pipes that you have found instead of the voice of Almighty God?' Who is that whom I see rising above the crowd with his head as white as Snowdon after a snow-storm, and clothed in shining black? He begins to address the people as if speaking in his sleep, and tells them that if they have any fears with reference to their state, it is because they are too unbelieving; and if they feel within them the motions of sin they must take comfort, for it has always been so with godly people. Is not this too much like lightly healing the bruise of the daughter of my people, and crying, Peace, peace, when there is no peace? From such cold, carnal way of speaking and hearing, *good Lord deliver us!* And yet I take comfort, for God has some oxen in London that pull a red furrow through the consciences of their hearers. May the Lord add to their number! Amen."[1]

John Elias was one of the first batch who were ordained in North Wales, and perhaps it is not too much to say that his sermons made a greater impression on the Principality than those of any other man who ever lived in it. He was a native of Caernarvonshire, but on his marriage settled in Anglesey, where he spent the remainder of his life. His parents were in humble circumstances, but greatly respected by their neighbours; and his paternal grandfather, who lived with them, was a member of the Church of England, and a very good and devout man. He took great pains to train the child in the right way, impressing upon his mind the evil of speaking bad words, swearing, taking the Lord's name in vain, and telling falsehoods, and teaching him to keep the Sabbath and to revere the ordinances of worship. By the faithful and persevering efforts of his good grandfather, John was able to read fluently while yet a little child. On one occasion they went together to hear a Methodist preacher, who did not arrive until the time when the service had been announced to commence had long passed. The old gentleman became impatient, and, addressing his little grandson, said,

'It is a pity that the people should be idling thus. Go up, John, and read a chapter to them;" and suiting his action to the words, he pushed the lad up into the pulpit and closed the door after him. The boy, with much diffidence, read a portion of the Sermon on the Mount, but, after reading on for a while, he ventured to withdraw his eye and to look aside, and lo! to his great dismay, there was the preacher waiting outside the pulpit door. He suddenly closed the book and quietly slipped downstairs. This was John Elias's first appearance in the pulpit, and no one dreamed at the time that he would ever be such a power in it as he afterwards became. He began to preach in 1794, when he was about twenty years of age, and it was very soon made evident that he was in truth a man of God. A very shrewd and popular preacher of those days, Dafydd Cadwaladr, remarked, after he had heard him the first time, "God help that lad to speak the truth, for he'll *make* people believe him." He became immensely popular at the outset of his ministry, and that popularity never waned. It was not to seek popularity, however, that he set out, but to serve his Master, and to serve Him especially by trampling down ungodliness. When he settled in Anglesey, that island had been already to a great extent blessed by the Gospel, but it still retained not a few of the relics of its former barbarism. He proclaimed war to the death against every one of these, and won over them a complete victory. Wherever there was held a periodical assembly of sinful men for ungodly purposes, Elias would go there with all the zeal and the power of his namesake of olden times, and invariably his God would thrust the enemy from before him, and give him the power to accomplish his destruction.

On Whitsunday in each year a great concourse of people were in the habit of assembling to burn ravens' nests. These birds bred in a high and precipitous rock called "Y gadair" (the chair), and since they were supposed to prey on young poultry, etc., the people thought it necessary to destroy them. But they always did it on the Sabbath, and in the most savage and revolting fashion. The nests were beyond their reach, but they suspended a fiery faggot by a chain. This was let down to set the nests on fire, and the young birds were roasted alive! At every blaze which was seen below, the triumphant shouts of the worse than brutal crowd would rend the air. God hears the young ravens when they cry, and they did not cry without cause on the rocky coast of Anglesey. When the savages had put the poor birds beyond the reach of their cruelty, they usually turned on each other, and wounds and bruises, broken heads and broken bones, were frequently some of the results of the day's "amusement." Elias resolved to make an attack on this revolting scene. He accordingly went to the place and proclaimed the wrath of God Most High against those who thus polluted His day and trampled upon every precept of His law, and with such effect as to fill the guilty crowd with terror; and the hideous custom was put an end to for ever.

At Rhuddlan, in Denbighshire,[2] there was an annual fair held *on the Lord's Day* in the season of harvest. It was chiefly for the sale of scythes, reaping-hooks, rakes, etc., and for the hiring of labourers for harvest-work. Elias went to the place to make a determined attack on this wicked assemblage. He stood on the horse-block, by the "New Inn," in the very thick of the fair, surrounded by all the implements of husbandry, and began the service amid the sound of harps and fiddles. He prayed with great earnestness and many tears, and took for his text the Fourth Commandment. The fear of God fell upon the crowd, harps and fiddles were silenced, and scythes, sickles, and rakes disappeared from the scene. The people stood to listen, and while they listened they trembled as if Sinai itself with all its thunder had suddenly burst upon them. One man who had purchased a sickle let it fall to the ground, thinking in his heart that the arm which held it had withered, and was afraid to pick it up again lest the same thing should happen to the other. He lost his sickle, but on that day he found salvation. The Sabbath fair was never afterwards held, and many were brought, through that marvellous sermon, to seek the Lord. This happened in the year 1802, when the preacher was only twenty-eight years of age, and there were many such customs and such assemblages which received their death-blow from John Elias.

He preached much in the open air, for it was not often that a building could be found large enough to contain the multitudes that would assemble to hear him. It was not a reed shaken with the wind nor yet a man clothed in soft raiment that they went out to see, but a prophet, and a very great prophet indeed. Referring to his oratorical powers, the late Rev. J. Jones, rector of Nevern, and one of the most eminent of the Welsh bards of his day, says in a letter to the author of *Eliasia:* "For one to throw his arms about is not action, to make this and that gesture is not action: action is seen in the eye, in the curling of the lip, in the frowning of the nose, in every muscle of the speaker. Mentioning these remarks to Dr. Pughe, when speaking of Elias, he said that he never saw an orator that could be compared to him; every muscle was in action, and every movement that he made was graceful, and highly oratorical... I never heard Elias without regarding him as a messenger sent from God. I thought of the Apostle Paul when I listened to him, and as an orator I considered him fully equal to Demosthenes."[3]

For many years he held the foremost place at the Associations. Those great Assemblies meet in the open air, and are attended by congregations varying from 5,000 to 30,000, according to the locality in which they are held. We should like to picture to our readers one of those meetings in the days of John Elias. A large raised and covered platform is erected on one side of a field; on this stands the preacher, while on either side, and behind him, sit some fifty or sixty of his brethren. Five or six services are held, on two succeeding days, and there are two sermons at each service. In front of the platform stand the great crowd, extending so far back that the first feeling of the preacher is that of despair of being able to make them all hear his voice. Elias generally preached last at ten o'clock on the second day, "the great day of the feast." While the minister who precedes him is preaching there are thousands who listen with rapt attention; but there is a restless semicircle in the outskirts of the crowd; some are walking to and fro, while others are standing in groups, and conversing. Beyond them are many lying on the grass, and beyond those there are some reclining against the hedge on the farthest side of the field. The first sermon finishes, and Elias stands up: he gives out a few lines of a hymn to sing, and his voice at once reaches the most distant of the loungers. The assembly very soon begins to contract itself; as he proceeds with his sermon the people come closer and yet closer together; there is no more walking to and fro, and no more conversing—not even a whisper—but all are listening as if for life. As the preacher waves his hand, the crowd is swayed backwards and forwards as a field of corn is swayed by a gentle breeze; copious tears are falling, there are not a few sobs and cries, and when he finishes his sermon the multitude find themselves wedged together as near the platform as they can possibly stand, having been for the time unconscious of everything in heaven and on earth but the everlasting truths to which they have just listened. Nor was this a transient feeling. Many and many were on those occasions turned to righteousness. The Rev. D. Charles of Carmarthen[4] says:—"In all my journeys through Wales I have never heard of any other preacher whose ministry has been so widely blessed to the conversion of sinners as that of John Elias. Almost in every neighbourhood, village, and town, some persons may be met with who ascribe their conversion to impressions received under one of his sermons." He died at his residence, Y Fron, Anglesey, on the 8th of June, 1841, in the sixty-eighth year of his age.

We pass to the South, and bring before our readers one of the first group who were ordained at Llandeilo in 1811—

namely Ebenezer Morris. He was the son of the David Morris of whom we have already spoken, and was born in the year 1769. The father was, in one particular, like Eglon, King of Moab,—a very fat man; and the son, though he never approached him in this respect, was himself large, and decidedly corpulent. He began to preach in 1788 at Trecastle, in Breconshire, where he had gone to teach a school; but a little more than a year after he had begun, he returned to his home in Cardiganshire. About a twelvemonth after his return his father died, in the forty-seventh year of his age, and great and general were the lamentations that were made for him; but it soon became evident that the son was qualified by the great Head of the Church to more than supply the loss that had been occasioned by his departure. A plain old exhorter in Glamorganshire, Jenkin Thomas, said to him while he was yet young, "When you first came this way, you rode your father's great horse; but I see you have quite as big a horse of your own. Take care that you don't fall, my dear boy."

Ebenezer Morris's private life was a reflection of the Gospel which he preached. His character was without spot or blemish, and sparkled with every Christian virtue and grace. He was neither gloomy nor morose, but free, open, and cheerful, and enjoyed a pleasant chat with a friend as much as any one; but he had the sternest sense of right, and we believe we can safely say that there never lived a man who was more completely than he under the dominion of his conscience.

The Calvinistic Methodists of those days had not learnt to believe that those who preach the Gospel should live by the Gospel, and it is rather slow progress that that great truth is making even now in some localities; but at the time of which we speak, good people were so deeply impressed with the privilege conferred on those who were permitted to preach the Gospel, that they were exceedingly careful not to deprive them of the full enjoyment of it by remunerating their labours, and consequently their best and greatest preachers were obliged to have recourse for the necessaries of life to some worldly business. Some of them kept shops, or rather their wives did, while they themselves devoted their whole time to the work of their Master. The memory of those holy women is worthy of being held in the highest veneration; for while the churches and the country enjoyed the ministry of their husbands, it was their self-denying labours behind the counter and elsewhere that furnished their families with the means of support, and stood between them and any worldly cares which might interfere with their great work.

Ebenezer Morris held a farm, and in his case the farmer was in every respect worthy of the preacher. His worldly transactions strove together with his ministry for the faith of the Gospel. He wanted to buy a cow, and finding one for sale which he thought would suit him, he at once bought it at the price named by the owner. A few days afterwards, Mr. Morris found that the price of cattle had gone up considerably, and meeting the previous owner of the animal, he said to him, "Look here, I find that you gave me too great a bargain the other day. The cow is worth more than I purchased her for. Here is another guinea; take that. There, I think we are now about right." One of his admirers offered him a valuable freehold farm as a present, but he respectfully declined the gift; and when a friend asked him his reason for refusing such an advantageous offer, his reply was, "I did not like to take it away from the rightful heir." Some people may be disposed to call this "softness"; but it was rectitude of principle. He was by no means a "soft" man in the sense in which that word is frequently employed; but while he was too shrewd to allow any one to take an unfair advantage of him, he was too honourable and magnanimous, too much above everything mean, little, and selfish, to profit at the expense of other people. Guineas and farms weighed with him as nothing in the balance against the strictest righteousness and truth.

In the pulpit, his fine majestic presence, powerful and commanding voice, complete mastery over the most appropriate words, and tremendous earnestness, made him one of the most effectual preachers that Wales ever knew. His delivery was inimitable. A single word from his mouth would often roll over the people like a mighty wave. It might be the word "eternal," and he would say it over again and again, "Eternal! *Eternal!* ETERNA-AL!" and on and on, six or seven, or perhaps more times, and it was as if some new light on the eternal flashed into the minds of the hearers each time the word was repeated. It rang in their ears, and sank into their hearts, and left an impression which it was easy to recall in after years, when all the sermon but that one word had been forgotten. "Look at that window," said an aged deacon in North Wales to a minister who had come to preach at a chapel to which the former belonged, "look at that window. It was there that Ebenezer Morris stood when he preached that great sermon from the words, 'The way of life is above to the wise to escape from hell beneath' and when all turned pale in listening to him." "Ah," said the minister, "do you remember any portions of that sermon?" "Remember?" said the old deacon, "remember! my good man, I should think I do, and shall remember for ever; but there was no flesh here that could stand before it." "What did he say?" asked the minister. "Say? my good man!" replied the deacon, "Say? why, he was saying, 'Beneath! *beneath!* BENEATH! Oh, my people, hell is beneath! *beneath!* BENEATH!' until it seemed as if the end of the world had come upon all in the chapel and outside." We have heard others attempting a similar style, but it would not do, for they were not Ebenezer Morrises.

At an Association at Capelnewydd in Pembrokeshire, he preached from Prov. iv. 18, and so mighty was the power of God which was then present, that upwards of a hundred joined the churches of the neighbourhood, and many more joined others at a distance under impressions received from that sermon. The Rev. W. Hughes, vicar of Caerwys, Flintshire, who was present on that occasion, says, "I was only about twelve years of age when I first heard Ebenezer Morris, at an Association at Capelnewydd, and now, after many years have passed away, I can say that that sermon was a flood of overwhelming eloquence. The effect produced upon the large congregation was thoroughly electrical. Great numbers were bathed in tears, while others were joyfully shouting 'Hosanna!' To myself it was that which the mount of transfiguration was to Peter. It was good for me to be there."

"I heard him afterwards," adds the same reverend gentleman, "when I was at school at Cardigan. His appearance in the pulpit was majestic, and all his actions were becoming the orator. The black velvet cap which he wore made him look like a bishop in his mitre. His manner made me think of the boldness of Luther, the perspicacity of Calvin, and the fervour of Knox. His sermons were not a mere voice; but there were found in them the depth of Chalmers, combined with the glowing eloquence of Stowell. His favourite subjects were the eternal purposes and love of God; the lost state of man through sin; redemption through grace, and regeneration and sanctification through the influences of the Holy Ghost. He knew how to pass mightily through the fire and smoke on Sinai, and would carry his hearers as if in his arms, and show them the New Jerusalem. His great standpoint was Calvary, and his darling theme the cross of our Lord Jesus Christ."

At an Association at Caernarfon he was appointed to preach at ten o'clock, after the Rev. John Evans of Llwynffortun. Mr. Evans was remarkable for his mild persuasive manner. He was a good man, and it was for goodness he searched everywhere, and it was upon that he delighted to gaze. We have heard him expatiate with surpassing pleasure on "the multitudes of good people that were in the world; many in the Church of England and other

Protestant denominations; many in the Greek Church; and many, no doubt, in the Church of Rome." We never heard him quote a divine without designating him "that great and good man." His remarkable facility of expression, unlimited command of words, loveable appearance, and evangelical spirit, gave him generally a complete mastery over the crowds who listened to him: and often have we seen the great majority of his audience bathed in tears. But on the occasion of which we speak, though the great mass of the congregation heard him with delight, there were many on the outskirts of the crowd who continued restless and disorderly throughout his sermon. Among these were some who called themselves "gentlemen," who had ridden into the field, and continued while Mr. Evans was preaching, to pace their steeds up and down among the people. Ebenezer Morris stood forward and took for his text Leviticus xvii. 11, "For it is the blood" (Welsh, *"this blood"*) "that maketh an atonement for the soul." When he had read the text, he fixed his eyes on the "genteel" equestrians before him, and in a loud commanding voice said, "Gentlemen! be so good as to be quiet for a little while to listen to the Word of God. I am going to speak of the soul, and of the way to make atonement for the soul, and *you* have souls." They *did* remain quiet, and listened attentively throughout the sermon. He spoke of the soul of man; of that soul as guilty before God; of all things on earth as insufficient to make atonement for the soul, and of the precious blood of Christ as all-sufficient for that purpose. He led his hearers to the valley of Achor, and they felt that they were there, but he showed them even there a door of hope, and shouts of joy at the prospect of deliverance arose from every part of the field. It is believed that some hundreds were converted under this sermon. For several weeks great numbers sought admission into the surrounding churches, who all ascribed the change in their minds to the feelings produced by hearing of "this blood." One woman who had pushed into the crowd "was a sinner," but the blood of which she heard was sprinkled upon her conscience, and she spent the remainder of her life to adorn the Gospel of Christ.

On an Easter Monday there were open-air services held at Ystrad, in the valley of the Aeron, Cardiganshire, and Mr. Morris preached both morning and afternoon. The platform faced the inn of the place, and the people stood on the plain between. An English family happened to be staying at the inn and occupying an upper room which looked out on the congregation. In the afternoon, while Mr. Morris was preaching, they sat in their window, and seemed greatly amused with the proceedings that were going on underneath. The preacher saw them, and at once turned to English and spoke a few earnest and affectionate words in that language. At the close of the sermon a messenger came from the inn asking him to tea "with the gentleman and lady upstairs," and the event gave good reason to believe that the latter at least became from that day a new creature.

The Rev. Rowland Hill had fixed upon a young Welsh Methodist preacher of great talent, Mr. Theophilus Jones, as his resident assistant at Wotton-under-Edge, and applied to the Association of South Wales for two ministers to take the leading part at his ordination. The Reverends David Charles of Carmarthen and Ebenezer Morris were appointed for that purpose, and, as the day of the ordination was drawing nigh, Mr. Hill promised his friends some amusement from the Welsh accent of one of the ministers who were about to visit them. He referred to Mr. Morris, for Mr. Charles spoke English "like a native." The day came, and the ministers. Mr. Morris prayed at the opening of the service, and no one was able to think of his "Welsh accent," for God was there. Mr. Charles delivered the charge to the minister from Acts xx. 26, 27, "Wherefore I take you to record this day, that I am free from the blood of all men: for I have not shunned to declare unto you all the counsel of God." The charge was worthy of the occasion, and of the man who delivered it. He was indeed a "master of assemblies." The Rev. William Howells of Longacre, who was himself for many years one of the most popular of the ministers of the metropolis, was wont to say, that for originality of conception and depth of thought, Mr. Charles was the greatest preacher he had ever heard. He was followed by Mr. Morris, who spoke to the Church from Psalm l. 5, "Gather my saints together unto Me, who have made a covenant with Me by sacrifice." He at once laid hold of the hearts and consciences of his hearers, and spoke of the day of judgement with such power, that many in the place felt as if that day had already come, and several gentlemen were so affected that they fainted away. Mr. Hill sat behind the preacher weeping, and saying now and then through his tears, "Amen!" "Go on, brother; give it them right well!" It is said that Mr. Hill, on subsequent visits to Wotton, when he found the people heavy and inattentive, was in the habit of saying,—"Well, we must have the fat minister from Wales here to rouse you again."

Mr. Morris's influence for good in his own country was immense. A neighbouring magistrate addressing him, said, "We are under great obligations to you, Mr. Morris, for keeping the country in order, preserving peace among the people. You are worth more than any dozen of us." On one occasion he was summoned to a court of justice to give evidence in a disputed case, and as the Book was handed to him that he might take the oath, the presiding magistrate exclaimed,—"*No, No!* There is no necessity that Mr. Morris should swear at all; *his* word is quite enough." But he was taken away in the midst of his days. On a visit to London in the spring of 1825, to supply at the Welsh Chapel, he caught a severe cold, and was only able to preach a few times after his return home. He was soon confined to his house, and then to his bed, where he lay in "perfect peace "until the 15th of August in the same year, when he fell asleep in the fifty-sixth year of his age. "I remember well," says Mr. J.

Thomas, Tŵr-gwyn, "the day on which Ebenezer Morris died. It was the time of harvest; and the sad news spread to the fields, and most of the reapers dropped their sickles and fell on their faces to the earth, weeping aloud. Oh, the mourning that spread through the whole country! Never did I see such a crowd at any other funeral, and on no other occasion did I hear such lamentations."[5]

Ebenezer Richard was a native of Pembrokeshire, but had settled at Tregaron, in Cardiganshire, in 1809, and had therefore been a fellow-labourer with Mr. Morris for sixteen years. He attended the funeral of his beloved friend, and returned home cast down in spirit; but there was yet one man in the county of whom he could think as able in some measure to fill up the great chasm which the departure of Ebenezer Morris had left. This was David Evans of Aberaeron. About eight o'clock on the Sabbath after the funeral, Mr. Richard was in his room preparing to go out to preach at a chapel at some distance, when a stranger came to the door requesting to see him. When he came down, the man said, "I am come, sir, to ask if you will please attend my master's funeral on Wednesday next?" "Who *is* your master?" asked Mr. Richard, in great agitation. "Mr. David Evans," was the reply. He almost fainted on the spot, and retired to his room, where he spent the morning in weeping and prayer. In the afternoon, the Rev. J. Williams, of Lledrod, who was to preach at Tregaron in the evening, came to the house, and Mr. Richard was apprised of his presence. He went down, and as he entered the room the venerable clergyman rose to meet him, and the two men flung themselves into one another's arms, and wept on one another's necks, sobbing aloud, and unable to utter a word. Mr. Williams was the first to speak. "O Eben, dear!" said he; "Eben, dear! what *shall* we do now?"[6]

As Elisha was to Elijah, so was Mr. Richard to Mr. Morris. The work of the departed prophet devolved upon the surviving one, and he did it faithfully and well. He was a complete man, and useful everywhere and with everything. To preach in the great assembly with demonstration of the Spirit and with power—to feed the flock of Christ—to organise and conduct every good and benevolent movement—to catechise the children, and to do everything belonging to the work of a minister—all these gifts and offices were his, and Wales, though eminently blessed with great and good men, has seen but a few who were equal to Ebenezer Richard. But his sun likewise went down while it was yet early. He died at his home, which he had only reached the day before from the visitation of the churches of his district, on the 9th of March, 1837, in the fifty-sixth year of his age.

The Rev. John Jones of Tal-y-sarn, Caernarvonshire, was born at Dolwyddelan, in the same county, on the 1st of March, 1796. He lost his good father when he was only ten years of age,[7] but his mother, who was equally devout, strove hard to bring up her children in the nurture and admonition of the Lord. John continued to attend the private meetings of the church with his mother until he was over eighteen years of age, although he had not so far given very satisfactory evidences of decision of character. About that time one of the deacons told him, in the presence of the Church, that it was of no use his hanging on with religion after that fashion, and that it was now full time that he should become religious out-and-out. He interpreted this speech to mean that he should be that, or not at all, and the effect of it was to determine him not to attend the members' meetings any more. There was a fair about to be held at Llan-rwst, about nine miles distant, and he had never in his life been at a fair. He knew that the older people went to fairs for business, and the younger ones for pleasure, and he wanted to know what that pleasure was like. His mother, fearing for his safety, did all she could to dissuade him from going, but his mind had been made up, and to the fair he went. With a number of other young people he went into a public-house, where each called for some beer. He had his half pint like the rest, and paid for it; but had scarcely tasted it when, disgusted by that which he saw and heard, he abruptly left the room and hastened towards his home, which he reached early in the afternoon. Observing his serious look his mother feared that he was unwell, but was reassured by his telling her, "You shall have no more trouble, mother, to prevent me from going to fairs; I never saw such a disagreeable place. What silly things they are that those young people call pleasures! The stupid fools! I will never go near them any more." Early in 1819 he came under the influence of the great revival which had in the preceding year [8] begun at Beddgelert, and had by this time reached Dolwyddelan, gave himself to the Lord, and from that day became religious out-and-out. He soon felt a desire to preach, and to gratify that feeling, he often retired to a lonely dingle in the neighbourhood, and there, under the shadow of a great rock, he often remained until late at night praying and preaching by himself. His first sermon in public was delivered at a dwelling-house, where a prayer-meeting had been announced. When the people had come together, and the time to commence had arrived, an old man stood up, and addressing him, said, "John, come on here and preach a little to us; thou hast preached enough to that old dingle." He complied, and it proved a mighty service, an unmistakable earnest of that which was to be. Soon after this he was received as a preacher by the monthly meeting of his county, and his fame spread through all the regions round about. He had scarcely been a preacher for six months, when the renowned John Elias had an opportunity to hear him, and was astonished and delighted. "I had heard of him," said he, "but had never imagined him to be such as he is. I felt in hearing him pray that there was something uncommon in him, but as soon as he began to preach, I saw at once that we had received a preacher from God."

He went on increasing in strength and growing in popularity for several years; but about 1833 a change came over the character of his ministry, which, although it did not in the least diminish, but rather increased its power, made it less acceptable to not a few of his brethren. At that time a spiritual deadness had spread over the whole country. A year or two before there had been a great revival, but now had come a reaction, and immorality, which had received a check from the cholera visitation of 1832, was again rising like a mighty flood, and bearing away with it many who had but recently given hopeful evidences of conversion. The question, "What is to be done?" came to press on Mr. Jones's mind, and so heavily, that for months together he had but little sleep. Many of his brethren thought that there was nothing to be done, but to wait for another wave of revival, which would come in God's own time, and with that they were tolerably well satisfied. But it did not satisfy him. Something *must* be done, and done at once. Souls in thousands were perishing, and the country was hastening towards moral ruin. He felt that the ministry of the time was not that which it ought to be. Great truths were enunciated; God's way to save sinners was fully brought before the congregations—fully, that is, as far as the Divine side of it was concerned. Sinners were told that God in His grace had made ample provision for them, and that that provision was revealed in the Gospel; but they were seldom told of the great responsibility under which they were placed by it, or of their bounden duty to receive it. Mr. Jones felt that this was a serious deficiency, and resolved in his heart that, in his own case, it should be so no longer. Convinced that it is an essential part of the ministry of the Gospel to "persuade men," and that God— who freely forgives transgression for the sake of His Son—"commands all men everywhere to repent," he impressed upon his hearers that if they continued to reject the Gospel the responsibility was theirs, and that if they perished at last the fault would be all their own. Let me give an example.

Preaching at the Bala Association in 1835, to a congregation numbering ten thousand or more, and in the hearing of many of the leading ministers of the Connexion from all parts of the Principality, he closed his sermon in words to the following effect;—"God has work for you to do, my people; work which is indispensably necessary, and it is useless for you to expect that any one else will do it in your stead, or that the Spirit of God will work upon you while you neglect to do it. 'But what can I do? I cannot believe.' Canst thou not read? Open the Bible. Go to the old Book; compel thy thoughts to come into contact with the great testimony concerning Jesus Christ, and pray the Spirit of God to give thee such light upon it as will enable thee to realise it in the depths of thy soul. 'But I cannot pray!' Canst thou try, my precious soul? Canst thou kneel? Is there not a joint in that knee of thine? Won't it bend? 'Well, yes, but it is necessary to pray from the heart, and such a heart I have not.' Wouldst thou give thy heart unto Him? Give thy body to Him. Give thy tongue. And if thou canst not give thy tongue; if thou hast not one word to say, go to Him, and remain mute in His presence. There is One above who can open His mouth for the dumb. My dear people, make a determined attempt to secure the salvation of your own souls. Do not, I beseech you, go headlong into perdition. In my very deed, I have resolved years ago that I will not do that whatever happens. If I must go there at last, I am determined that I will not go there straight ahead, I will linger much about the garden of Gethsemane, I will give many a turn around mount Calvary, I will try the throne of grace every day of my life, and if I must go to hell at last— but no, *no;* blessed be God! we have the most undoubted assurance that that is the way to heaven. Hell was never reached by any one along that path, and never, never shall be. Are you for trying it, my dear people? Shall I tell Him that you wish to come unto Him this day? 'O Lord, our Lord, here are thousands of souls before Thee, resolved, many of them for the first time, to come unto Thee this day; receive them, Lord Jesus, and place Thine own infinite merits between them and the curse which they have deserved, and give Thy Holy Spirit to enable them to trust in Thee, and in Thee only for their everlasting life.'"[9] The effect was overpowering; an intense feeling, expressing itself in sobs and cries, spread through the vast congregation as that magnificent voice, loud and clear like that of a trumpet, rose higher, and still higher in earnest, beseeching cadences, saying, "Try, my dear people, *try!*" and there is good ground for believing that a large number on that very evening *did* try, and that they succeeded in finding salvation.

But there were not a few of the elder brethren who did not like it at all, for it seemed to them that it was going against doctrines which they had always believed and taught. It was true that he had not said anything against those great and much-cherished doctrines; but did not the things which he had said imply a contradiction of them? Suspicions spread that the great preacher was going astray from the faith. Other men, of less note, began to preach in the same strain, and there was trouble. The subject was discussed at several Associations in North Wales, conferences were held, and things seemed to be approaching a serious crisis. A Representative Meeting was convened at Mold, to consider the cases of three or four younger brethren, who had been charged with heresy in this particular. It was expected, and perhaps hoped, by some men of more slender gifts and smaller influence, that the accused would be condemned, but the event proved otherwise. Their explanations were deemed quite satisfactory by the eminent men who had come together to make the inquiry, and from that day Calvinistic Methodist ministers, while holding fast all the leading doctrines of Calvinism, have felt at perfect liberty to earnestly persuade their hearers to seek their own salvation. To the inexpressible grief of thousands, the Rev. John Jones died on the 16th of August, 1857, at the comparatively early age of sixty-one years.

The Rev. Henry Rees was another of those men whom the Lord raised to adorn the ministry of the Gospel in Wales, and to be a blessing to thousands. He was born at Llansannan, Denbighshire, February 15th, 1798.[10] He feared the Lord from his early childhood. "I was religious," says he, "before I can remember; at least, I would often, when alone, think of death, was afraid of doing anything sinful, and very fond of preachers and preaching. When those workings of my mind began I cannot say. In my childhood I used to retire to a solitary place, to repeat to myself such portions as I could remember of sermons to which I had listened. I continued that habit in my youth, and, for that reason, was glad to have something to do far away on the fields, or in the woods, where I could be quite alone." When he was between ten and twelve years of age his family were struck with his deep seriousness, and specially noticed his preaching habits. He preached in the stable, the cowhouse, and the barn, and on the slopes of the mountain where he was sent to watch over the sheep. I heard it from an aged relative of his that sometimes, when any of the family would come on the scene, they would find him praying or preaching, and the sheep "nowhere." He began to preach to men and women when he was about twenty-one years of age, and it is said that his father, who was an able man and a deacon, and who heard his first public sermon, upon being asked whether he thought Harry would make a preacher, replied, "I do not know about that, but I am sure that he will never make anything else in the world." A few months after he made this beginning, his neighbour, the Rev. Peter Roberts, finding himself unable to fulfil a Sabbath's engagement which he had at Mold, sent him to supply his place. At that town there was a good old deacon, Mr. Foulkes by name, who, failing the usual pulpit supply, would generally preach himself. Mr. Roberts, being an eminent man, had been announced to preach on Saturday evening. Mr. Foulkes watched and waited for him, and as he did not make his appearance went through the service himself, taking little or no notice of the modest young stranger, who sat near him in the pulpit pew. At the close of the service one of the brethren told him that that young man had come to supply on the morrow instead of the expected preacher. Mr. Foulkes did not like it, and though he took the young preacher to stay at his house, was very dry to him. But soon after the Sunday morning's sermon had begun, the stern old deacon began to melt, and before it had finished, his tears were running fast. "Look here," said he to one of the brethren at the close of the service, "that young lad is a far better and greater preacher than Peter Roberts." He was advised to learn the trade of bookbinder, that he might have something to live upon, for living by the Gospel was at that time, in Wales, quite out of the question. He accepted the advice, and did a little in that way, but not much; for his heart was in a far greater work. His eminent brother, Dr. William Rees, who has but recently gone to his rest, referring to this episode in his life, said, "Instead of the lad binding books, the books bound the lad."[11]

He lived amply to fulfil the promise of his youth. For many years he stood foremost among his brethren. For unwearied industry, for purity of taste, for elegance of diction, for wealth of illustration, for ability to analyse the deepest thoughts and feelings of the human heart, and for that mysterious unction which gives a peculiar power to the ministry of the Gospel, he was never surpassed in Wales, and scarcely ever equalled, and it was the honest conviction of some of the leading men of the Body to which he belonged, that, until he died, the greatest Welsh Methodist preacher that had ever existed was still living. Having left his home at Liverpool, where he had resided for many years, to attend the funeral of a friend in Anglesey, he was taken ill on his journey, and turned to rest at the residence of his only child, the wife of Mr. Richard Davies, M.P. for Anglesey, and died there on the 18th of February, 1869, when a few days over seventy-one years of age.

The Rev. David Howell of Swansea was for many years one of the foremost ministers of South Wales. He became a professed disciple of Christ while yet a child, and when he removed from his native place in Carmarthenshire to Swansea, he was known in the town as "the godly boy." He began to preach when he was about nineteen years of age, and there never lived a more faithful and indefatigable labourer in the vineyard of Christ than he. Very early in his ministry he was sent to a field of labour from which many would have retired in despair. Radnorshire was at that time about as heathenish as it could well be. Thither he was sent to find places to preach in, and to get, if he could, people to listen to him, and many were the discouragements which he met, and the difficulties which he had to encounter. One incident will serve to give some idea of the character of this district at the time when he entered it. He had obtained permission to preach in the penthouse of a blacksmith's forge. There was a public-house opposite, where a number of men were drinking and shouting while he conducted the service. One of them looked out, and seeing a man in the penthouse opposite, talking to a few people, got up, and pint in hand, went to the preacher, and said to him, "Here, man, drink; you have been talking for a long while, you must be very dry." But undaunted by the ignorance and indifference of the people, he persevered, and by God's blessing on his labours, the face of the district was completely changed, and it is now as decent and religious as any average place in the Principality. He returned to Swansea, where, with the exception of one or two short intervals, he resided for the remainder of his life. For many years his influence was paramount at the South Wales Association. People listened to that which he said, for in every conscience there was the conviction that he honestly cared for the cause of Christ. The day before his death, the writer who was about to leave for an Association called to see him, and asked whether there was any message which he would like to send to the assembled brotherhood. He replied, "Remember me to the brethren. Tell them that I am sorry not to be with them, but that is impossible—*I suppose.* Bid them keep the words of truth and soberness in their proper places,—the word of the kingdom in the place where it has always used to be." The ruling passion was, with him, strong in death, and that ruling passion was jealous care for the truth of the Gospel and the best interests of immortal souls. "I am persuaded," said he afterwards, "that I shall never recover, but I feel sure that I shall be for ever with the things which have been my delight in this world. The great Person of the Mediator, the might of His offices, the value of His sacrifice, the infinite sufficiency of His atonement, the efficacy of His blood, and His faithfulness to His word,— these are immovable things—*immovable things.*" Resting on those immovable things, and talking of them to the very last, he fell asleep, August 4th, 1873, when seventy-six years of age.

There are many more whom we would have been glad to bring before our readers. We would speak of Evan Richardson, the gentlemanly schoolmaster and eloquent preacher of Caernarfon, who taught pupils to live, and lived to preach the gospel of Christ; of Thomas Richard, the brother of Ebenezer, who appeared like a prince among his brethren, and was all that he appeared to be; of William Morris, of St. David's,[12] whose every sermon was a string of sparkling gems; of David Jones, brother of John Jones, almost his equal in power, but his superior in pathos; of John Hughes, the fine preacher, and the accomplished author of *Methodistiaeth Cymru;*—of Thomas Phillips, who chose for his motto the words, "Bibl i bawb o bobl y byd,"[13] and did more, perhaps, than any living man towards putting that motto in practice, and was removed in the autumn of 1870; of _____. But we forbear. There are many, many more names rising before our mind. They are a great cloud from which countless blessings were rained on our dear country. But now they are all gone. It is comforting to feel that there are some of like spirit still left among us, and it gives stronger comfort to know that He who anointed them has an inexhaustible supply of that Spirit. May He abundantly descend on the existing and on the rising ministry! It is that only that can enable us to retain the ground which our fathers won with their sword and their bow, and to march on to greater and still greater victories over ungodliness and sin.

NOTES

1. The original Welsh letter is in the National Library of Wales (MS 4836E). It has been printed in Emyr Roberts ac E. Wyn James, *Robert Roberts: Yr Angel o Glynnog* (Pen-y-bont ar Ogwr: Llyfrgell Efengylaidd Cymru, 1976), pp.40-42.

2. Rhuddlan was actually in Flintshire when the book was first published, but as a result of local government reorganisation it is now included within Denbighshire.

3. "Bleddyn" [William Jones], *Eliasia, neu rai Sylwadau ar... John Elias* (Merthyr Tydfil: 1844), p.50.

4. This quotation is not from either David Charles of Carmarthen (one being the brother and the other the nephew of Thomas Charles), but from the David Charles of Bala, grandson of Thomas Charles, referred to on p.230-1. Edward Morgan, *John Elias: Life, Letters, and Essays* (1844, 1847: revised edition in one volume, Edinburgh: Banner of Truth Trust, 1973), p.123.

5. Williams acknowledges his indebtedness for most of this information to an article on Ebenezer Morris by Roger Edwards in *Y Gwyddoniadur Cymreig* (The Welsh Encyclopaedia), ten volumes (Dinbych: Gee, 1854-79).

6. E. W. Richard and H. Richard, *Bywyd y Parch. Ebenezer Richard* (Llundain: 1839), pp.88-89.

7. Eleven, not ten. Owen Thomas, *Cofiant y Parchedig John Jones, Talsarn* (Wrexham: Hughes, 1874), pp.17, 24.

8. See note 2, p.188.

9. Owen Thomas, *John Jones, Talsarn*, pp.234-5.

[10] Llansannan was in Denbighshire when the book was first published, but is now in Conwy.

[11] *Y Drysorfa*, 1869, p.121.

[12] Also known as William Morris, Cilgerran.

[13] "A Bible for every one of the people of the world." The original motto in the revised Welsh orthography reads as follows: 'Beibl i bawb o bobl y byd'.

APPENDIX A

William Williams and
Welsh Calvinistic Methodism[1]

Dr. D. Martyn Lloyd-Jones

I

Let me start by giving some kind of explanation as to why I
am dealing with this subject; it is quite a simple one. Last
year I should have been doing what I am going to do tonight,
because it was the 250th anniversary of the birth of William
Williams. He was actually born at the end of 1717. But I felt
constrained to deal with the question of Sandemanianism
first.[2] It came in a kind of logical sequence in my own mind
with regard to the addresses that I have been delivering at
the close of this Conference, and I suddenly realised that it
would make quite a good introduction to this subject
tonight, because the greatest opponent of Sandemanianism
in Wales was none other than William Williams. So it has
seemed to me to be right to give this address this year. It
does also serve, I trust, as an interesting link with what has
been before us almost throughout this Conference because
I shall be dealing with Calvinism and Methodism and what
I shall say will, in a sense, perhaps, help to sum up the
various matters that we have discussed together.

I am not going to say very much about William Williams
himself. One could not attempt to deal with him without
taking a whole evening, because he was such a many-sided
man, who stands out as one of the three, or perhaps four,

great leaders of Methodism in Wales in the eighteenth century. Daniel Rowland was the outstanding preacher, as we heard last year. Howel Harris was the great exhorter and the great organiser. But William Williams was a many-sided man.

We think of him instinctively first and foremost as a great writer of hymns, and he was, I would say, supreme in this matter. Certain literary authorities in Wales, who are not Christian themselves, are ready to grant that he is, in their judgement, the greatest of all Welsh poets. This is something of very real significance, because here you have such an outstanding, natural poet, now, under the influence of the Spirit, writing these incomparable hymns. An indication of his place as a writer of hymns, and indeed a writer of prose in addition, is the fact that the University of Wales Press are in process of republishing Williams' *Complete Works*. Two volumes have already appeared.[3] So we are dealing with a very remarkable man, a man of very unusual ability.

In addition to being an outstanding poet and writer of hymns he was also, we can say, the theologian of Welsh Calvinistic Methodism. He showed that in his attack upon Sandemanianism, but he showed it in many other ways positively. He was the theologian of this group of three or four men, and he showed great ability there. He would give his theology sometimes in verse and sometimes in prose. But in many ways I would say that the greatest of all his gifts was the gift which he had of instructing the little societies or companies of Methodists that used to meet together. He was acknowledged by everybody to be supreme in this matter. He wrote a book which he called *Drws y Society Profiad* or *The Door to the Experience Society*, or *The Door to the Society in which experiences are dealt with*.[4] It is quite a classic. I had intended at one time to devote my whole paper to that, because it might be very useful and instructive for us in this phase through which we are passing at the present time, when we have little groups of Christians meeting together for fellowship in different parts of the country. The early Methodists had to face that problem. They had new converts whom they formed into societies. The question, then, was, how could they be instructed? They needed leaders; they might be good men but still they would not know how to handle people. Well, Williams wrote the book in order to instruct them and to guide them as to how to do this all-important work.

There, then, are the outstanding characteristics of this man. He was born, as I have said, in 1717, and was converted while quite young under the ministry of the great Howel Harris. Williams intended to be a doctor, and he was preparing to become a medical student. As he was going home one day, quite heedlessly and thoughtlessly, he saw a crowd of people listening to a man. He joined them; it was Howel Harris preaching. There and then he was converted and immediately, almost, felt a call to the ministry. Eventually he was ordained as a deacon in the Church of England, and as such he was one of the men present at the first great Association held by the Calvinistic Methodists in Wales in 1743 with Whitefield presiding.[5]

II

These are the main facts about Williams. You can see how easily one could spend the whole time with him, but I propose to look at him as one of the leaders of the Calvinistic Methodists, and particularly in Wales. Our theme, then, is going to be 'Calvinistic Methodism'.

I have often found during the years that people, both Arminians and Calvinists, have regarded this term as a contradiction in terms. 'Calvinistic Methodism?' they say; 'this is impossible, it is a contradiction'. I remember speaking at an anniversary in a church not so far from here about twenty-five years ago. I said I was glad to be present as a Methodist and as the representative of Whitefield and

Calvinistic Methodism. And the then minister of that church said that he regarded this as a contradiction in terms. Well, that was because he was seriously defective in his understanding of the term Methodism. But there are others, on the other side, who have been astounded at this. The term 'Methodism' on the Continent in particular is a dirty word, and there are Calvinists who dislike any association between Calvinism and Methodism. Again this is due to a serious defective understanding, as I hope to show, of both Calvinism and Methodism. So it is clear that this is a subject that has a good deal to tell us at the present time.

The best way of approaching it, I think, is for me, first of all, briefly to outline how Calvinistic Methodism ever came into being. We have to start, of course, with the rise of Methodism. Consider first the condition of England at that time, when Methodism really began in the 1730s. The Church of England was generally Arminian. You remember the famous dictum of the great Lord Chatham with respect to the condition of the Church of England. He said that she had a Calvinistic creed, a Popish liturgy, and an Arminian clergy. And that was an accurate description. She was not only Arminian but also spiritually asleep.

What about the other Churches? Presbyterianism had ceased to be. There had been a Presbyterianism in England, but it had become Arian in its doctrine. The Westminster Confession of Faith does not guarantee that you cannot go wrong doctrinally. It was the Presbyterians who went most astray and became guilty of Arianism, and Presbyterianism literally died. The Presbyterian Church of England which we have today is something quite new which only started in the last century. As regards Congregationalism, these Arian tendencies for a while even affected people like Isaac Watts and Philip Doddridge. The Congregationalists had also been affected by Hyper-Calvinism, to which reference has been made, and we have been reminded also that among the Baptists there was this teaching.

That was the condition of England in general. In Wales it was very similar. The Church of England was in the same condition in Wales as in England. In the Nonconformist bodies there was an occasional good man here and there; we must not depreciate them. The Methodists in their enthusiasm, and perhaps William Williams himself, tended to do so. In his elegies on the death of Rowland and of Harris he tends to give the impression that there was no light at all. There were good men, but unfortunately these good men were given to argumentation and disputation among themselves. So that from the standpoint of a live spirituality they did not count very much.

It was into that kind of condition in England and in Wales that Methodism came. How did it come? I cannot, obviously, go into detail. As regards England the real origin and genesis are to be found in the Holy Club that was founded in Oxford, mainly at the instigation of Charles Wesley. The story is well-known. However, the Holy Club in and of itself would never have led to Methodism. The real beginning of Methodism is found in the mighty experience through which Whitefield passed in 1736, and through which the Wesley brothers passed in May 1738. In Wales Methodism was quite independent and spontaneous. Welsh Methodism owes nothing to English Methodism. It started before that in England, in 1735, with the conversion of both Howel Harris and Daniel Rowland, and again, quite independently. They had never heard of each other and knew nothing at all about each other. But the Spirit of God dealt with these two men in a most amazing way, and it was only in 1737 that they met and came together.

That is how Methodism began. At first they were all one— in England and in Wales when they eventually met and came together. There was one Methodism, including all these men to whom I have referred. But then, as we have already been reminded, a division came in and Methodism divided into two groups, Calvinistic and Arminian. In Wales they were all Calvinists. In England they were not all Calvinists. On the Calvinistic side you have the great names, Whitefield, Berridge, Toplady, Romaine, and the two Hill brothers, Rowland Hill and Sir Richard Hill, and also the Countess of Huntingdon. On the Arminian side there were the Wesleys, John Fletcher, Thomas Olivers, and various others.

These are historical points which are of considerable interest. The Methodism of Wales was entirely Calvinistic. The Wesleys visited there but they did not have any churches there until the beginning of the nineteenth century. But again I would emphasise this fact—that we have a Methodism that is common to both. This is a basic point. Actually the term 'Calvinistic Methodist' in Welsh emphasises this very strongly, for it is not Calvinistic Methodism, but Methodism-Calvinistic. And so you have Methodism-Wesleyan. The Methodism comes first, and the other is an adjective describing the particular type. At first they all worked together, but, owing to the division, it was Whitefield who became most intimately associated with the men in Wales, and he was actually the Moderator of their first Association in 1743.[6]

III

We must now face this question—What then is Methodism? Let me first answer negatively. It is not primarily a theological position or even a theological attitude. Methodism was not a movement designed to reform theology. It was not that at all. Actually in Welsh Calvinistic Methodism they did not have a Catechism or a Confession of Faith until the following century—emphasising this point, that it was not primarily a theological movement. We must not think of it in terms of theological reform.

What was it then? Well, Methodism is essentially experimental or experiential religion and a way of life. I think that is an adequate definition of it. What produced this? How did this ever come into being? The answer is that it was born of a number of things. The first was the realisation that religion is primarily and essentially something personal. This was the thing that came to all of them. They all became aware of their own personal sinfulness; they underwent conviction of sin, and it was an agonising process. But they all experienced this terrible need of forgiveness. This became a burden to them—both parties. Then there was also a great desire for a knowledge of God—a direct knowledge of God: not to believe things about God—they had already got that—but the desire to know God. 'This is life eternal, that they might know thee the only true God, and Jesus Christ, whom thou hast sent' (John 17:3). All this led on then to a desire for assurance of sins forgiven.

Many have probably read the account of the first meeting between Whitefield and Harris in Cardiff in 1739. The first question that George Whitefield put to Howel Harris was this: 'Mr Harris, do you know that your sins are forgiven?' He did not ask him, 'Do you believe that sins can be forgiven?' or 'Do you believe that your sins are forgiven?' for various reasons, but, 'Do you *know* that your sins are forgiven?' And Harris was able to say that he had rejoiced in this knowledge for several years. This again was a point that was common to all of them—assurance of salvation, assurance of sins forgiven.

The next thing that was common to all types of Methodism was the desire for 'new life'. So you had that great emphasis on the doctrine of regeneration and rebirth. You know how they were all influenced by the book of Henry Scougal, *The Life of God in the Soul of Man*. This was their longing and desire. Whitefield preached constantly on regeneration, and so did the others. You remember that he even had to be corrected on this point, actually by the Wesleys, though he had gone before them. They felt that he was not making enough of justification by faith. There was this tremendous emphasis on the need of a new birth, a new beginning.

The next thing I have to stress is the emphasis which they all placed on 'feeling'. They were very concerned about what Whitefield once called a 'felt' Christ. They were not content with orthodoxy, correct belief; they wanted to 'feel' Him. They laid tremendous emphasis upon the place of feelings in our Christian experience. This I could illustrate at great length. Unfortunately there are only two of Williams' hymns in the *Congregational Hymnary*, and they are translations, of course. You get there no true idea of his greatness as a hymn-writer and as a poet. He cannot be translated. In his hymns you have an incomparable blend of truly great poetry and perfect theology. We have, 'Guide me, O Thou great Jehovah', and 'O'er the gloomy hills of darkness', but one of the greatest of all his hymns has been translated like this, and it is so typical of Williams:

> *Speak, I pray Thee, gentle Jesus!*
> *O, how passing sweet Thy words,*
> *Breathing o'er my troubled spirit*
> *Peace which never earth affords!*
> *All the world's distracting voices,*
> *All the enticing tones of ill,*
> *At Thy accents mild, melodious,*
> *Are subdued, and all is still.*

And he goes on:

> *Tell me Thou art mine, O, Saviour,*
> *Grant me an assurance clear,*
> *Banish all my dark misgivings,*
> *Still my doubting, calm my fear.*
> *O, my soul within me yearneth*
> *Now to hear Thy voice divine;*
> *So shall grief be gone for ever,*
> *And despair no more be mine.*

Now that is so typical of him. There are endless hymns by him on that theme in the Welsh hymn-book. He wanted to 'feel' these things. He believed, but he was not satisfied with that; he wanted to *know*.

Of course you get the same note in the English Methodist hymn writers in exactly the same way. Let me give one example out of the writings of Toplady:

> *Object of my first desire,*
>   *Jesus crucified for me;*
> *All to happiness aspire*
>   *Only to be found in Thee:*
> *Thee to please, and Thee to know,*
>   *Constitute my bliss below;*
> *Thee to see, and Thee to love,*
>   *Constitute my bliss above.*
>
> *Lord, it is not life to live*
>   *If Thy presence Thou deny;*
> *Lord, if Thou Thy presence give,*
>   *'Tis no longer death to die:*
> *Source and Giver of repose,*
>   *Only from Thy smile it flows;*
> *Peace and happiness are Thine;*
>   *Mine they are, if Thou art mine.*
>
> *Whilst I feel Thy love to me,*
>   *Every object teems with joy;*
> *May I ever walk with Thee,*
>   *For 'tis bliss without alloy:*
> *Let me but Thyself possess,*
>   *Total sum of happiness:*
> *Real bliss I then shall prove,*
>   *Heaven below and heaven above.*

And as you read Toplady's diaries you find this kind of

thing emphasised repeatedly.

That brings me to say just a little more about this whole question of assurance, because in many ways it was the distinguishing mark of Methodism and the same thing that was common to Methodism. They divided over holiness teaching, as we have already been reminded, and over other matters, but here there was this great unity, this teaching concerning assurance. What was it? It was this, that our assurance of salvation is not only, and not merely, something that is to be deduced from the Scriptures. They agreed that that was part of it. I would say that the bulk of evangelical people today, in this and other countries, stop at that. That is their only assurance, that which you deduce from the Scriptures. 'Whosoever believeth in Him is not condemned.' So they say, 'Do you believe in Him?' 'Yes.' 'Very well, you are not condemned, and there is your assurance. Do not worry about your feelings,' etc. etc.

Now Methodism taught the exact opposite. That is the point at which you start, and you can go on and test yourself in terms of the teaching of the first Epistle of John. As you do so you will get a better assurance, an assurance which will save you from a kind of 'believism', or an intellectualism that just says that it believes and accepts all this, and which emphasises the importance of evidences of new life. But these men were concerned to go on to a further source of assurance, which to them was the one that they desired and coveted above everything else. That was the direct witness of the Spirit himself to the fact that they were the children of God. So they made much, of course, of Romans 8:15 and 16; and also of Galatians 2:20: 'The Son of God, who loved me, and gave himself for me', etc.

This, I repeat, was common to all of them. We are all familiar with the experience of John Wesley in Aldersgate Street on May 24, 1738. 'My heart was strangely warm, and I did know that my sins, even mine, had been forgiven.'[7] William Williams made a great deal of this. Let me give two quotations to establish this point. I am translating out of his book, *The Door* (or 'Entry' if you like) *to the Experience Meeting—the Experience Society*. He was giving instructions to the men in charge of the societies as to how they should question and catechise and cross-examine the people who were anxious to be admitted to the societies, and, indeed, how they should examine the experiences of those who belonged to the societies. He drew a distinction between the way in which you questioned and catechised young members, new members, and the way in which you catechised older members. He says: 'You must not expect as much of the light of faith, and certainly amongst those whom you are receiving for the first time, as you must expect amongst those who have been in for some time'—although he goes on to say that 'sometimes you will get a shock and you will find that people's early experiences are very much better than their later experiences'. However, that is his main point of distinction—that you do not expect as much light and clarity and certainty from the young convert as you do from the older one.

How, then, do you question and examine the young convert? This is one of his ways of putting it—that the examiner is to say to the young convert, 'Though you have not yet received the testimony of the Spirit (to your salvation), nevertheless, are you seeking God with your whole heart, and with this as the main rule of your life? Not by fits and starts or occasional touches of conviction—Is this the main thing in your life?' But notice how he starts: 'Though you have not yet received the testimony of the Spirit.' Then when he comes to the way in which they should question the older men he says, 'You must examine them concerning the clarity or the clearness of their testimony, how they first received their testimony, whether they have lost any of it or not.' Then he tells them to ask: 'Has this testimony which you have in your own spirit been doubled by the Holy Spirit?' That is the term he used—'doubled'. In other words, that was Williams' view of 'the Spirit himself also beareth witness with our spirits that we are the children of God' (Rom. 8:16). Our spirit tells us this, 'the Spirit of adoption, whereby we cry, Abba, Father'. But the Spirit, as it were, doubles it, seals it, guarantees it, gives an extra, an overplus on top of it, confirms it. That is the term which he uses with regard to these older converts.

That was their teaching, and, of course, it was their own experience. This comes out very clearly in the case of Daniel Rowland, who having come to see the doctrine of justification by faith as he had heard it preached by Griffith Jones at Llanddewi Brefi, still did not have certainty about it. But one day when he was reading the litany at the communion service in his own church in the village of Llangeitho, suddenly the Spirit came and did this 'doubling'; and he knew. And it was from then on that he began to preach in that amazing way and with that amazing power, of which Ryle writes in his famous book, *Christian Leaders of the Eighteenth Century*.[8] The same thing is very clear in the case of Howel Harris. Howel Harris, being convicted of sin on the Sunday before Good Friday 1735, got an assurance at Whitsun. But it was only three weeks later that he had this 'doubling' by the Spirit, and that was the thing that made him an evangelist. They taught this, and they taught people to expect this, not to be satisfied with anything less, as my quotation from Williams' book has already shown you.

I go on from this to add another vital point about them all—Methodism in England and in Wales and in all parties. They met together in little groups or classes; whatever you may like to call them. What did they do there? Well, the main thing they did was to state their experiences to one another, and to examine one another's experiences, and to discuss them together. They told of the Lord's dealings with them, what had happened to them since they last met, of anything remarkable that had occurred to them, and so on.

This was the main element in these societies; that is the thing that Williams treats of in that book to which I have referred—this great emphasis on experience, and on assurance, on this 'felt' element. They were primarily 'experience' meetings. Indeed I think we are justified in using this term, that the thing that characterised Methodism was this pneumatic element. Over and above what they believed there was this desire to feel and to experience the power of the Spirit in their lives.

All this was expressed in their lives, about which they were so careful and so meticulous. They were taught to be so, and were examined in order to make sure that they were so. That is the picture of their life in their societies. These people, under the preaching, had undergone an experience, and they had made application to join the Society, and they had been received; and that is how they went on.

One other great thing we have got to emphasise is their evangelistic zeal; and again it was common to all of them. Who can decide as to which had the greater evangelistic zeal, John Wesley or George Whitefield? You cannot answer the question. They both had it. And it seems to me that both these branches or divisions of Methodism showed exactly the same zeal and enthusiasm in this desire to bring their fellow men and women to a knowledge of God's salvation in Christ Jesus, and that they were equal also in the success which they attained.

All this was common to all Methodism. Then there came the division. When I say that they had these things in common, 'and then', it sounds as if I were saying that from there on they did not have them in common. But they did. After the division all that went on, all that remained common; but they became divided into those two groups, the Arminian and the Calvinistic.

The question has often been asked as to why this ever happened. I remember it being asked in a final meeting at this Conference a number of years ago. The answer is very difficult. I suppose in a sense it cannot be answered. Dare I make one suggestion? (We might very well have this as a topic for discussion some time.) Is there even a national element in this? I mean by that, that it may have something to do with national characteristics. I am not going to go into this, I am simply asking a question. What is the place of nationality in these matters? Can you allow it any place at all?

Let me just say this before I leave the matter. I have always felt that John Wesley was about the most typical Englishman of whom I have ever read. I could substantiate what I am saying. However, we do know this, and we have been reminded of it already, the Church of England at that time was thoroughly Arminian. The Wesley family, the father and mother, had become Arminians, and were proud of it. Not only that, there is very interesting evidence brought forth by Professor Geoffrey Nuttall to show that Arminianism had had a particular vogue in the village of Epworth, where the Wesleys lived. So they had been brought up and nurtured in a thoroughly Arminian atmosphere. No doubt that has a great deal to do with it. But in Wales, as I have reminded you, the whole thing was entirely different, and they were all Calvinistic.

It is interesting to notice that they only became Calvinistic after a while. They all started as Methodists, but in Wales they became Calvinistic. Howel Harris tells us this quite plainly, in his own diary, as to how he became a Calvinist. The same thing is true of Whitefield. Whitefield 'became' a Calvinist. I am not going into the details as to when, but the fact is that he became a Calvinist. I believe that in the case of Rowland and Harris in particular, and probably also in the case of Whitefield, it was their study of the Thirty-Nine Articles and of the Puritans that brought them to this position. However, the fact is that they became Calvinistic, and in Wales they remained purely Calvinistic until the end of the century.

IV

We come now to look at the characteristics of Welsh Calvinistic Methodism. These are quite clear. First and foremost there was the great preaching. That was the outstanding characteristic. I am one of those who believes that Calvinism should always lead to great preaching; and when it does not I query the genuineness of the Calvinism. You cannot have great preaching without a great theme; and they had that great theme, and so you had great preaching all over the country. And the great characteristic of the preaching, as of the life, was warmth, and enthusiasm, and rejoicing. Some of them went through an early phase in which they tended to be a bit legalistic; but it did not last long and the other element came through.

Welsh Calvinistic Methodism was also characterised by singing. Williams produced most of the hymns, and the people would sing them to old tunes and ballads. Moreover there was often great shouting during the preaching. They would interrupt the preacher, they would cry out their 'Amens' and 'Hallelujahs', and sometimes the excitement was quite marked. This joy and rejoicing and singing and assurance were the great characteristics of Welsh Calvinistic Methodism.

The other thing that one must mention, because it is of such vital importance, is that they had a succession of revivals. I trust it is not necessary for me to define and describe the word 'revival'. I know that in some countries the word 'revival' has now come to mean the holding of an evangelistic campaign. This is not revival! In a sense I cannot think of anything that is further removed from revival than just that—a man-made, man-organised series of meetings. That is not it! Revival is 'a visitation from on High', an outpouring of the Holy Spirit. They had a whole succession of them. One of the great revivals in that eighteenth century broke out as the result of the publishing of a new hymn-book by this man William Williams in 1763.[9] The very publication of the hymns and the fact that the people began to sing them led to one of these new outbursts. There had been a period of dryness and of aridity, because, unfortunately, there was a quarrel even amongst the Welsh Calvinistic Methodists. It is a blot on their story. It was almost entirely a personal matter: not entirely so. But it seems to me, the more I have read about it, that it was a clash of personalities, as so often happens, alas, in the church, between Rowland and Harris. Harris undoubtedly had also been going astray somewhat in his doctrine, and this had happened about 1751-53. Following that there had been this period of dryness, but then William Williams' new hymn-book came out and as the people began to sing these great expressions of theology a revival broke out.

The hymns of William Williams are packed with theology and experience. That is why I once, in giving a lecture on Isaac Watts, ventured to say that William Williams was the greatest hymn-writer of them all. You get greatness, and bigness, and largeness in Isaac Watts; you get the experimental side wonderfully in Charles Wesley. But in William Williams you get both at the same time, and that is why I put him in a category entirely on his own. He taught the people theology in his hymns; as they sang the hymns they were becoming familiar with the great expressions of the New Testament doctrines of salvation and the glory of God. But this element of 'revival' is something I want to emphasise, because it was a peculiar feature of 'Calvinistic' Methodism. You also had activity amongst others, and occasions when there was a movement of the Spirit; but they were much less frequent and they were not so clearly 'special' visitations as was the case amongst the Calvinistic Methodists.

Those, then, were the great characteristics of Calvinistic Methodism. It seems to me that it might be of some help if we now considered this question: Was this an entirely new phenomenon? Is the Calvinistic Methodism of the eighteenth century something without antecedents? I suggest that it is not and that there were precursors of it. Again I think we are dealing here with a most interesting point—the relationship of this Calvinistic Methodism to what had gone before. Where do we get hints or adumbrations of this previously? Well, I have always felt that you get a good deal of it in the saintly Hooper, Bishop of Gloucester, martyred in the time of Queen Mary I. The same is true also of John Bradford. You get there the same stress upon feeling and the same warmth. Let us not forget that these two were really the first two Puritans, though the name was not then used. We are in grave danger of forgetting the Puritans of the 16th century in our concentration on those of the 17th century, yet let us never forget that but for them the 17th-century Puritans would probably never have come into being. I find in these first Puritans something more akin to Calvinistic Methodism than one finds even in those who are sometimes described as the 'Pietistic' Puritans, such as William Perkins and others like Lewis Bayly, and so on. These were men who put their emphasis on practical and pastoral theology. They were interested in the application of the Law of God in the life of the believer. They put this great emphasis upon 'practising' it. So you get their 'casuistry' and their dealing with 'cases of conscience'. That does lead to a kind of piety, but it is not the same thing as you have in Calvinistic Methodism. There, the emphasis was on the teaching of the Law and its application in the daily life of the Christian—of course I am not excluding the other element altogether, I am talking about the main emphasis—whereas in Calvinistic Methodism the great emphasis and stress was upon 'experience'.

When you come to the next century you get something that is similar to, though not identical with Calvinistic Methodism, in people like Walter Cradock and Morgan Llwyd (Lloyd, as he is called in English). But they were more mystical.[10] It is wrong to say of these Calvinistic Methodists that they were mystics. There is a mystical element in them; you cannot exclude it; but you cannot classify them with the mystics. They were suspicious of and opposed to mysticism, as was shown in their opposition to the quietism that became such a characteristic of the Moravians. And yet, surely, there is a true Christ-mysticism which we must not exclude, and which I maintain you get in the Apostle Paul himself, as well as in many others throughout the centuries.

There is much about people like Walter Cradock and Morgan Lloyd that seems to suggest what blossomed so fully in the eighteenth century. They were entirely different from the Quakers. They did not just believe in an 'inner light' and tend to depreciate the Scriptures. No, they had this great theological content as well. I have often felt that you get something of the same thing appearing here and there in John Flavel and Thomas Brooks—touches of it. But it seems to come in as 'touches'; it is not given the centrality that it is given in the Calvinistic Methodists. Personally, I would not hesitate to describe the Jansenists, including the great Blaise Pascal, as Calvinistic Methodists before their time. And certainly I would say that there is more of an affinity with some of the men in Scotland, such as William Guthrie and even before him, Robert Bruce and John Livingstone, than there is with the bulk of English Puritans.

This is a most interesting point. We know that these Calvinistic Methodists read the Puritans a great deal. They fed on them. Puritan writings were their food next to the Bible, and they learned a great deal from them. Yet I am suggesting that Calvinistic Methodism was not a mere continuation of Puritanism. A new element has come in—this emphasis upon the feeling aspect, the revival aspect, and this whole matter of assurance, all the things I have been describing as the essence of Calvinistic Methodism. I venture again to suggest that Jonathan Edwards must be called a Calvinistic Methodist. You have the same combination in Edwards. I know the brilliant intellect tended to obscure this at times, but I would say that essentially Jonathan Edwards as a type was a Calvinistic Methodist, though actually a Congregationalist.

When you come to the Continental Pietists, again we are in a slight difficulty. There were affinities, clearly in the case of Spener, Francke, and people like that, and the Moravians. We know the association between the Moravians and the Methodists, especially at first. They did separate and go apart for certain reasons, but from the beginning they were aware of something in common, and, what was in common was again this very thing which I have been trying to emphasise as being the main characteristic of Calvinistic Methodism.

V

Let us now attempt some kind of assessment, or attempt to draw out some lessons from all this. We have been dealing with the history of this Methodism that split in two directions, and yet in a sense kept together right through and in spite of the divisions. What are the lessons?

The first, it seems to me, is the grave danger of hardening our terms. We are ever in danger of so 'hardening' the terms that in the end they come to stand for something which is no longer true of the original. It is assumed today that if you use the word Methodist you are speaking of Arminians. That is the general assumption, that you are speaking of John Wesley and his followers. It is to me ridiculous that a religious denomination in this country should call themselves The Methodists. They have no right to do this. It is not true historically. But this is the sort of thing that happens and terms become hardened.

It also shows us the danger of party spirit. Labels generally lead to a spirit, and we must avoid this as Christian people. We must avoid this hardening and rigidity which leads to a wrong spirit and lands us eventually in a position in which we are tempted to ask, as people have asked before us: 'Can any good come out of Nazareth?' God save us and preserve us from ever becoming victims of that terrible spirit!

But there is another lesson that may be of great value to us at this present time through which we are passing. We are in an age of change, and there is no doubt that in a few years the religious situation in this country is going to be very different from what we have known, and there will be new groupings of Christian people. The many will doubtless be in one 'Territorial Church' together, or even in a 'World Church'. There will be others who will not. And the problem will arise for those who do not belong to a 'Territorial Church' as to what they are going to call themselves—the problem of 'denominations'. We are familiar with all these terms—Congregationalists, Presbyterians, Baptists, and so on—and the multiplicity of divisions and names that our friends in America know so much better than we do. But I am raising this question now: Is it not time that we put an end to all this, and that we cease to use and to bandy about these names of men? I know the difficulty. The argument is: 'Well, you have got to call the church something, you have got to show how one differs from another.' But I am raising the question as to whether you should do that; whether we should not merely as the result of all we have been considering in this Conference, and all we know about the history of these matters, decide that in future all we put on the notice-boards of our buildings is—'Christian church'.

If a man should come and say to me, 'But what do they teach in there?' I would reply, 'Go in and listen'. Why should we put up a notice that is going to exclude people? Let it be known that the gospel is going to be preached here. That is what a church is for. Let them go in, let them listen; they will soon find out what is being preached and they can then decide for themselves whether they are going there again or whether they are not. Why is it necessary that we should harden the things about which we disagree, and on which we differ, and harden them to the extent of 'placarding' the thing? It has caused great confusion to the world outside always. And we know that it is doing so at this present time. Is not this one of the greatest hindrances of all in evangelism? In other words, are we not guilty of the sin of schism in this very respect? And we are adding to it by putting up these labels. All we need to announce is that this is a Christian church, a place where the gospel is preached. Can we not leave it at that?

But having said that, let me come to more particular statements with regard to my assessment of Calvinistic Methodism. First of all I would say that Calvinistic Methodism is true Methodism, and the only 'true' Methodism. Why do I say that? I say so because I assert that Arminian Methodism is inconsistent with itself in the following ways. It starts by emphasising 'grace'. The Arminian Methodists claimed and still claim that they were preaching 'grace'.

> *His only righteousness I show,*
> *His saving grace proclaim,*

says Charles Wesley in a well-known stanza. They laid great claim to this. But then it has become equally clear, has it not, that they introduce works again with their whole notion of free will, and the part that the man himself plays. I have never found an Arminian who can satisfactorily interpret I Corinthians 2: 14: 'The natural man receiveth not the things of the Spirit of God: for they are foolishness unto him: neither can he know them, for they are spiritually discerned.' Their difficulty is this. They say, 'Quite right: all men by nature are sinners.' They believe in depravity. But then they go on to say that God in His grace has given this power to believe and accept the gospel to 'all men'. That, therefore, means this, that all men now are spiritual, whereas Paul says quite plainly that all are not spiritual, that you have 'carnal' and 'spiritual' men. So if you say that grace is given to 'all', it must follow that all are spiritual, because it is the only grounds on which they can possibly believe and accept this gospel and not regard it as 'foolishness'. So while they start with grace they go on to deny it.

Secondly, though they emphasise—I am dealing still with Arminian or Wesleyan Methodism—the re-birth and regeneration, they then go on to deny it by saying that we can lose it. Re-birth is the action of God, and yet they say that we can undo this and we can lose it. From this it follows— and you get it in its extreme form, of course, in the Salvation Army, which came out of Arminian Methodism—that you can be regenerate today and unregenerate tomorrow, and regenerate again, and back and forth. This whole notion of 'falling from grace', and coming in and out of salvation, is surely a fundamental denial of the doctrine of regeneration.

The same thing applies to their teaching concerning assurance. What is the value of an assurance that you can lose? I mean by that, what is the value of an assurance of salvation if you can lose your salvation? If your persistence in grace and in salvation is dependent upon you, where is your assurance? Can you rely upon yourself? Would any man be eventually saved if it were left to us to persevere in grace? It is not a doctrine of assurance. It leaves it all back with me, and I am in all the uncertainty that I was in before. Of course, that is why so many turn to the Church of Rome, where you hand it over and the Church looks after it for you. It is because you cannot possibly do it yourself. The Church of Rome does not offer you assurance of salvation. What she says is, You cannot get it, but leave it to us and we will put it right for you. And then you get all the paraphernalia that characterises that Church, by which they tell you they are going to do this. So the whole emphasis of the Arminian Methodist upon assurance is nullified.

I would sum up this section like this. One of the greatest proofs of the truth of the doctrines emphasised by Calvin, what is known as 'Calvinism'—though I have already said I do not like these terms—is John Wesley. He was a man who was saved in spite of his muddled and erroneous thinking. The grace of God saved him in spite of himself. That is Calvinism! If you say, as a Calvinist, that a man is saved by his understanding of doctrine you are denying Calvinism. He is not. We are all saved in spite of what we are in every respect. Thus it comes to pass that men who can be so muddled, because they bring in their own human reason, as John Wesley and others did, are saved men and Christians, as all of us are, because it is 'all of the grace of God' and in spite of us.

Calvinistic Methodism is the true Methodism for those reasons. But in addition to that, Calvinistic Methodism saves Methodism from degenerating into mysticism. There is always this danger. Put your emphasis on feeling, upon the 'felt' aspect, and you are already in danger of degenerating into mysticism, or into a false asceticism, or into a kind of 'illuminism'. And all these, of course, have made their appearance in history. But Calvinistic Methodism saves us from that because of its great emphasis upon the doctrines. Here, you have got the doctrines, but in addition you have got this other element, the 'felt' element; It is a perfect combination of both. Not only does it guarantee our doctrinal correctness, it also saves us in the realm of experience itself from many aberrations, which have often ended in what seems to me to be nothing but a kind of Spiritism. Calvinistic Methodism saves us from that. So I argue that Calvinistic Methodism is true Methodism.

Secondly, I argue that Calvinistic Methodism is also true Calvinism. I want to show that a Calvinism that is not Methodist as well is one which we need to examine carefully. Calvinism without Methodism has certain dangerous tendencies, which we must recognise. If we do not we are in a very dangerous position.

Calvinism without Methodism tends to lead to

intellectualism and scholasticism—that is its peculiar temptation. The result is that men talk more about 'the Truth we hold', rather than about 'the Truth that holds us.'

Another danger which Calvinism without Methodism is prone to is that Confessions of Faith, instead of being subordinate standards, tend to be the primary and supreme standard, replacing the Bible in that position. I am only talking about tendencies, and not saying that this happens to all Calvinists. Officially we say that these Confessions are the 'subordinate standard'; the Bible comes first, then these. But there is always a danger that the Calvinist may reverse the order.

A question arises here—it has already been suggested in one of our discussions. It is the whole question of the rightness of preaching from and through the Catechism rather than preaching through and from the Bible itself. I am simply putting it up as a question which we need to examine. The Calvinistic Methodists did not preach through the Catechism. Their whole tendency was to say—as was the tendency of Charles Haddon Spurgeon—that you should not even preach a series of sermons, but that each sermon should be 'given' to you, that you look to God for your sermons. I mean by that, that you look to God for your text and the message you are to deliver. That was the emphasis of Calvinistic Methodism. So I put it in this general way by saying that there is at any rate a danger that we may change the position of the Confession, and it ceases to be the 'subordinate' standard.

A third danger always, as a tendency in Calvinism unless it is corrected by Methodism, is to discourage prayer. This is a very serious matter. The Calvinistic Methodists were great men of prayer, and their churches were characterised by prayer-meetings—warm, moving prayer-meetings, which would sometimes last for hours and where great experiences would come to people. I am suggesting—and I could produce facts—that Calvinism without Methodism tends to discourage prayer. I have known Calvinistic churches in which they have no prayer-meeting at all, and in which prayer is really discouraged.

Lastly, Calvinism without Methodism tends to produce a joyless, hard, not to say a harsh and cold type of religion. I am saying that this is a tendency. All this results from intellectualism of course; and the more the intellect dominates the less joy there will be, and a hardness, and a coldness, and a harshness, and a bigotry tend to come in. I had almost said that Calvinism without Methodism tends to produce 'dead Calvinism'. But I am not saying that. Why not? Because I regard the term 'dead Calvinism' as a contradiction in terms. I say that a dead Calvinism is impossible, and that if your Calvinism appears to be dead it is not Calvinism, it is a philosophy. It is a philosophy using Calvinistic terms, it is an intellectualism, and it is not real Calvinism.

Why not? Because true Calvinism not only does justice to the objective side of our faith and our whole position, it does equal justice to the subjective; and people who cannot see this subjective element in Calvinism seem to me never to have understood Calvinism. Calvinism of necessity leads to an emphasis upon the action and the activity of God the Holy Spirit. The whole emphasis is upon what God does to us; not what man does, but what God does to us; not our hold of Him, but 'His strong grasp of us'. So Calvinism of necessity leads to experiences, and to great emphasis upon experience; and these men, and all these older Calvinists, were constantly talking about 'visitations', how the Lord had appeared to them, how the Lord had spoken to them—the kind of thing that we have seen Toplady expressing in the hymn already quoted and in his diaries. They also talked about 'withdrawings'. Why have those terms disappeared from amongst us modern Calvinists? When have you last spoken about a 'visitation' from the Spirit of God? When did Christ last make Himself 'real' to you? What do you know about 'withdrawings' of the Spirit, and the feeling that your Bridegroom has left you and that He has not visited you recently? This is of the essence of true Calvinism; and a Calvinism that knows nothing about visitations and withdrawings is a caricature of Calvinism, I object to its using the term with respect to itself.

But more, Calvinism leads to assurance, and assurance of necessity leads to joy. You cannot be assured quietly and unmoved by the fact that your sins are forgiven, and that you are a child of God, and that you are going to heaven: it is impossible. Assurance must lead to joy. Not only that; knowing this leads to prayer. God is my Father. I am adopted. I know Him. I have an entrance, and I want to go there. I want to speak to Him and I want to know Him. This is true Calvinism. And that, of course, leads to a love of His Word. You meet Him in the Word. The Word instructs you as to how to find Him; it helps you to understand the visitations and the withdrawings. You live on the Word. Nothing so drives a man to the Word of God as true Calvinism.

Then, in turn, as I have been trying to say, true Calvinism is bound to emphasise the element of revival, the 'givenness' of the activity of God, the visitations of God. It is only since the decline of Calvinism that revivals have become less and less frequent. The more powerful Calvinism is, the more likely you are to have a spiritual revival and re-awakening. It follows of necessity from the doctrine. You cannot work up a revival. You know that you are entirely dependent upon God. That is why you pray to Him and you plead with Him and you argue, and you reason with Him. These Fathers used to do this. How different is our approach to the condition of the church today from that which was true of these Fathers and their successors for several generations. Today we look at the situation and we say—'Well, things are very bad, everything is going down—what shall we do? We had better have an evangelistic campaign.' So we call a committee together and we begin to organise, and to talk about what is going to happen in a year's time or so.

Calvinistic Methodists did not look at the problem like

that. This is how they looked at it. They said, 'Why are things like this? What is the matter? We have offended God, He is grieved with us, He has turned His back on us. What can we do about this? We must get down on our knees and ask Him to come back, we must plead with Him.' And so they would use the kind of arguments you find Moses using in praying to God in Exodus 33, or such as you get in Isaiah 63. They would reason and argue with God, and say, 'After all, we are Your people, not those others. Why do You not come back to us? We belong to You, Your name is involved in all this'. They would plead the 'promises' with God, they would agonise in prayer until God heard them and visited them again.

This is Calvinism. Nothing so promotes prayer as Calvinism. Calvinists who do not pray, I say, are not Calvinists. These things follow the one the other as the night follows the day. The true Calvinist is concerned about revival. Why? Because he is concerned about the glory of God. This is the first thing with him. Not so much that the world is as it is, but that the world is behaving like this, and that God is there. It is God's world, and they are under God. The glory of God! This is the great thing which dominates all the thinking of the Calvinist. So he is waiting, and longing, and pleading with God to 'show' this glory, to show this power, to arise and to scatter His enemies, and to make them like the dust, and to show the might of His almighty arm. This is Calvinism. They want this. They are zealous, and they are jealous, for His name.

At the same time, having an understanding, through their doctrine, of the condition and the state of the unregenerate, they become burdened about them also, and they are anxious to do everything they can to bring them to a knowledge of salvation in Christ Jesus. And when this happens it ends in— what? Well, in great praise and thanksgiving.

My argument is, that cold, sad, mournful, depressing Calvinism is not Calvinism at all. It is a caricature; something has gone wrong somewhere. It is mere intellectualism and philosophy. Calvinism leads to feeling, to passion, to warmth, to praise, to thanksgiving. Look at Paul, the greatest of them all. We should not talk about 'Calvinism'; it is Paul's teaching. He tells us that he wept. He preached with tears. Do you? When did we last weep over these matters? When did we last shed tears? When have we shown the feeling and the passion that he shows? Paul could not control himself, he got carried away. Look at his mighty climaxes; look at the way in which he rises to the heavens and is 'lost in wonder, love, and praise'. Of course, the pedantic scholars criticise him for his *anacolutha*. He starts a sentence and never finishes it. He starts saying a thing and then gets carried off, and forgets to come back to it. Thank God! It is the truth which he saw that led to these grand climaxes of his; and it is bound to do so. If we understand the things we claim to believe we are bound to end in the same way. 'Who shall separate us from the love of God?' And the answer is, 'I am persuaded'—and in the language of the Welsh Calvinistic Methodists it is much better and stronger—'I am certain'. It is sure, it is certain, 'that neither death, nor life, nor angels, nor principalities, nor powers, nor things present, nor things to come, nor height, nor depth, nor any other creature, shall be able to separate us from the love of God, which is in Christ Jesus our Lord'. Or listen to him again at the end of Romans 11, 'O the depth of the riches both of the wisdom and knowledge of God.' How often have you had that 'O' in your preaching—you Calvinists? Calvinism leads to this 'O'!—this feeling, this passion. You are moved to the depths of your being, and you are filled with joy, and wonder, and amazement. 'O the depth of the riches both of the wisdom and of the knowledge of God! how unsearchable are his judgements, and his ways past finding out!'—and so on. Or take the same thing at the end of Ephesians 3. These are men dominated by a sense of the glory of God, and who are concerned about His praise.

In other words I am arguing that the first Christians were

the most typical Calvinistic Methodists of all! I am just describing them to you. Not only the great apostles—Paul and others—but the people, the ordinary people—joy and rejoicing, praising God and thanking Him always 'from house to house' as they ate their bread together. Peter can say of them: 'Whom having not seen, ye love; in whom, though now ye see Him not, yet believing, ye rejoice with joy unspeakable and full of glory.' That is first century Christianity! It is also the very essence of Calvinistic Methodism. It leads to praise and thanksgiving and rejoicing. It always leads to something like this:

> We *praise, we worship thee, O God,*
> *Thy sovereign power we sound abroad:*
> *All nations bow before Thy throne,*
> *And Thee the Eternal Father own.*
>
> *Loud alleluias to Thy Name*
> *Angels and seraphim proclaim:*
> *The heavens and all the powers on high*
> *With rapture constantly do cry—*
>
> *'O holy, holy, holy, Lord!*
> *Thou God of hosts, by all adored;*
> *Earth and the heavens are full of Thee,*
> *Thy light, Thy power, Thy majesty.'*
>
> *Apostles join the glorious throng*
> *And swell the loud immortal song;*
> *Prophets enraptured hear the sound*
> *And spread the alleluia round.*
>
> *Victorious martyrs join their lays*
> *And shout the omnipotence of grace,*
> *While all thy church through all the earth*
> *Acknowledge and extol Thy worth.*

Glory to Thee, O God most high!
Father, we praise Thy majesty,
The Son, the Spirit, we adore,
One Godhead, blest for evermore.[11]

* * *

Glory be to God the Father,
Glory be to God the Son,
Glory be to God the Spirit,
Great Jehovah Three in One,
Glory, glory—[that was the great shout of the
                    Calvinistic Methodists]
While eternal ages run.

NOTES

[1] The lecture was first published in 1969 in *The Manifold Grace of God*, the collection of papers given at the 1968 Puritan and Reformed Studies Conference. It was subsequently included in D. Martyn Lloyd-Jones, *The Puritans: Their Origins and Successors* (Edinburgh: Banner of Truth Trust, 1987), pp.191-214. Further light on Dr Lloyd-Jones's view of Calvinistic Methodism may be found in Iain H. Murray, *The Life of D. Martyn Lloyd-Jones. Volume 1: The First Forty Years, 1899-1939; Volume 2: The Fight of Faith, 1939-1981.* (Edinburgh: Banner of Truth Trust, 1982, 1990), 412pp., 862pp.

[2] The lecture on Sandemanianism is to be found in D. M. Lloyd-Jones, *The Puritans*, pp.170-190. It first appeared in 1968 in *Profitable for Doctrine and Reproof*, the collection of papers given at the 1967 Puritan and Reformed Studies Conference. Welshmen attracted to Sandemanianism included J. R. Jones, Ramoth, and (for a while) Christmas Evans.

[3] The two volumes are: Gomer M. Roberts, *Gweithiau William Williams Pantycelyn*, I: *Golwg ar Deyrnas Crist; Bywyd a*

Marwolaeth Theomemphus (Caerdydd: Gwasg Prifysgol Cymru, 1964), 400pp. and Garfield H. Hughes, *Gweithiau William Williams Pantycelyn, II: Rhyddiaith* (Caerdydd: Gwasg Prifysgol Cymru, 1967), 303pp.

4 This book is now available in English (trans. Bethan Lloyd-Jones) as *The Experience Meeting: An introduction to the Welsh Societies of the Evangelical Awakening* (Vancouver: Regent College Reprint, 1995; distributed in UK by Gwasg Bryntirion Press, Bryntirion, Bridgend, CF31 4DX.)

5 Whitefield was not present at the first official Association held by the Calvinistic Methodists in Wales in January 1742. The occasion referred to in the text is the joint Association of Welsh and English Methodists held in January 1743. See Note 8, p.74.

6 See Note 5 above.

7 Wesley's words as recorded in his Journal are as follows: "In the evening I went very unwillingly to a society in Aldersgate Street, where someone was reading Luther's preface to the *Epistle to the Romans*. About a quarter before nine, while he was describing the change which God worked in the heart through faith in Christ, I felt my heart strangely warmed. I felt I did trust Christ, Christ alone, for salvation; and an assurance was given me that he had taken away my sins, even mine, and saved me from the law of sin and death." Robert Backhouse, ed., *John Wesley's Journal* (Sevenoaks: Hodder & Stoughton, 1993), p.56.

8 Republished Edinburgh: Banner of Truth Trust, 1978, 432pp.

9 The year in question, as regards both the revival and the publication of the hymn-book, was 1762. Eifion Evans, *Daniel Rowland*, p.309.

10 This statement does not perhaps do full justice to Cradock. There were admittedly certain mystical tendencies in Morgan Llwyd (although these have been overemphasized by modern writers seeking to portray Llwyd as less orthodox than his fellow-Puritans), but they were not shared by Cradock.

11 Quoted from Philip Gell's Collection (1815).

APPENDIX B

A list of books quoted in the text

Charles Alfred Ashburton, *A New and Complete History of England*. London, [1791-94].

'Bleddyn' (William Jones), *Eliasia, neu rai Sylwadau ar . . . John Elias*. Merthyr Tydfil, 1844.

Richard Davies, *An Account of the Convincement, Exercises, Services, and Travels of . . . Richard Davies*. 1710; 5th ed., London, 1794.

John Evans, *A Sketch of the Denominations of the Christian World*. 1795; 14th ed., 1821.

Howell Harris, *A Brief Account of the Life of Howell Harris Esq., Extracted from Papers Written by Himself* [by Benjamin La Trobe]. Trevecka, 1791. (Republished as *Howell Harris: His Own Story*. Chepstow: Bridge Publishing, 1984.)

T. B. Howell, *A Complete Collection of State Trials*. London, 1816.

John Hughes, *Methodistiaeth Cymru*, 3 volumes. Wrexham, 1851, 1854, 1856.

Griffith Jones, *Welch Piety, or, a Collection of the Several Accounts of the Circulating Welch Charity Schools*. London,1740 f.

The Life and Times of Selina [Hastings], Countess of Huntingdon, by a Member of the Houses of Shirley and Hastings [A.C.H. Seymour]. 2 volumes. London, 1839.

Rhys Prichard, *The Morning Star, or the Divine Poems of Mr Rees Prichard . . . Translated into English Verse by the Rev. William Evans.* 1771; new edition: Merthyr, 1815.

Lord Raymond, *Reports of Cases Argued and Adjudged in the Courts of King's Bench and Common Pleas, in the Reigns of the Late King William, Queen Anne, King George the First, and King George the Second.* I, 4th ed., corrected by John Bayley, 1792.

T. Rees, *A Topographical and Historical Description of South Wales.* London, 1819.

Thomas Rees, *History of Protestant Nonconformity in Wales from its Rise to the Present Time.* London, 1861; second ed., 1883.

E. W. Richard and H. Richard, *Bywyd y Parch. Ebenezer Richard.* Llundain, 1839.

Erasmus Saunders, *A View of the State of Religion in the Diocese of St David's about the Beginning of the 18th Century.* London, 1721; republished Cardiff: University of Wales Press, 1949.

A Short Narrative of the Proceedings against the Bp. of St. A[saph] [by Robert Wynne]. London, 1702.

John Stoughton, *History of Religion in England from the Opening of the Long Parliament to the End of the Eighteenth Century. V: The Church of the Revolution.* 1874; revised edition: London, 1881.

A Summary View of the Articles Exhibited against the Late Bishop of St David's. London, 1701.

Ioan Thomas, *Rhad Ras*. Abertawe, 1810; republished, ed. J. Dyfnallt Owen, Caerdydd: Gwasg Prifysgol Cymru, 1949.

Owen Thomas, *Cofiant y Parchedig John Jones, Talsarn*. Wrexham, 1874.

A. M. Toplady, *The Posthumous Works of the Late Reverend A. M. Toplady*. London, 1780.

Ellis Wynne, *Gweledigaethau y Bardd Cwsg, gyda nodiadau eglurhaol gan D. Silvan Evans*. 1853; new edition, Caerfyrddin, 1878.

APPENDIX C

A selection of recent publications in English on aspects of Calvinistic Methodism in Wales and beyond

Some older works and books in Welsh have been mentioned in the Notes and in Appendix C. Relevant articles, some of which are in English, also appear regularly in the *Journal of the Historical Society of the Presbyterian Church of Wales.*

The Background to Methodism

Geraint H. Jenkins, *Literature, Religion, and Society in Wales, 1660-1730.* Cardiff: University of Wales Press, 1978. 351pp. (This scholarly survey emphasizes religious activity in Wales before Methodism, and is therefore more sympathetic to the viewpoint of Thomas Rees than to that of William Williams.)

Idem, *The Foundations of Modern Wales: Wales 1642-1780.* Oxford: Clarendon Press and Cardiff: University of Wales Press, 1987, 490pp. (The standard introduction to the period, but again unsympathetic towards Methodism.)

Calvinistic Methodism in Wales

Richard Bennett, *Howell Harris and the Dawn of Revival.* Bridgend: Evangelical Press of Wales, 1987. 210pp. (First published in Welsh in 1909, and subsequently in English under the title *The Early Life of Howell Harris*. London: Banner of Truth Trust, 1962.)

Roger L. Brown, *The Welsh Evangelicals*. Tongwynlais: Tair Eglwys Press, 1986. 200pp. (Excessively sympathetic to Anglicanism both before the advent of Methodism and afterwards.)

Thomas Charles, *Spiritual Counsels, selected from his letters and papers by Edward Morgan*. 1836; republished Edinburgh: Banner of Truth Trust, 1993. 520pp.

George E. Clarkson, *George Whitefield and Welsh Calvinistic Methodism*. Lewiston, New York/Queenston, Ontario/Lampeter, Ceredigion: Edwin Mellen Press, 1996. 148pp.

Eifion Evans, *Daniel Rowland and the Great Evangelical Awakening in Wales*. Edinburgh: Banner of Truth Trust, 1985. 416pp.

Idem, *Fire in the Thatch: The true nature of religious revival*. Bridgend: Evangelical Press of Wales, 1996. 240pp.

Idem, *Howel Harris, Evangelist, 1714-1773*. Cardiff: University of Wales Press, 1974. 75pp.

Idem, *Pursued by God: A selective translation with notes of the Welsh religious classic* Theomemphus *by William Williams*. Bridgend: Evangelical Press of Wales, 1996. 192pp.

Idem, *Revival Comes to Wales*. Bridgend: Evangelical Press of Wales, 1979. 132pp. (Previously published in 1959 as *When He Is Come: An Account of the 1858-60 Revival in Wales*.)

Howell Harris: His Own Story. Chepstow: Bridge Publishing,

1984. 92pp. (First published in 1791 under the title *A Brief Account of the Life of Howell Harris Esq., Extracted from Papers Written by Himself.*)

Glyn Tegai Hughes, *Williams Pantycelyn*. Cardiff: University of Wales Press on behalf of the Welsh Arts Council, 1983. 137pp. (A literary and critical study.)

Hugh J. Hughes, *Life of Howell Harris, the Welsh Reformer*. 1892; republished Stoke-on-Trent: Tentmaker Publications, 1996. 394pp.

David Jones, *The Life and Times of Griffith Jones of Llanddowror*. 1902; republished Clonmel: Tentmaker Publications, 1995. 200pp.

Hywel Rees Jones, *Daniel Rowland: Man of Truth and Power*. Cardiff: Evangelical Library of Wales [1972]. 27pp.

Owen Jones, *Great Preachers of Wales*. 1885; republished Clonmel: Tentmaker Publications, 1995. 528pp.

R. M. Jones & Gwyn Davies, *The Christian Heritage of Welsh Education*. Bridgend: Evangelical Press of Wales, 1986. 134pp. (This work includes material on, and by, Griffith Jones, Llanddowror, and Thomas Charles.)

R. Tudur Jones, *John Elias: Prince Amongst Preachers*. Bridgend: Evangelical Library of Wales, 1975. 33pp.

H. Elvet Lewis, *Sweet Singers of Wales: The story of Welsh hymns and their authors with original translations*. 1889; republished Clonmel: Tentmaker Publications, 1994. 104pp.

Derec Llwyd Morgan (trans. Dyfnallt Morgan), *The Great Awakening in Wales*. London: Epworth Press, 1988. 323pp.

(This is a stimulatiing and not unsympathetic account by a prominent Welsh academic, although some aspects of his interpretation might be questioned.)

Edward Morgan, *John Elias: Life, Letters and Essays*. 1844, 1847; republished Edinburgh: Banner of Truth Trust, 1973. 432pp.

Iain H. Murray, *The Life of D. Martyn Lloyd-Jones. Volume 1: The First Forty Years, 1899-1939; Volume 2: The Fight of Faith, 1939-1981*. Edinburgh: Banner of Truth Trust, 1982, 1990. 412pp., 862pp. (These volumes shed light on the decline of Calvinistic Methodism in Wales in the twentieth century.)

John Owen, *A Memoir of Daniel Rowlands of Llangeitho*. 1848; republished, *Banner of Truth Magazine*, 215-6 (Aug-Sept 1981), 80pp.

Thomas Phillips, *The Welsh Revival: Its origin and development*. 1860; republished Edinburgh: Banner of Truth Trust, 1989. 168pp. (The revival in question is that of 1858-60.)

Emyr Roberts & R. Geraint Gruffydd, *Revival and its Fruit*. Bridgend: Evangelical Library of Wales, 1981. 40pp.

J. C. Ryle, *Christian Leaders of the 18th Century*. 1869; republished Edinburgh: Banner of Truth Trust, 1978. 432pp. (This book, part of which was issued previously by the same publishers as *Five Christian Leaders*, contains biographies of Daniel Rowland and other leading Methodists.)

William Williams (trans. Bethan Lloyd-Jones) *The Experience Meeting: An introduction to the Welsh Societies of the Evangelical Awakening* (Vancouver: Regent College Reprint, 1995; distributed in UK by Gwasg Bryntirion Press, Bryntirion, Bridgend, CF31 4DX.) 62pp. (A translation of *Drws y Society Profiad*.)

William Williams, *Songs of Praises: English hymns and elegies of William Williams, Pantycelyn, 1717-1791* (with introduction by R. Brinley Jones). 1991; republished by Drovers Press, 1995. 124pp.

Calvinistic Methodism Beyond Wales

The aim of the following brief list is to locate Welsh Calvinistic Methodism within its wider context. In some of the works there are references to contemporary developments in Wales. No account has been taken of the voluminous literature on Wesleyan Methodism.

Faith Cook, *William Grimshaw of Haworth*. Edinburgh: Banner of Truth Trust, 1997. 368pp.

C. H. Crookshank, *Days of Revival*. 1885; republished Clonmel: Tentmaker Publications, 1994. 220pp. (A history of Methodism in Ireland.)

Arnold Dallimore, *George Whitefield*. 2 volumes. London, Edinburgh: Banner of Truth Trust, 1970, 1980. 612pp, 620pp.

Idem, *George Whitefield - Evangelist of the eighteenth century*. London: Wakeman Trust, 1990. 224pp. (This is an abridged form of the two-volume work mentioned above.)

Arthur Fawcett, *The Cambuslang Revival: The Scottish evangelical revival in the eighteenth century*. London: Banner of Truth Trust, 1971. 256pp.

John H. Gerstner, *Jonathan Edwards - Evangelist*. Morgan, Pennsylvania: Soli Deo Gloria, 1995. 192pp. (Previously published by Westminster Press, Philadelphia, as *Steps to Salvation: The evangelistic message of Jonathan Edwards*.)

John Gillies, *Historical Collections of Accounts of Revival*. 1754/ 1845; republished Edinburgh: Banner of Truth Trust, 1981. 604pp. (There are a few references to early Methodism in Wales.)

Helen C. Knight, ed., *Lady Huntingdon and her Friends*. 1853; republished Grand Rapids, USA: Baker, 1978. 292pp.

Iain H. Murray, *Jonathan Edwards*. Edinburgh: Banner of Truth Trust, 1987. 536pp.

Idem, *Revival and Revivalism: The making and marring of American evangelicalism, 1750-1858*. Edinburgh: Banner of Truth Trust, 1994. 480pp.

Nigel R. Pibworth, *The Gospel Pedlar: The Story of John Berridge and the Eighteenth-Century Revival*. Welwyn: Evangelical Press, 1987. 313pp.

John Pollock, *George Whitefield and the Great Awakening*. 1973; republished Tring: Lion, 1982. 272pp. (A lively account, but not as perceptive as that of Dallimore.)

Graham Thomas, ed., "George Whitefield and his Friends", *National Library of Wales Journal*, XXVI, 3 (Summer 1990), 251-280; XXVI, 4 (Winter 1990) 367-396; XXVII, 1 (Summer 1991), 65-96; XXVII, 2 (Winter 1991), 175-203; XXVII, 3 (Summer 1992), 289-318; XXVII, 4 (Winter 1992), 431-452.

Joseph Tracy, *The Great Awakening: A history of the revival of religion in the time of Edwards and Whitefield*. 1842; republished Edinburgh: Banner of Truth Trust, 1976. 464pp.

W. R. Ward, *The Protestant Evangelical Awakening*. Cambridge: Cambridge University Press,, 1992. 370pp. (A generally sympathetic academic survey of the eighteenth-century revival in Europe and America.)

Michael Watts, *The Dissenters. Volume 1: From the Reformation to the French Revolution; Volume 2: The Expansion of Evangelical Nonconformity, 1791-1859.* Oxford: Clarendon Press, 1978, 1995. 543pp., 911pp. (As with Ward above, an academic but generally sympathetic - and comprehensive - discussion.)

Edwin Welch, *Spiritual Pilgrim: A reassessment of the life of the Countess of Huntingdon.* (Cardiff: University of Wales Press, 1995). 233pp.

George Whitefield, *Journals.* 1738f; republished London: Banner of Truth Trust, 1960. 596pp.

Idem. *The Journals of George Whitefield* (ed. Robert Backhouse). Sevenoaks: Hodder & Stoughton, 1993. 256pp. (An abridged version.)

Idem, *Letters, 1736-1742.* 1771; republished Edinburgh: Banner of Truth Trust, 1976. 584pp.

General Works on Revival

Brian Edwards, *Revival! A people saturated with God.* Darlington: Evangelical Press, 1990. 303pp.

Jonathan Edwards on Revival. 1736, 1741, 1743; republished London: Banner of Truth Trust, 1965. 160pp. (The three treatises contained in this volume - *A Narrative of Surprising Conversions, The Distinguishing Marks of a Work of the Spirit of God,* and *An Account of the Revival of Religion in Northampton, 1740-1742* - are also to be found in his *Works,* 2 volumes. 1834; republished Edinburgh: Banner of Truth Trust, 1974. The second treatise has been abridged and modernised in *God at Work?* published by Grace Publications.)

Eifion Evans, *Revivals: Their Rise, Progress, and Achievements*. 1960; republished Bridgend: Evangelical Press of Wales, 1986. 36pp.

W. Vernon Higham, *The Turn of the Tide*. Cardiff: The Heath Trust & Wheaton, Ill., USA: International; Awakening Trust, 1995. 124pp.

Erroll Hulse, *Give Him No Rest: A call to prayer for revival*. Darlington: Evangelical Press, 1991. 144pp.

D. M. Lloyd-Jones, *The Puritans: Their Origins and Successors*. Edinburgh: Banner of Truth Trust, 1987. 421pp. (A number of the addresses in this volume are concerned with the nature and history of revival; an address on 'Howell Harris and Revival' is to be found on pp. 282-302.)

Iain H. Murray, *Pentecost—Today?* Edinburgh: Banner of Truth Trust. (Forthcoming)

Richard Owen Roberts, *Revival!* Wheaton, Ill., USA: International Awakening Press, 1991.

I. D. E. Thomas, *God's Harvest: The nature of true revival*. 1956; rev. edition Bridgend: Gwasg Bryntirion, 1997. 64pp.

Various authors, *The Revival of Religion: Addresses by Scottish evangelical leaders delivered in Glasgow in 1840*. 1840; republished Edinburgh: Banner of Truth Trust, 1984. 468pp.

INDEX

PEOPLE

PLACES

OTHER MATTERS